New directions for criminology

New directions for criminology
Notes from outside the field

Edited by

Ronny Lippens
Patrick Van Calster

Maklu
Antwerpen | Apeldoorn | Portland

Cover photo taken by Annelies Vanlandschoot in Le Lonzac (France)

Ronny Lippens/Patrick Van Calster (eds.)
New Directions for Criminology. Notes from outside the field
Antwerpen | Apeldoorn | Portland
Maklu
2010

218 pag. - 24 x 16 cm
ISBN 978-90-466-0219-5
D/2009/1997/42
NUR 824

Maklu-Publishers
Somersstraat 13/15, 2018 Antwerpen, Belgium, info@maklu.be
Koninginnelaan 96, 7315 EB Apeldoorn, The Netherlands, info@maklu.nl
www.maklu.eu

USA & Canada
International Specialized Book Services
920 NE 58th Ave., Suite 300, Portland, OR 97213-3786, orders@isbs.com,
www.isbs.com

Table of Contents

Introduction

Ronnie LIPPENS and Patrick VAN CALSTER
Keele University (UK) and University of Leyden
(the Netherlands)

Why Criminal Law? Why Break It? If Broken, Then What?

Some time ago Stanley Cohen achieved quite formidable a feat by capturing the task of criminology in just nineteen words. Criminologists ask themselves the following questions: 'Why are laws made? Why are they broken? What do we do or what should we do about this?' (1988: 9). In a slightly modified form these questions sound like 1) 'why do definitions of crime change and vary across time and space?', and 'why do particular behaviours and even whole groups or populations get to be criminalized in the first place?'; 2) 'why do people offend against norms, including legal norms such as the Criminal Law?'; and '3) what should we do with offenders or, more broadly, what should be done about crime?'.

Criminologists have in the course of a century and a half produced quite a varied smorgasbord of answers to these questions. This book is not the place to rehearse them. Indeed, the book in your hands is no introduction to criminology. It is meant to be read by students of criminology who have already read at least one or a few books or textbooks that deal with the aforementioned questions, and who are familiar with the concepts, theories, theoretical frameworks, and overall perspectives which the criminological community – if there is such a thing – has made its own. If you are such a student, then you will probably have realised that many, if not most of the attempts made by criminologists to grapple with either of the three basic criminological topics or questions could be ranged according to their focus on either *micro* dynamics or *macro* dynamics underpinning processes of criminalization (first question), criminogenesis (second question), and crime control (third question). There have been theories and perspectives where the concrete *micro* actions and minute interactions of and between concrete actors, on the very ground of everyday life, as it were, are assumed to be determined by the dimensions of broader, all-encompassing dynamics that, at a *macro* level (e.g. in the global political economy) set the conditions for concrete actions and interactions to unfold. At the other side of the micro-macro spectrum one will find explications and explanations of criminalization, crime and crime control that point to the very minute actions, interactions and exchanges between concrete actors – each with their own motives, intentions, strategies, tactics, and so on – which are then said to ultimately produce macro effects. The American sociologist C. Wright Mills (writing in

1959) was one of those who urged sociologists (and criminologists alike) to imagine the connections between the micro and the macro. It took criminologists of the stature of Ian Taylor, Paul Walton, and Jock Young to attempt just that. In their seminal *The New Criminology* (published in 1973) they envisaged a *fully social theory* of crime and crime control. Combining inspiration gleaned from the Marxist study of political economy (*macro*) and from symbolic interactionism (*micro*) the *New Criminologists* set the agenda for the integrated ("fully social theory") explanation not just of crime, but also of the "social reaction" to crime. This "fully social" explanation would focus, in one and the same effort, on both macro and micro dynamics in the "immediate origins" (micro) and "wider origins" (macro) of both crime and "social reaction". But this project remained, to a large extent, what it was: a mere project.

Criminological theories of criminalization, crime and crime control could also be arranged according to their preference for either structural explications and explanations of criminalization, crime, and crime control, or, as the case may be, explications and explanations that are much more interested in how the particular agency of actors –acting and interacting individuals and groups – generate, perpetuate, modify, or change the structural determinants of criminalization, crime, and crime control. It is fair to say that a significant part of the criminological enterprise has, on the whole, focused more on structural determination rather than on action. The British sociologist Anthony Giddens made a serious attempt – in his *structuration theory* (e.g. Giddens, 1984) – to combine both perspectives. Structural conditions (or the combination of structural possibilities and constraints), he claimed, are the (result of the) intended and unintended consequences of that which *knowledgeable actors*, who constantly monitor and interpret the conditions and constraints they perceive, decide to do. These decisions, in turn, may, or may not, perpetuate or, as the case may be, change these very structural conditions and constraints. Structural conditions and constraints, in short, are *structured* (this word is a verb), while, at the very same time, the actions through which structures are structured, are themselves structured by their structural conditions. Criminologists such as Stuart Henry and Dragan Milovanovic would build on Giddens' structuration theory in order to demonstrate, in their path-breaking *Constitutive Criminology* (1996), how processes of structuration underpin both the production of crime and forms of crime control. But Henry and Milovanovic went beyond mere structuration theory. Inspired by what we now know as post-structuralism, and by complexity theory (or chaos theory), they argued that the outcome of structuration (whether it be in processes of criminalization, or in crime, or crime control) tends to be, to a large extent, unpredictable, contingent, indeed indeterminate.

In the above sentence we mentioned the word 'post-structuralism'. Having largely dissolved the boundaries between the subject and the self, on the one hand, and their environment, on the other, authors working from this perspective are usually able to think by way of notions such as 'emergence', 'assemblage', 'event', 'self-organisation', or 'dissipation'. Subjects and selves *are* not. They emerge; they come into the world; they *become*; they change continuously. Campaigns to criminalize particular behaviours or groups of people are not just the result of interacting subjectivities acting within contexts; they are, first and foremost, assemblages of desire. The killing of an 'anti-globalization' protester during a demonstration is not the mere effect of global developments and local context. It is an 'event' whose productive energies stretch out, *rhizomatically* (to borrow from Gilles Deleuze and Felix Guattari) in-between the local and the global. The actions of a lynch mob are not so much determined by structural conditions, as they are forms of action that self-organize around attractors that are already on their way to dissipation. One way of looking at 'events', or actions, or behaviours, or subjects and selves, or still: forms of governance, for instance, is to situate them within the *form of life* (a Nietzschean, and later also Foucauldian concept; but see Luis Lobo-Guerrero's contribution to this volume) of which they form part. Such forms of life – ways of seeing, ways of thinking, ways of life, basically – are emergent, ever-becoming anew, always on the move. They are, at least to some extent, open, and open-ended, and it is in this openness, or in this contingency, that subjects, selves, actions, behaviours, indeed 'events' (such as, e.g. instances of criminalization, crime or crime control) form, that is, emerge, assemble, crystallize, and again dissipate.

It should then come as no surprise that authors such as Henry and Milovanovic extended Giddens' structuration theory using theoretical work by authors such as Jacques Lacan (who, in his psychoanalytical work, dissolved the boundary between the fractured self and world; but see, on Lacan, Veronique Voruz's contribution to this volume), complexity theory (or 'chaos' theory) and work on self-organization and dissipation (on complexity theory, see Patrick van Calster's contribution). Dragan Milovanovic would later go on to focus on the work of Gilles Deleuze and Félix Guattari (e.g. in Milovanovic, 2007; see Jamie Murray's contribution on the work of Gilles Deleuze).

Much effort has been made, ever since the publication of *Constitutive Criminology*, to use work of post-structuralist inspiration in applications within the broader field of crime and criminal justice studies. But much, if not all of this applied work appeared sporadically, either in single journal articles or book chapters, or in highly specialized edited collections (e.g. Milovanovic, 1997; Arrigo & Williams, 2006), although there are exceptions where a more didactic approach is noticeable (e.g. Arrigo, Milovanovic, and Schehr, 2005). More importantly, however, much of this work remains locked up, as it were, in a scholarly 'niche'. It never succeeded in drawing, much less capturing the attention of the mainstream in criminology and criminal justice studies. Only few students are aware, if at all, of this body of literature and where they *do* have access to these ideas and insights, it seems to be very hard for them to get to grips with them. The time has therefore come, we thought, to make an effort to gather the more basic insights from the post-structuralist canon in a highly accessible format. This is where this book comes in. The book at hand introduces basic ideas, concepts, and theories from these 'new theories' in a number of short, introductory chapters that were written with an undergraduate readership in mind. That readership, we assume, is likely to be largely unfamiliar with the 'niche' materials and literatures mentioned above. This book, then, aims to introduce students to these materials and literatures – at least to some of them – in a didactically appropriate format that should allow them to venture further afield on their own initiative should they wish to do so.

The Outside

The introduction of, and integration into criminology and criminal justice studies, of the 'new' theories, that, roughly since about the latter half of the 1970s, have come to be known as post-structuralism, as said, never really reached the mainstream. We are, well into the 21st century, still talking about 'niche', or perhaps worse, 'fringe' activity. And this is where criminology differs from other fields of study and disciplines such as legal theory, political science, governance studies, international relations and diplomacy studies, management studies and organization theory, sociology and social theory, urban studies, philosophy and philosophy of law, and so on. These have allowed post-structuralism to make much deeper inroads into 'their' mainstream. In the criminological and criminal justice communities much of the effort has been resting – and still does – on a small group of niche-workers. But much more could be done. Hence this book which, we hope, reaches out to the heart of the criminological and criminal justice community, i.e. its undergraduate student population.

But let us say a few more words on the 'niche' we mentioned. The mere fact that this niche is peopled, mostly, by scholars and researchers – such as the editors of this volume – who have a background in criminology and criminal justice studies, has coloured the translation and application, of the 'new' of post-structuralism, into the 'old' of the criminological enterprise. Indeed, we, the editors, have felt ourselves the need – and still do – to make a constant effort, for instance, to translate or at least direct the most important tenets of post-structuralist thought toward the three basic questions which we mentioned at the very beginning of this introduction. And we asked the contributors to this volume to do similarly, even though we were, and remain, aware of the quite artificial character of the whole exercise. 'Artificial', since, of course, post-structuralist thought itself doesn't know 'crime', 'criminalization', or 'crime control' as objects of study. That said, however, we *did* make an effort to prevent our own criminological and criminal justice backgrounds to determine or even colour the form and content of the translation and application effort. We did this, quite simply, by asking scholars and researchers working in *other* fields of study to introduce and translate post-structuralist thought for us. Indeed, Gilles Deleuze – whose name has been mentioned a few times already – has, on a number of occasions (e.g. in his book on *Foucault*, 1988), stated that newness in thought can only come about in and through a confrontation with "the Outside"; it can only come from the unfamiliar, from beyond the outer limit of our horizon (in this case: our criminological and criminal justice horizon). In a way this statement is similar to the one once made by the philosopher Thomas Nagel, who, in 1974, claimed that, as soon as one steps outside one's world – it takes some imagination – and one notices the *circularities* of the reasoning and justifications in it, or its *particularities*, one is immediately struck by the *absurdity* of it all (Nagel, 1979, 11-23). It therefore pays to allow the Outside to work its ways into one's own world. And it pays to open up one's own world to the Outside. This is what we attempt to do here, in some small measure, in this book.

So we asked scholars and researchers from *other* backgrounds to tell us, criminologists, how post-structuralist thought might be applicable to problems and issues that usually form the staple of criminology and criminal justice studies. Most, if not all contributors, have a firm foot in another discipline or domain of study. Allow us to be very honest here. All contributors to this volume do *also* have some idea about what it is that preoccupies criminologists. Indeed nearly all contributors regularly cooperate with criminologists and some have even taught the subject. So, rather than ask criminologists themselves to contribute chapters on cutting edge developments *within* criminology, we decided to consult authors *outside* the criminological community to demonstrate how the latest theoretical work in *their* field could be made fruitful for criminology. All contributors however are well placed to make the connections between the cutting edge of *their* field of research and scholarship, and its potential for criminology, clear. This, by the way, goes some way to explaining why we chose 'New Directions *for* Criminology' as the title for our collection, rather than 'New Directions *in* Criminology'.

The contributions are divided between on the one hand papers – in Part 1– that elaborate on the usefulness of particular theories, perspectives and concepts for criminology and, on the other, papers – in Part 2– that outline particular research topics or themes which we believe could be of interest to those working within the broader criminological community. Part 1 includes introductory chapters on theoretical models or perspectives, such as complexity theory (by philosopher and criminologist Patrick van Calster), Jacques Lacan's psychoanalytical work (by legal theorist Veronique Voruz), Gilles Deleuze's philosophical work (by legal theorist Jamie Murray), assemblage theory, which itself is a hybrid assemblage of Deleuzianism, elements of actor-network theory, and complexity theory (by sociologist and criminologist Don Crewe), and Paul Virilio's idiosyncratic work on *dromology* (by philosopher Gijs van Oenen). In Part 2 readers will find more applied chapters on themes and topics which criminologists will have some affinity with, as well as chapters that attempt to rethink the criminological enterprise altogether. Each of the chapters in Part 2, however, also focuses on one or a few particular theories, theorists, or theoretical models. Part 2 thus includes chapters on the importance of the notion, or concept, of 'forms of life' for criminological scholarship and research (by political scientist Luis Lobo-Guerrero), with a particular focus on work by Michel Foucault; on 'foundations' as criminological objects (by philosopher of law Claudius Messner), with a focus on phenomenology and on (Luhmann's) systems theory; on 'monstrosity' as an object of criminal justice and governance (by legal theorist Luciano Nuzzo), with, here also, a focus on Luhmannian theory; on tribal dynamics as the criminological problematic *par excellence* (by criminologist Ronnie Lippens), with most attention here directed at what is known as 'actor-network theory'; and on the work of the late 19th century sociologist Gabriel Tarde as a source of inspiration for urban sociology and for urban criminology's much needed 21st century renewal (by criminologists and philosophers Patrick van Calster and Mark Schuilenburg). All contributions to Part 2 are, they too, very much inspired by theoretical developments of the post-structuralist kind. These contributions, and therefore this collection, by no means pretend to exhaust our problematic. On the contrary. It is probably best to consider this work here as a 'taster' collection. Students may be able to draw inspiration from this book. Many, we hope, will want to find out more about 'New Directions for Criminology' and explore the vast literature that's 'out there' on their own initiative and at their own leisure. If and when they do so, we will have achieved our goal. Allow us now to introduce the contributions in some more detail.

The Contributions

Contributions to part one of this volume revolve around the observation that the traditional way of thinking about crime and crime control has hit its limitations. Mainstream (social) science, Patrick Van Calster argues in the opening chapter, is steeped in principles of systemic thought. Referring to the work of the 18th century philosopher Immanuel Kant, the author argues that this approach is quite useful for the study and analysis of *complicated* systems, but unable to grasp *complex* systems which are characterized by non-linearity, uncertainty, and unpredictability. Drawing on the work of sociologist Norbert Elias and complexity scientist Stuart Kauffman, Van Calster argues that social science actually generates ideological and political statements, rather than scientific ones. Moreover, social sciences often address the problems they observe very poorly. 'Systemic' thinking has also led to the fragmentation of social science. This in turn has made them unfit to grasp the complexity of the dynamics, transformations and movements of life.

Don Crewe asks the question about the object of criminological research. This question must be posed since criminology supposes that its object is, basically, 'crime'. However, what goes under the heading 'crime', always caught up in processes of transformation, is the result of many interactions between and across a variety of social landscapes. Crewe argues that Gilles Deleuze's (and others') assemblage theory is of significant use in understanding the way transformations, and emergence of the new, work. Assemblage theory goes beyond social science as we know it. It transcends the more traditional questions which start from a well-defined object. Assemblage theory invites criminologists not to restrict themselves to a particular object of research. The focus is on processes and interactions in and through that which is known as 'crime' of 'deviancy' emerge as assemblages.

Jamie Murray takes up this point. The work of Gilles Deleuze (and Félix Guattari) is of extreme importance for any adequate understanding of social reality. The author begins with a short introduction to the highly complex and engaging theoretical work of Deleuze and Guattari, on the basis of which he explores criminology's three questions. Murray argues that a Deleuzoguattarian approach to criminology might not so much be interested in the question about the causes of crime, or in the question about the particulars of the criminal justice system and its workings and functioning. Life is, first and foremost, a question of *desire*. And desire carries within itself potential for the new. Using Deleuzoguattarian terminology, one could phrase it as follows: life, potentially, is *germinal* deviance. Germinal deviance is deviance in itself. It is not deviance as departure from or transgression of a norm. This position leads Murray to explore the profound and creative operation of germinal deviance in terms of the problematic of social organisation.

Gijs van Oenen takes the most incisive characteristic of modernity, i.e. speed, to show where western societies seem to be heading for, and argues what this may mean for criminology. Drawing on the work of Paul Virilio, van Oenen is interested in how the hectic speed and the abundance of impressions characteristic of modern life influence our perception of the world. People are overloaded with information and choice all the time. This could – and in some instances already *has*- lead to paralysis. In the light of this, Van Oenen explores a number of issues which criminologists may want to think through in years to come, e.g. nodal policing, the demands of logistics, and the rise of Ambient Intelligence.

Veronique Voruz introduces us to the work of psychoanalyst Jacques Lacan. She identifies a number of ways in which Lacanian psychoanalysis can cast a different light on criminological concerns. The Lacanian perspective is one of those which focus on singularity – singularity of the self or subject, in particular. Voruz explores Lacan's insistence on subjective responsibility and shows that his insistence is based upon a specific conception of the subject of the unconscious. This conception allows Voruz to trace some elements for a theory of the criminal act.

Part two, with its focus on themes and topics, opens – in Luis Lobo-Guerrero's contribution – with the idea that crime and crime control are fully implicated in the emergence and transformation of *forms of life* and in the measures taken to secure or protect those very forms of life. Definitions of crime and processes of criminalisation, the emergence and spread of crime and criminality, as well as strategies of crime control and reactions to crime, are all related to the forms of life they seek to secure. This approach abandons the idea that 'crime' is a nicely delineated research object. 'Crime', rather, poses an intellectual problem that relates to the promotion and protection of ways of being in the world. This implies power. What we call 'crime' (or 'disorder', and so on) is embedded in relations and interactions of power. As Lobo-Guerrero argues, the task of criminologists could be to reflect on these relations and interactions of power.

Building on an intricate etymological analysis of the common root of words such as 'crime', 'crisis' and 'critique', Claudius Messner explores Robert Musil's novel *The Man without Qualities* – and the passages therein on the murderer Moosbrugger in particular – for illustrations that show how the almost unlimited amounts of possible interpretations of events open up equally unlimited possible contexts and avenues for action (and vice versa). Musil's novel contrasts many different interpretations of events and contexts that seem to share no common thread or plot that would lend them overall coherence. Musil's approach, says Messner, encourages us to question the way we acquire, indeed produce knowledge. Knowledge is the result of observation. Observations inevitably take place in a localised and specifically coded space of judgment. Observations, and the knowledge based on them, are therefore unavoidably partial representations of that which is observed. The issue for criminologists, then, is to observe 'crime' in such a way – to paraphrase Messner – as to be 'critical' in the sense of causing a 'crisis' of signification, that is, to be 'critical' in such a way as to help bring about the collapse of fixed regimes of judgement.

Luciano Nuzzo's contribution has more than one issue in common with Messner's chapter. Not only does it seek inspiration in art, it also addresses the problem of first-order and second-order observation in criminology (and the social sciences more broadly). Art, Luciano Nozzo argues, allows us to see that which we cannot see from within the bounds of 'scientific' observation. Art may help the observing criminologist to escape – albeit temporarily – the 'blind spots' of his or her own observations. The author makes a strong case with his analysis of Fritz Lang's *'M' the Monster of Düsseldorf* (1931), a film about a 'murderer among us', as was the initial title of the film. The narrative of the movie seems to suggest that, ultimately, there never is a fundamental distinction between 'outside' (any putative outside) and inside (any putative inside) to be made. Drawing on Foucault's writings on monstrosity (his lectures on the *Abnormals* at the Collège de France in 1974-1975 in particular), Nuzzo concludes that criminology will only be able to produce useful knowledge if it fully recognizes that it is itself implicated in the constitution of its observed object.

The next chapter by Patrick Van Calster and Marc Schuilenburg revisits the work of 19th century sociologist Gabriel Tarde. Tarde was a contemporary of Emile Durkheim and one of the founders of French sociology. Unlike Durkheim, however, Tarde focuses on small changes and details in everyday social life. This 'micro perspective' seeks to draw the criminologist's attention to the complex processes of interaction from which 'order' emerges. Van Calster and Schuilenburg argue for criminologists to become more aware of the need to analyse human action and interaction *within* social processes. Emphasis should be placed on perceptions, world views and interaction styles of all those who participate *in* (rather than *with*) those processes. Criminal activity and attempts to control it, for instance, are not just a matter of wilful and 'rational' decision, or of 'functional' emergence, but are, rather, effects of complex processes operating on a micro level over which no single entity or force could ever have full and complete control.

In the concluding chapter, Ronnie Lippens reflects on the way change, or newness, seem to emerge in criminological knowledge and practice. Drawing on actor-network theory, Lippens elaborates on the slightly provocative idea that novelty is all to do with image (in many senses of the word). Criminological newness could be considered as the result of tribal processes of assembling and circulating images. Such processes simultaneously constitute academic communities, academic selves, as well as knowledge. Communities, selves, and their knowledges all emerge simultaneously. Newness, then, emerges from such processes. Lippens illustrates this thesis with 'criminological' examples taken from art history and anthropology.

List of References

Arrigo, B., Milovanovic, D., and R. Schehr (2005) *The French Connection in Criminology. Rediscovering Crime, Law and Social Change.* New York: SUNY Press.

Arrigo, B. & C. Williams (eds) (2006) *Philosophy, Crime and Criminology.* Chicago: University of Illinois Press.

Cohen, S. (1988) *Against Criminology.* New Brunswick: Transaction.

Deleuze, G. (1988) *Foucault.* London: Athlone.

Giddens, A. (1984) *The Constitution of Society.* Cambridge: Polity Press.

Henry, S. & D. Milovanovic (1996) *Constitutive Criminology.* London: Sage.

Mills, C. Wright (2000) [1959] *The Sociological Imagination.* Oxford: oxford University Press.

Milovanovic, D. (1997) Chaos, *Criminology and Social Justice. The New Orderly (Dis)Order.* Westport: Praeger.

Milovanovic, D. (2007) 'Diversity, Law and Justice: A Deleuzian Semiotics View of 'Criminal Justice', *International Journal for the Semiotics of Law* 29, 1: 55-79

Nagel, T. (1979) *Mortal Questions*. Cambridge: Cambridge University Press.
Taylor, I., Walton, P. and J. Young (eds) (1973) *The New Criminology*. Routledge and Kegan Paul.

Studying Society, Safety and Security: Notes on Observer Involvement

Patrick VAN CALSTER
University of Leyden (the Netherlands)

Introduction

According to Ulrich Beck (1986), Zygmunt Bauman (2006) and David Garland (2001), our society is moving towards a risk-obsessed society of control[1]. One of the more recent developments in this evolution is the so-called precautionary principle, and precautionary measures based on it (Pieterman, 2008; Ericson, 2007). These measures differ in significant aspects from preventative ones. The main difference is in the degree of uncertainty on which the measures are based (Ewald, 2002). Prevention aims to prevent a real proven danger, while precautionary measurers aim to avert *possible,* not yet proven problems that could or might pose a threat, sometime in the future (Pieterman, 2008: 40). The idea behind this is that not all dangers or threats can be known, or proven. Therefore, a lack of clear evidence of threats and danger does not necessarily mean there is a lack of danger. A lack of evidence is no reason to forsake precautionary measures. This shows that knowledge (or the lack of it) actually plays a rather minor role in our precautionary risk society.

This chapter tries to establish the extent to which science has contributed to the development of a precautionary culture such as ours, and what the role of science is or should be in these developments. I will argue that the scientific debate generates political and ideological statements, rather than scientific ones. I will argue that this is due to the particular systems-theoretical reason, logic and methods used. These methods led to the fragmentation in the social sciences also. Scientific research (and social sciences are included here) address selective and clear-cut problems that are often posed in a wrong way. In order to state my case, I will undertake excursions into the epistemology of Immanuel Kant, Norbert Elias's long-term research, and Stuart Kauffman's pioneering research on complexity theory.

1 The phrase 'risk society' here does not refer to an actual increase of risk in society, but, rather, to a society which aims to prepare and equip itself against risks.

Scientific Discourses as System Perspectives on (Social) Reality

In his *Problems of Involvement and Detachment* Norbert Elias (1956) makes a distinction between two ways of addressing reality. The first he calls *involvement*. It reflects the way nature was (or is) experienced in a pre-scientific era. Nature here is experienced as a collection of mysterious forces to which one is exposed. People did (or do) not understand nor control these forces, and were afraid of them. They were *involved* in what they experienced and had plenty of trouble trying to maintain themselves. The questions they asked themselves were mostly personal ones: "what danger does this flash of lightning pose *for me*?" As a result, they tried to allay these fears in a magical or mythical manner. Nature, it was believed, was populated with ghosts and other personalized forces. The only way to control nature was through sacrifice, including human sacrifice.

The second approach, Elias calls detachment. Scientific method enabled man to conquer his fears and to reflect on nature as something that can be controlled, even mastered. By approaching nature in a *detached* way, and by acting as a (supposedly) *objective* observer, man felt less emotionally involved in his experience of nature. His fears disappeared to a large extent and, one could argue, led him, to some extent, to a level of mastery of nature. Questions asked were: "what is it?", or "how does it work?". Successes in physics led to its application to the study of *social* reality. The German philosopher Immanuel Kant played a significant role in this process of application.

Immanuel Kant was an 18th century philosopher who, amongst other things, thought through the conflict between free will and determinism. The scientific method as developed by Bacon, Galileo, Newton and Leibniz (see Buchdahl, 1971) is, basically, about observation. Hypotheses are tested by measuring the actual movements of an object (Chalmers, 1999: 23-40). Such tests suggest causal relations between the movements of an object and the nature of the object. This way of thinking immediately draws attention to the connections between cause and effect using an "if (cause)... then (effect)" structure which is then applied to one or a few particular parts of the whole. In other words, the method isolates causal relations (in an attempt to achieve efficiency of explanation). Therefore, this method is *reductionist*. The attention is focused on (some of) the parts of a phenomenon or object. The parts are supposed to act in a predictable manner. Little or no attention is given to interactions between parts. As one can imagine, Immanuel Kant was very intrigued by this method. However, he had to face, immediately, its flaws. Causality of a "if... then" type left no room for human freedom and morality. In other words, this method could not be applied to *social* reality. After all, humans have free will (Kant, 2003: 48; 129-131; 137-157). Therefore, humans must be subject to a causality based on freedom, not on determinism. Kant had to reconcile autonomy of the individual (freedom) with the context within which the individual is defined (determinism).

In trying to resolve the problem Kant accepted different forms of causality. Besides the causality of nature, he also accepted two other forms of causality, i.e. one for humans, and another for organisms (Heinrichs, 1986; Kemp-Smith, 1984). Kant argued that organisms should be studied as systems. He distinguished a formative process in the course of which parts work together in a functional way to form the whole, or the end product. This is no mere "if... then" idea whereby one takes the parts separately in order to study the essence, or nature of each part, to then put them back together in order to understand the whole. The logic here assumes that the system, the whole, moves towards its final state or end condition which somehow can be known in advance (Brittan, 1978). The parts *function* to form the whole, or end condition (Kant, 2003: 296). The identity of the organism (its end condition) is somehow fixed in advance, and the organism in formation moves towards it.

Although Kant knew that this approach could not explain the emergence of newness (i.e. could not explain novel and unknown forms) the method, he believed, could be useful for the study of social reality. However. Kant also argued that this form of causality could never be applied to (individual) human beings, because *they* have free will. If they hadn't, there would be no sense in having ethics; the world would be reduced to an a-moral place. Therefore, Kant claimed, human actions should be understood according to another form of causality, i.e. one based on rationality.

So the conflict between free will and determinism was resolved by accepting two kinds of causality. One for organisms which are represented as systems that move towards an end form. And rationality for humans who have free will, and who can decide autonomously what they will do. This solution had an important implication. Kant (2003: 129-132) actually argued that humans can not know reality as such. They can only know reality as it *appears* to humans (Brittan, 1978; Friedman, 1968; Parrini, 1994). Kant therefore postulated that nature as such is, by no means, a system. It is humans (e.g. researchers) who can think *as if* nature is a system.

The success of this way of looking at the world led to the abstraction of systemic models which, eventually, came to be considered as reality itself (Van Calster, 2005a; Van Calster & Vander Beken, 2004: 13). This way of looking at reality is of extreme importance today. It has developed into a dominant paradigm in science. It has also deeply impacted upon the social sciences. I will call this way of looking at the world the dominant scientific perspective. I hasten to add that there are – and have been – many scientific attempts to escape from this Kantianism. The work of Michel Foucault (1975; 1988), or Anthony Giddens's structuration theory (1976; 1979; 1984; 1991) may come to mind here (see Van Calster, 2005a). But I shall not deal with those here.

The Dominant Scientific Perspective ...

Social scientists, like all researchers, tend to break down reality into parts in order to then focus their attention on isolated and controllable matters. They draw boundaries around that which they research or investigate. Doing this they make their object of research discernible from the rest of the world. That which counts as the more or less undisputed research program of a particular discipline is then what determines such boundaries (Hoogenboom, 1996: 142; see also Foucault, 1988; Kuhn, 1962). This research program will narrow down the focus of attention to a few recurring research questions.

Typical for this way of doing research is the 'outside' position of the researcher who, furthermore, focuses on functionality. Let us take research on organised crime as an example. Elsewhere I have noted how the body of organized crime related research could broadly be divided into three dominant perspectives (Van Calster, 2006). Researchers in all three perspectives however construct organized crime as a distinct phenomenon, or as an object, and then try to find relations between 'it' and its environment. In each of these perspectives the focus is on organized crime as a goal-driven object. Researchers study each of the parts, such as individuals, organizational structures, tasks and working methods, as a function of the end goal or end product. The *raison d'être* of these parts is the end result and the need to maintain the 'it' of the criminal organization. 'Organized crime' is thus reified as 'a thing' with characteristics of its own. Most researchers therefore tend to distinguish between 'organized crime' as a goal-driven object and its parts. As Vander Beken (et al, 2002: 795–796) argue, the nature of organized crime is not the crime itself, it is the way of its execution. 'Organized crime' exists separately from its activities. In other words 'organized crime' is assumed to be more that the sum of its parts. The characteristics of 'organized crime' are not reducible to those of the parts. Moreover, 'organized crime' functions according to particular principles which are different from those of its parts. As a result, researchers are sometimes obsessed with functionality. Let us have a look at some recent organized crime related research literature pertaining to, e.g. steroid hormone mafia (De Ruyver, et al, 1999), trafficking in human beings (Foster, 1997), car fraud (De Bruyn, 1997), drug cartels (Bullington, 1991; de Kort & Korf, 1992; Jenkins, 1992), violent organizations (Van San et al, 2002), fraudulent criminal organizations (Bologna, 1993; Clarke et al, 2001), smuggling organizations (Jamieson, 1998; Junninen & Aromaa, 1999; Saba et al, 1995), laundry organizations (Beare & Schneider, 1990;Santino 1988; Shana, 1988) and blackmail organizations (Catanzaro, 1994; Nelli, 1976; Roache, 1988). In research such as the above the goals and tasks held by criminal organizations determine their form and nature. Consequently, researchers tend to analyze organized crime and criminal organizations from a *macro* point of view.

In this dominant view processes of functional determination are supposed to underlie the execution and performance of criminal projects. Organizational goals are determined and, in a way, given beforehand, and will in turn determine criminal activities. In this view it is assumed that a determined criminal plan or idea exists before criminal activity – functional to the plan or idea – takes place. This dominant view is capable of explaining stability as well as change, but the pattern of change is always somehow predetermined. No significant change can emerge at the level of the organization itself. This mechanism of determination cannot explain the emergence of protean[2] transformations; it can only explain (slight) variations in performance and execution. This dominant view can only explain the origin of newness and fundamental change by pointing, *ex machina*, to the exceptional qualities or visions of particular individuals (leaders, entrepreneurs, brokers, and so on) who happen to appear within the criminal organization or network. Such individuals, it is then believed, initiate and control new projects and are therefore not subjected (and quite enigmatically so) to mechanisms of determination. This view implies that such individuals actually stand *outside* organizational dynamics, evaluate them, devise a new plan, and prescribe appropriate action, rationally and autonomously. It seems to me that this dominant macro-level approach presents a clinical and mechanical description of life in general and human behaviour in particular. It often ignores complex *micro*-dynamics between individuals and criminal organizations.

However, this dominant scientific perspective achieved many practical successes. Norbert Elias (1990) noticed that these successes tend to produce a growth of complexity[3] in human interactions. For example, more institutions get to be established and become ever-more complicated and more tightly interwoven (Elias, 1956: 232). Take the information wave at the end of the 20th century, which had – and still has – an important impact on the way of (everyday) life (Castells, 1996; 1997; 1998). Because of these changes, people become more dependent on one another (Elias, 1956; 1990). Knowledge grew rapidly en transformed human relations and interactions. Indeed, an increase of technology and prosperity brings about extensive social organisation (Elias, 1990). This in turn had – and has – as a consequence that more social groups – and therefore more individuals – become interdependent for the fulfilment of their needs en their safety. More importantly, all happens in ways that seem to be beyond most people's comprehension. Norbert Elias (1956: 232) uses the metaphor of a chain: 'It is as if first thousands, then millions, then more and more millions walked through this world their hands and feet chained together by invisible ties. No one is in charge. No one stands outside. Some want to go this, others that way. They fall upon each other and, vanquishing or defeated, still remain chained to each other. No one can regulate the movements of the whole unless a great part of them are able to understand to see, as it were,

2 Evoking here the many metamorphoses of Proteüs, the Greek sea god.

3 In this chapter, I will use the concept of 'complexity' as it is used by complexity science.

from outside, the whole patterns they form together.' In other words, the scientific method which aimed for control and mastery over nature, brought about other types of insecurity, uncertainty and powerlessness (see also Nowotny et al, 2001: 1-29). These new problems are an unintended consequence of human interactions: caused by people, but not intended as such (Elias, 1956: 232).

... and Complexity

Elias's description resembles what scientists such as Stuart Kauffman (1993; 1995) and Gregoire Nicolis en Ilya Prigogine (1989) call *complexity*. The latter remark that complexity can not be located in one identifiably place in a system (Nicolis & Prigogine, 1989: 5). Stuart Kauffman (1993; 1995) discovered that complexity is the result of *interactions* between the different components of a system. It manifests itself on the level of the system itself. There is a difference to be noted here between *complexity* and *complication*. Some systems have a large number of components and carry out varied, sophisticated tasks, albeit that they do so in a quite linear manner that can be accurately analysed and precisely described. Such systems are *complicated*. Other systems include intricate sets of *non-linear* relations and feedback loops. Only a few of their aspects can be analysed. The analyses themselves, moreover, always create distortion. These are *complex* systems. On the basis of computer simulations researchers uncovered a few basic principles of *complex* adaptive systems. They discovered that complex adaptive systems constantly produce unexpected results and opposite effects (see Mainzer, 1997). They also found that in complex adaptive systems it is difficult to establish the relation between 'cause' and 'effect'. It is very hard to say what exactly is causing what. The problem gets even worse with coincidental events which look like causes, but are actually relational by nature. This makes it really hard to make specific predictions, regarding complex systems, of future events in a specific place over a specific period of time.

The work of Stuart Kauffman suggests that complex adaptive systems are not built according to a predetermined design, but emerge and evolve through processes of spontaneous self-organisation that produce *emergent* outcomes. If there is a design in complex adaptive systems, it is the design principles of that kind of system itself, i.e. its network type features. Such systems are networks of agents, each driven by iterative, non-linear interactions in the course of which they produce *emergent* outcomes which form patterns. There is an inherent order in complex adaptive systems though, albeit one which nobody could possibly know what it is until it actually emerges. Agents interacting in a complex system may produce newness, but nobody can predict what it will be. In other words, complex systems are best described as self-organising processes which lead to emergent coherence. All attempts to predict long-term futures of (or in) complex adaptive systems, or to change their culture and behavioural patterns, may, or will generate resistance. Little of the planned changes will therefore be achieved. More often than not, such attempts will start unintended changes.

Now, in what way is the dominant scientific perspective dealing with these relatively new and complex problems? As I argued earlier, the dominant perspective developed two ways of dealing with these problems. Each is based on the types of causality. First, there is determinism. This means scientists search for those systems that (seem to) determine human interactions. The causes of what people do are then located in a system which is supposed to determine human behaviour, e.g. economic dynamics, culture, values, mentality, and so on. They are supposed to *precede* interactions, i.e. that through which these interactions develop in a knowable and predictable way. An impression is cultivated here that provided these basic systems are optimal, human actions and interactions could be directed in an orderly (and controllable) fashion. But there is, as we have seen, also 'rationality', and thus individual autonomy. Here the hope is to be able to control the individual action through e.g. incentives. In this perspective many are convinced that it is possible to intervene in human systems in such a way that aims and goals (e.g. in policies envisaged) can be achieved in a controlled way. Unfortunately however, such interventions very often achieve only very little of what was intended. This often leads interveners with no other alternative than to create yet more, or and stronger interventions. These interventions often do produce outcomes, but very often they will be less than effective and efficient (Van Calster, 2005a; 2006). Let us take again the example of organised crime. Neither scientific research, nor criminal policy seems to fully understand what it is. Whichever way scientists, researchers and policy makers try to get a grip on it (in both senses of the term), it seems to elude them, it transforms and shifts, it pops up elsewhere and in other forms, and it constantly changes its MO. It never fails to surprise. Organized crime seems to be a protean phenomenon. As a result, some researchers suggest that an arms race seems to be going on between criminal organizations and governments. McIntosh (1975) suggests that powerful governmental intervention often results in the (unintended) professionalization of organized crime. The fight against organized crime, then, resembles a never-ending cycle in which it becomes necessary to deploy ever more and stronger strategies and measures in an attempt to break the relentlessly inventive resistance of criminal networks. This is not to mention the fact that such strategies often have side effects, such as endangering fundamental rights and liberties, that are perhaps less than desirable (Onsea, 2002). The reason for all this mishap is that the dominant perspective, which was developed and which does an excellent job *for complicated systems,* is seriously lacking when it comes to complex adaptive systems. As I discussed earlier, the researcher in this dominant perspective is assumed to be an objective observer, whose role enables him or her to distinguish stable patterns in 'objects' out there. It is, moreover, this 'outside' position which gives the researcher the impression of control. The focus of research is on the 'whole'. Consequently, the parts, such as individuals, organisational structures, culture, interactions, ... are studied as *functions* of this whole. The parts exist for the sake of the whole and in order to maintain the whole. Problems are defined restrictively e.g. as 'police' and 'justice' matters, which in turn leads to well-defined system-theoretical concepts on for example organized crime. The research 'object' is thus nicely delineated and research is almost invariably characterised by a confirmation of what we already know.

But it seems to me that *complexity* sciences provide us with an important insight. Stuart Kauffman's work (1993; 1995) for example makes us see how many, if not most relations are non-linear and are subject to unpredictable patterns which are in continuous transformation. The development of what has become known as 'chaos theory' during the 1970s was an important eye-opener. 'Chaos' was a powerful metaphor that brought unpredictability under attention, in sciences as well as in governmental matters and everyday life (Gleick, 1989). Chaos theory had an enormous impact. Suddenly 'expert' knowledge appeared to be limited. As a result, the political, social, economic... distance between e.g. government and citizen was reduced even further and traditional power hierarchies erode. Chaos theory seemed to suggest that many 'expert' opinions on determinism and predictability were not tenable (Broer et al, 1995). These insights and findings are completely in line with the work of Ulrich Beck (1986). This sociologist argues that political debates on the topic of safety and security amongst other things are quite hypocrite, since most of the problems which threaten life and society are an additional (and often unintended) product of rules and regulations themselves. Each and every 'solution' unleashes new problems. Interventions and measures often have undesirable, indeed even opposite effects (Van Calster, 2006b). According to Beck (1986) it has become very difficult, if not impossible, to manage new problems with 'old school' laws, regulations and structures. Politics then tends to be reduced to a collection of merely symbolic gestures and manoeuvres that aim to spread the impression that all is under control. Beck argues, just as Elias did in 1956, that western societies in particular produce – in their very attempts at control – all kinds of unintended consequences or side effects over which there is very little control. These side effects were at first hardly noticed, but the increase in the number of relations and interactions, and thus the interdependence and complexity between people, institutes and even nations made them more visible.

The problems mentioned by Beck and Elias ask also attention from a philosophical point of view. One could argue that all kinds of supposed remedies (e.g. penal law) are an important element in the emergence or exacerbation of that which they intend to control. Take risk seeking behaviour. The danger inherent in, and the ban on specific behaviour can themselves be a trigger for engaging in that behaviour. Risk seeking behaviour can become attractive precisely because of the ban that rests on it. The ban plays a role in the construction of enjoyment and danger, which in turn plays a role in the increase on said behaviour, which in turn leads tot more stringent interventions, which in turn ... (and so on). It seems that linear solutions to problems often generate opposite effects. In many western societies we have now reached a point where everyday behaviour is being criminalized (Presdee, 2000) and where measures are taken with an eye on the precautionary prevention of hypothetical, potential, not yet proven problems which might cause damage in the future (Pieterman, 2008).

Let us recap. First, there is the nuisance of non-linearity and complexity. Problems as described by Beck answer to the criteria of complex adaptive systems. Think about the rich interactions that exert influence on each element in the system and which in return become influenced (see Kauffman, 1993; Cillier, 1998). Then there is the assumption of the 'outside' observer. Many researchers tend to assume that their own role is merely one of an observer who does not have any influence at all on what he or she observes. Of course, researchers may take a step backwards, in order to reflect upon what happens. But however sophisticated the level of reflective observation may be, models of the observed system will always be partial. Any model of a system will necessarily neglect *details* and focus on what itself finds important. The model will never comprise the full complexity of the system. As a matter of fact, the system is itself always in constant formation and evolution. Furthermore, such models in turn will act as resources for others to react (upon). A researcher may for instance develop specific insights into the nature of crime and disorder. These insights however will in turn evoke many reactions not just in the scientific community, but also in police services, in politics, or in society more broadly... Let us take the example of organised crime once more.

During the conversations Winlow (2001: 167) had with his 'organized crime' respondents, he noticed, for example, how many of them would imitate Robert de Niro's character in *Goodfellas*. He was told about a raid on a truck, just as the one Joe Pesci and Ray Liotta did in the movie. Remnick (1994: 316–317) reports a similar experience. It came to his attention that one of his respondents imitated the laughter of Robert de Niro's character in *Mean Streets*. Van de Port (2001: 146–156) noticed how the alleged violence of East Europeans as described by academic researchers is often copied by the former. Bovenkerk (2001: 48) writes about Dutch criminal Klaas Bruinsma and the interest he had in books about the mafia. Taussig (1993: 78) calls this "a space (...) in which it is far from easy to say who is the imitator and who is the imitated, which is copy and which is original." Gangsters imitate the characters of Robert de Niro, Joe Pesci and Marlon Brando and in turn provide new material for criminal fictitious heroes (see also Bovenkerk & Yesilgöz, 1998; Mangione & Morreale, 1992; Rudolph, 1993). The same goes for criminal practices and methods (Bovenkerk, 2001). According to Van de Port (2001: 51) criminals are interested in what is written about them and they conscientiously follow up journalistic publications. Criminological knowledge finds its way to criminal milieus and becomes a part of the self-image of criminals who subsequently confess their exploits in these new terms to police and press, whence it returns to academics and criminologists (Van de Port, 2001: 54). Criminological knowledge, as well as policy efforts, structure what organized crime is and how it develops. Consequently, researchers and their work do not stand 'outside' the phenomenon they observe. They could never be mere 'observers'. Researchers inevitably participate in what they research. This is not too extraordinary an insight. The physicist Heisenberg (1962: 19) already claimed that even physicists inevitably participate in the phenomenon they (supposedly) 'objectively' study. Researchers can form certain ideas concerning the nature of criminal organizations, the nature of leadership, the roles in and between criminal networks, and so on. But these are mere interpretations and, indeed *actions* which themselves will call forth particular responses from others, offenders included. This calls for an interpretative methodology.

It seems to me that complexity sciences have uncovered a fundamental shortcoming of systemic (i.e. Kantian) thought and method. Complex adaptive systems are accomplished in and through the interactions between their components, not by the sum of their components, nor by cooperation of parts that produce a pre-determined end product (Goodwin, 1994; Holland, 1998; Gell-Mann, 1994; Kauffman, 1993; 1995). By delineating and dividing the system – any system under observation – the dominant though reductionist method demolishes what it tries to understand. By focusing on functionality and on end products, it neglects the many 'non- functional' transformations and the emergence of newness.

Scientists like Stuart Kauffman (1993; 1995) and Tom Ray (1992) point to the possibilities offered by technology to study non-linear interactions. Technology enables us to study things which we do not fundamentally understand. According to Cilliers (1998) powerful computers are able to simulate the behaviour of complex systems without understanding the complexity of it. In Kauffman's and Ray's computer simulations, each phenomenon consists of a large number of agents, and each agent behaves according to its own interests, intentions, behavioural patterns, and so on. Because the focus lies on an agent-based approach, the object of their research is expressed as a population of agents which interact according their own local "if... then" rules (Mainzer, 1997; Lewin, 1993). Research on complexity does not work with rules, laws or regulations that are deemed valid for the whole population, but, rather, with rules for individual entities that together form a population or system. No agent has ultimate control over the interactions and reactions of others, nor over the behavioural patters of the system, or the way in which the system develops. This approach makes no appeal to someone or something 'outside' the system, who then impose their, or its will.

Stuart Kauffman (1995: 63–64) demonstrates that systems which consist of a large number of randomly interacting agents will develop into connected, autocatalytic networks (see also Mainzer, 1997: 97). In other words, when entities interact with each other randomly, some entities will start to play a part in the constitution of other entities. This is catalysis. Eventually the strings of emerging catalytic interaction will fold back and form autocatalytic networks. This means that entity X will play a part in the construction of entity Y which will play a part in the construction of Z that will play a part in the construction of X[4]. There is no design or blueprint for this network. Interactive cooperation has the intrinsic capacity to produce both transformation and coherence. Both, however, are unpredictable (Mertens, 2000: 91–96). According to Kauffman, variation simply emerges in interaction between entities. The amount and strength of the connection(s) between the entities in a network make up the dynamics of the network (Taylor, 2001: 188).

Notice the difference with the dominant systemic approach. Typical for the systemic approach is the process of reification by which one reduces phenomena to 'things'. Rules of conduct, for example, are supposed to exist outside the system from which they structure and determine the behaviour of the system. As a result, culture for example becomes individualised and attributed with values and motives. The conduct of the members of a system, such as an organisation, is supposed to be determined by the values, or 'culture', of that organisation. Put slightly differently, reification idealises the collective, which is depicted as a personality that structures the conduct of its members. This idealisation, however, distracts attention from the crucial importance, for the emergence of conduct, of everyday interactions. Let me illustrate this with the example organised crime, as observed by Mattijs van de Port (2001: 51).

He noticed that criminals study newspaper and other media coverage conscientiously. "Repeatedly, they told me about television programmes" (translation: PvC). Van de Port mentions a detective who told him that criminals find it very important to be mentioned in television programmes. Many of the criminals studied by Van de Port carry newspaper articles in their pockets. Van de Port tries to explain it with mechanisms such as *blow back* (Naylor, 1997), imitation (Taussig, 1993) en *self-fulfilling prophecy*. However, he admits that these concepts do not fully and adequately describe reality (van de Port, 2001: 55). He places these (dominant) systemic concepts within what he calls the imaginary space (Van de Port, 2001: 45-55). He argues that the world of organized crime is characterized by *not-knowing*. Every question asked by researchers about criminals' motives, about the why of their actions, about the violence in criminal projects, or about the shared life histories of criminals, lead to the imaginary space (the space of not-knowing). This not-knowing should have a central place in the analysis of data collected by researchers, Van de Port claims. "I am convinced that this starting point will eventually lead to a more faithful interpretation of the data collected (...)" (Van de Port, 2001: 55) (translation: PvC). What Van de Port intimates, but fails to put in words, is that all described processes are self-referential. Culture, for example, could not be captured by terms such as 'feedback'. Simply because there is no fixed, external

4 Notice the connection with what I mentioned earlier on the topic of risk seeking behaviour.

point of reference, i.e. 'culture' (see for example Baumann, 1998: 11; Cohen, 1998: 135). Self-reference is a process that tries to provide an answer to the question of how a phenomenon becomes what it is by referring to itself. All given examples (Van de Port, 2001; Van San et al, 2002; Siegel & Bovenkerk, 2000; Winlow, 2001) are self-referential. This suggests that rules of conduct (and therefore values and norms) are functionalized in everyday interactions. Because of that, conflicts are emerging all the time. Those conflicts are constantly negotiated and contested.

Research of complex adaptive systems focuses attention on the processes of interaction in which all, researchers as well government as police and criminals, are involved. As I stated earlier, the researcher can not escape the fact that he or she is part of what he researches. And nobody is able to put in words what the researched phenomenon exactly is, or how it is interwoven with society, myths, research findings, and so on ... All research attempts are bound to lead to so much interpretations.

The Magical-Mythical Nature of the Dominant Scientific Perspective ...

I have so far been arguing that research is often characterized by a dualism between on the one hand attention for systems which (supposedly) explain concrete interactions and behaviours. It is then often assumed that there must be someone or something (e.g. culture, values, or 'mentality') that precedes those behaviours and interactions and that make the latter knowable and predictable. On the other hand, there is also room in such explanations for 'rational' (i.e. cognitive, autonomous) capacities of individuals. I also argued that the practical success of the dominant perspective led to ever more complex forms of interaction, in the course of which ever more people became (and become) interdependent for the satisfaction of their needs and safety. This in turn led to new types of problems emerged. More often than not these new problems were unintended consequences of the aforementioned complex interactions (Elias, 1956). Many attempts to solve these new types of problems generate opposite effects, which often leads to more problems.

With the assumption of the existence of systems that guide behaviour and interaction it seems to me that many social scientists are actually fetishists (see also Van Calster & Verfaillie, 2007). As I argued earlier, the main reason for this is that they tend to reify what they research. Berger and Luckmann (1967: 106-109) defined reification as a way of approaching reality by which social phenomena are seen as being 'apart' from concrete human interactions. When actions are objectified and people experience those actions as being 'outside' themselves, reality may indeed be experienced as something 'out there'. Structures, cultures, rules... are then seen as 'natural' and 'necessary'. Roles and identities also may be the object of 'reification'. In the first case, people identify strongly with the roles they act. As a result they often tend to restrict their degrees of freedom and choice because they assume they have to act according to the position or role they hold. If that happens, identity boils down to the identification of the individual with a particular type. According to Berger and Luckmann, reifications are the result of a process of objectification that is taken too far. Reifications are forms of modern idolatry (Elias, 1956; Van Calster, 2006b). Organisations, culture, organisational structures, laws and regulations are such idolatries, which are idolised as something inevitable and necessary. As a consequence, people tend to believe that dynamics and even change are subject to forces outside their reach on which they can exercise little influence (see also Van Calster, 2005a, 2005c; 2006a; 2006b). They then often assume that human interactions are driven by e.g. economic principles, or by a certain organisational culture, or a regulation, and so on. Responsibility is placed within those systems that are supposed to be in the driving seat. Actors are merely victims and have no or little responsibility for what happens. As a result, it is often believed that human actions can be controlled and steered if these systems are (to an extent inexplicably so) changed. This dominant scientific research perspective has taken a specific form for which Immanuel Kant himself, long ago, warned us. Kant after all argued that humans could never be the subjects of this kind of causality, because it would make ethics and morality impossible.

The dominant perspective has – in the words of Norbert Elias – magical-mythical features. Researchers talk about the economy (e.g. supply and demand market dynamics) and culture as if those are systems which determine behaviour and interactions. This reminds us of the pre-scientific, magical-mythical era: the world is a bundle of forces to which people are relentlessly subjected. This magic-mythical nature is now represented in a rational, scientific language that conceals its mysterious aura. Very few seem to find it odd that the 'economy', 'culture' and all the other systems are considered to be 'things' that, from the outside, determine human interactions. Now this could of course be an effective way to suppress fears, uncertainties and anxieties. However, as Elias (1956) and Beck (1986) observe, the world nowadays is experienced as more capricious, and uncertainty is growing. All attempts to control this capriciousness generate even more problems. And yet, most researchers seem to retain the dominant perspective in an attempt to try and understand social reality.

Research on complex adaptive systems showed that the dominant systemic methods mentioned above are successful for understanding phenomena with a low degree of organisation, but are unsuitable for understanding more complex phenomena with higher levels of organisation, and that are characterised by processes of emergent order. Scientists such as Stuart Kauffman (1993; 1995), John Henry Holland (1995), Murray Gell-Mann (1994) and Tom Ray (1992) made clear that complex adaptive systems that are characterised by a certain level of openness, and by emergence, ask for a different approach. Such characteristics (i.e. emergence, openness, complexity, and so on) can not be derived from the characteristics of the parts. Applying the dominant perspective to complex adaptive systems will only lead to more and new problems.

Now, let us go back to the precautionary principle mentioned at the beginning of this chapter. Just because these new problems are difficult to understand and cannot be controlled, governments and researchers try to intervene even before these problems (including imaginary ones) emerge. Let us take the *collective shop ban* (in Dutch: *Collectieve Winkel Ontzegging*) in the Netherlands. In The Hague, shopkeepers have recently introduced safety measures under the guise of precaution. They are reasoning: since there is no certainty about future threats (or about the lack of them), it is legitimate to intervene now, e.g. by banning particular groups of individuals from shops (Wesselink et al., 2009). In other words, unproven danger gives cause for precautionary measures. One of the implications is that indicidυals and activities are held to be dangerous, unless proven otherwise. Van Gunsteren (2008: 19) puts it this way: "it is not because everybody wants to do harm, but because it is not known who won't" (translation: PvC). Against this background all kinds of security mechanisms are now being deployed. They focus on the prevention of crime and the reduction of fear. To that end techniques such as identification and classification of individuals according to (supposed) degrees of dangerousness are used (Feeley & Simon, 1994; van Swaaningen, 1995). Attention hereby seems to be shifting to the control of potential risks and to interventions before any problem occurs.

Note that the main reason for introducing precautionary measure is based on the assumption of Kant's dualism between determinism (formative process) and 'rationality' (autonomy). Since governments (or other institutions) have little or no grip on non-linear interactions and the choices people make, they expand the system of control as extensively as possible. We now see the genesis of all kinds of models that try to assess potential risks. The profiling of risk is one such model. Profiling assesses specific characteristics of individuals that might classify them as potential offenders. To wit, 'male', 'coloured skin', 'baseball cap' (and so on) ... (Schuilenburg, 2007: 50). It subordinates human action (and thus free will) to a formative, organizing principle. As I argued earlier, this method shows magical-mythical features. It reminds me of the Aztecs who thought that there were certain periods in time when the sun (which they worshipped as a god) would disappear and abandon them (see also Elias, 1956). They tried to persuade the sun to stay with ritual and human sacrifice. Compare this with the way we try to secure safety (our new god) by excluding vagrants from public spaces such as shopping malls. These are also, in a way, human sacrifices.

... Leads to Pseudo-Detachment and Bad Science

Scientists such as Kauffman and Ray compel us to rethink the nature of knowledge and the way we obtain it. Many of today's researchers rarely scrutinise the methods they use and seldom ask themselves whether those methods are able to cope with the problems they address. There is a kind of hardboiled habit among researchers to cling to the dominant, 'systemic' method. But this also leads to a misconceived formulation of problems and to a restrictive selection of research problematics (e.g. with an eye on quick short-term solutions).

The practical success of the dominant systemic perspective and method has led to an increase of levels of interdependence between people (see again Elias, 1956; 1990). This involves strain, tension and conflict. Emerging changes that are the product of concrete human interactions, and that often have forms which were not intended, can have advantages for some, but will be to the detriment of others (see also Elias, 1956). As I have suggested above, the systemic approach assumes that order is imposed by something or someone 'outside' the system[5]. Therefore, the person or group that are facing disadvantage will tend to look for the person or the group that (supposedly) imposed the order. Often overwhelmed by uncertainty, fear, and feelings of vulnerability, they are unable to study the problems in a detached way, like beta scientist do (Elias, 1956: 234). They believe they have little or no control on developments. It is therefore difficult for them to master their emotions. According to Elias (1956: 233), it is precisely this heightened emotionality, in connection with the acute social and political tensions, that block the progress of research in the social sciences. On the one hand there is pressure to bring solutions to problems in the short term, while on the other it is realized that these problems can not be resolved in the traditional (i.e. old style, 'systemic') way. Also, there is this increasing complexity of human relations and interactions. Many researchers resort to a flight in small, nicely delineated research topics. After all, short term solutions to problems ask for quick fixes. But the downside of this is that the acute difficulties posed by the consequences of unmanageable forces of social change, and the mutual frictions and conflicts that go hand in hand with them, keep on emerging (see also Elias, 1956).

Social scientists are very much involved with the problems of the society they observe. Often quite literally so: they try to secure the prosperity of their society; they feel responsible for well-being and welfare they want to protect their own lifestyle (and so on). Norbert Elias (*et al.*, 1997: 152) writes about double binding: a high level of perceived danger or threat leads to high levels of emotionality in human relations and interactions, which, however, hamper a realistic analysis of the dangers and threats, and eventually undercut control efforts.

---

5 Note the difference with complexity science, where order emergence spontaneously.

The researcher's involvement inevitably has an impact on the questions he or she asks. In the debate on security one could distinguish between two opposite positions. On the one hand, there is the position that emphasizes human freedom and its protection by means of human rights interventions and safeguards. Here, we hear once again the argument about individual rationality and autonomy. Authors such as Britta Böhler (2004), Herman van Gunsteren (2004) and Benjamin Barber (2003) point emphatically to the infringement on human freedom and civil rights. On the other hand, there is a focus on the rights and obligations of individuals in society. Here society, or the collective, is considered more important than its individual citizens. This is clearly a formative argument, which puts the collective first. The parts (the individuals) have to accomplish the whole (safety) which is paramount. In other words, the answers given are not so much scientific as ideological. Within their own internal 'logic', both positions make sense. But since they are ideological, discussions never stop, with hardly anyone persuaded by the other position.

These discussions keep generating tensions and conflicts because they continue to turn around the question of what the relation between individual and society should be (an attitude which expresses the observer's involvement), rather than the question of what the relation between individual and society actually *is* (a question that would betray the observer's detachment). The latter is the question with which sociology began. And it is this question that resides at the heart of complexity (social) science. The incapacity to isolate this question from the ideological and political debate is perhaps the most important reason why social sciences are unable to let go of the dominant 'systemic' perspective and method. The dominant perspective and method pose the wrong questions. Theirs is a *pseudo*-detachment. A I argued earlier scientists such as Kaufmann, Holland and Gell-Man teach us that some problems can not be solved and understood properly because they are posed the wrong way. What can reifications tell us when we know they are reifications, magical-mythical constructions?

Exit

In this chapter I argued that scientific debates generate mostly ideological and political statements, rather than scientific ones. This is largely due to the dominant, 'systemic' perspective and method. It is used for the study of *complex* adaptive systems, while it is applicable only to the study of *complicated* systems. This same perspective and method also led to the fragmentation of social research, whereby much, if not most research focuses on selected, delineated problems and issues that are, moreover, often wrongly posed. In the chapters to come, each of the authors will elaborate on alternative perspectives.

References

Barber, B.R. (2003) *Fear's Empire: War, Terrorism and Democracy*, New York: Norton

Bauman, Z. (2006) *Liquid Times: Living in an Age of Uncertainty*, Cambridge: Polity

Baumann, G. (1998) *Contesting Culture. Discourses of Identity in Multi-Ethnic London*, Cambridge: Cambridge University Press

Beare, M.E. & S. Schneider (1990) *Tracing of Illicit Funds: Money Laundering in Canada, User Report 1990-5*, Ottawa, Solicitor General Canada

Beck, U. (1986) *Risikogesellschaft; auf dem Weg in eine andere Moderne* Frankfurt am Main: Suhrkamp

Berger, P.L. & T. Luckmann (1967) *The Social Construction of Reality*, London: Allen Lane, The Penguin Press

Böhler, B. (2004) Crisis *in de Rechtsstaat. Spraakmakende Zaken, Verborgen Processen*, Amsterdam: De Arbeiderspers

Bologna, J. (1993) *Handbook on Corporate Fraud: Prevention, Detection, and Investigation*, Boston: Butterworth-Heinemann

Bovenkerk, F. (2001) *Misdaadprofielen*, Amsterdam: Meulenhoff.

Bovenkerk, F. & Y. Yesilgoz (1998) *De Maffia van Turkije*, Amsterdam: Meulenhoff/Kritak

Brittan, G.G. (1978) *Kant's Theory of Science*, Princeton: Princeton University Press

Broer, K., J. van de Craats & F. Verhulst (1995) *Het Einde van de Voorspelbaarheid. Chaostheorie, Ideeën en Toepassingen*, Utrecht: Aramith

Buchdahl, G. (1971) 'The Concept of Lawlikeness in Kant's Philosophy of Science' *Synthese*, 23, p. 24-46

Bullington, B. (1991) 'Smugglers Paradise: Cocaine Trafficking Through the Bahamas', *Crime, Law and Social Change*, 16, 1, p. 59-83

Castells, M. (1998). *End of Millennium, The Information Age: Economy, Society and Culture Vol. III*. Oxford, UK: Blackwell

Castells, M. (1997) *The Power of Identity, The Information Age: Economy, Society and Culture Vol. II*. Oxford, UK: Blackwell

Castells, M. (1996). *The Rise of the Network Society, The Information Age: Economy, Society and Culture Vol. I*. Oxford, UK: Blackwell

Catanzaro, R. (1994) 'Supply and Demand of Protection in Interpretations of the Mafia: A Reply to Gambetta', *Polis*, 8, 3, p. 456-468

Chalmers, A. (1999) *Wat Heet Wetenschap*, Amsterdam: Boom

Cilliers, P. (1998) *Complexity and Postmodernism. Understanding Complex Systems*, London/New York: Routledge

Clarke, R.V., R. Kemper & L. Wyckoff (2001) 'Controlling Cell-Fraud in the U.S. Lessons for the U.K. 'Foresight' Prevention Initiative' *Security Journal*, Vol. 14, 1, p. 7-22

Cohen, A. (1998) *Self Consciousness. An Alternative Anthropology of Identity*, London: Routledge

De Bruyn, A. (1997) *Firma Fraude. Een Handleiding tegen Oplichters*, Zutphen: Stichting Preventie Economische Criminaliteit

De Kort, M. & D. Korf (1992) 'Development of Drug Trade and Drug Control in the Netherlands: A Historical Perspective', *Crime, Law and Social Change*, 17, 2, p. 123-144

De Ruyver, B., F. Bullens, T. Vander Beken & N. Siron (1999) *Anticorruptiestrategieën. De Aanpak van Corruptie en Beïnvloeding bij de Bestrijding van de Hormonendelinquentie en de Vleesfraude: Een Case-Study*, Antwerpen: Maklu

Elias, N., S. Mennell & J. Goudsblom (1997) *On Civilization, Power and Knowledge*, Chicago: University of Chicago Press

Elias, N. (1990) *Het Civilisatieproces: Sociogenetische en Psychogenetische Onderzoekingen*, Uitgeverij Het Spectrum

Elias, N. (1956) 'Problems of Involvement and Detachment', *The British Journal of Sociology*, 7, 3, p. 226-252

Ericson, R.V. (2007) *Crime in an Insecure World*, Cambridge: Polity Press.

Ewald, F. (2002) 'The Return of Descartes' Malicious Demon: An Outline of a Philosophy of Precaution' in: Baker, T. & J. Simon (eds.) *Embracing Risk. The Changing Culture of Insurance and Responsibility*, Chicago & London: The University of Chicago Press

Foster, T. (1997) 'Trafficking in Human Organs: An Emerging Form of White-Collar Crime?', *International Journal of Offender Therapy and Comparative Criminology*, 41, June, p. 139-150

Foucault, M. (1988) *De Orde in het Vertoog*, Amsterdam: Meppel

Foucault, M. (1975) *Surveiller et Punir. Naissance de la Prison*, Paris: Gallimard

Feeley, M. & J. Simon (1994) 'Actuarial Justice: the Emerging New Criminal Law', in Nelken, D. (ed.) *The Futures of Criminology*, London, Sage, p. 173-201

Friedman, M. (1968) *Kant. Ontology and the A Priori*, Evanston, Ill.: Northwestern University Press

Garland, D. (2001) *The Culture of Control. Crime and Control in the Contemporary Society*, Oxford: Oxford University Press

Gell-Mann, M. (1994) *The Quark and the Jaguar: Adventures in the Simple and the Complex*, London: Abacus

Giddens, A. (1991) 'Structuration Theory : Past, Present and Future', In: Bryant, C.G.A. & D. Jary (eds.) *Giddens' Theory of Structuration. A Critical Appreciation*, London/New York: Routledge, p. 201-221

Giddens, A. (1984) *The Constitution of Society: Outline of the Theory of Structuration*, Cambridge: Polity Press

Giddens, A. (1979) *Central Problems in Social Theory: Action, Structure, and Contradiction in Social Analysis*, London: Macmillan

Giddens, A. (1976) *New Rules of Sociological Method*, London: Hutchinson

Gleick, J. (1989) *Chaos: The Making of a New Science,* London: William Heinemann Limited

Goodwin, B. (1994) *How the Leopard Changed its Spots,* London: Weidenfeld and Nicolson

Gunsteren, H. van (2008). 'Risicoburgers. Veranderende Opvattingen over Burgerschap en Veiligheid', in: Boutellier, H. & R. van Steden (red.). *Veiligheid en Burgerschap in een Netwerksamenleving.* Den Haag: Boom Juridische Uitgevers, p. 11 – 30

Heinrichs, J. (1986) *Die Logik der Vernunfskritik: Kants Kategorientafel,* Tübingen: Francke Verlag

Heisenberg, W. (1962) *La Nature Dans la Physique Contemporaine,* Paris : Gallimard

Holland, J.H. (1995) *Hidden Order: How Adaptation Builds Complexity,* Reading, Mass: Addison-Wesley Publications Co

Holland, J.H. (1998) *Emergence from Chaos to Order,* New York, Oxford University Press

Hoogenboom, A.B. (1996) 'Crisis in de Misdaadanalyse', In: Bovenkerk, F. (red.) *De Georganiseerde Criminaliteit in Nederland,* Deventer, Gouda Quint bv, p. 141-152

Jamieson, R. (1998) 'Contested Jurisdiction Border Communities' and Cross-border Crime. The Case of Akwesasne,' *Crime, Law and Social Change,* 30, 3, p. 259-272

Jenkins, P. (1992) 'Speed Capital of the Worlds: Organizing the Methamphetamine Industry in Philadelphia 1970-1990', *Criminal Justice Policy Review,* 6, 1, p. 18-39

Junninen, M. & K. Aromaa (1999) *Crime Across the Border: Finnish Professional Criminals and Estonian Crime Opportunities,* National Research Institute of Legal Policy, Helsinki, Finland

Kant, I. (2003) *De Drie Kritieken. Een becommentarieerde Keuze,* Amsterdam: Uitgeverij SUN

Kauffman, S.A. (1995) *At Home in the Universe,* New York: Oxford University Press

Kauffman, S.A. (1993) *Origins of Order: Self-organization and Selection in Evolution,* Oxford: Oxford University Press

Kemp-Smith, N. (1984) *A Commentary to Kant's Critique of Pure Reason,* London: Macmillan

Lewin, R. (1993) *Complexity: Life at the Edge of Chaos,* London: J.M. Dent

Mainzer, K. (1997) *Thinking in Complexity. The Complex Dynamics of Matter, Mind, and Mankind,* Heidelberg, New York: Springer-Verlag Berlin

Mangione, J. & B. Morreale (1992) *La Storia: Five Centuries of Italian American Experience,* New York: Harper

McIntosh, M. (1975) *The Organization of Crime,* London: The Macmillan Press

Mertens, R. (2000) *De Ge-heel-de Mens. Een Nieuw Denkkader*, Leuven: Davidsfonds

Nelli, H.S. (1976) *The Business of Crime: Italians and Syndicate Crime in the United States,* New York: Oxford University Press

Nicolis, G. & I. Prigogine (1989) *Exploring Complexity: An Introduction*, New York: W.H. Freeman & Company

Nowotny, H., P. Scott & M. Gibbons (2001) *Re-thinking Science. Knowledge and the Public in an Age of Uncertainty*, Cambridge: Polity Press

Onsea, I. (2002) *De Bestrijding van Georganiseerde Criminaliteit in het Belgische Strafrecht: De Subtiele Grens Tussen Waarheidsvinding en Grondrechten*, unpublished PhD thesis

Parrini, P. (ed.) (1994) *Kant and Contemporary Epistemology*, Dordrecht: Kluwer

Pieterman, R. (2008), *De Voorzorgcultuur. Streven naar Veiligheid in een Wereld vol Risico en Onzekerheid,* Den Haag: Boom.

Pieterman, R. (2006). 'Onzekere Voorzorg Bedreigt Rechtszekerheid', *Nederlands Juristenblad*, 7(1), pp. 2-8

Port, M., van de (2001) *Geliquideerd. Criminele Afrekeningen in Nederland,* Amsterdam: Meulenhoff

Presdee, M. (2000) *Cultural Criminology and the Carnival of Crime*, London en New York: Routledge

Ray, T.S. (1992) 'An Approach to the Sythesis of Life', In: Langton, G.S., C. Taylor, J. Doyne Farmer & S. Rasmussen (eds.) *Artificial Life II, Santa Fe Institute, Studies in the Science of Complexity*, vol. 10, Reading, MA: Addison-Wesley

Remnick, D. (1994) *Lenin's Tomb. The Last Days of the Soviet Empire,* New York: Vintage Books

Roache, F.M. (1988) 'Organized Crime in Boston's Chinatown', *Police Chief*, 55, 1, p. 48-51

Rudolph, R. (1993) *Mafia Wiseguys: The Mob That Took On The Feds,* New York: S.P.I.

Saba, R.P., T.R. Beard, R.B. Ekeland & R.W. Ressler (1995) 'The Demand for Cigarette Smuggling', *Economic Inquiry*, 33, 2, p. 189-202

Santino, U. (1988) 'The Financial Mafia: The Illegal Accumulation of Wealth and the Financial Industrial Complex', *Contemporary Crises*, 12, September, p. 203-243

Schuilenburg, M.B. (2007). 'Een Politiek van Versplintering. Over Enclaves, Denizens en Margizens', in: Boutellier H. & R. van Steden (red.). *Veiligheid en Burgerschap in een Netwerksamenleving*. Den Haag: Boom Juridische Uitgevers, p. 31-52

Shana, A. (1988) *The Pizza Connection: Lawyers, Money, Drugs and the Mafia,* New York, NY: Weidenfeld

Siegel, D. en F. Bovenkerk (2000) 'Crime and Manipulation of Identity Among Russian-Speaking Immigrants in the Netherlands', *Journal of Contemporary Criminal Justice*, 16, 4, p. 230-251

Swaaningen, van, R. (1996) 'Justitie als Verzekeringsmaatschappij'. *Justitiële Verkenningen*, 22(5), 18 p., 80-97

Taussig, M. (1993) *Mimesis and Alterity. A Particular History of the Senses*, New York: Routledge

Van Calster, P. & K. Verfaillie (2007) 'Het Strafrechtsysteem als Narratief Proces. Over de Illusie van Maakbaarheid en Controle', in Van Calster, P., J. Christiaens, E. Enhus, A. Nuytiens, S. Snacken (eds.) *Liber Amicorum Christiaen Eliaerts*, Brussels: University Press Brussels, p. 319-332

Van Calster, P. (2006a) 'Re-visiting Mr. Nice. On Organized Crime as Conversational Interaction', *Crime, Law and Social Change*, 45, 4/5, p. 337-359

Van Calster, P. (2006b) 'Naar een Criminologie van het Lichaam? Over Angst, het Nemen van Risico's, Belevingen en Identiteit', *Justitiële Verkenningen*, 32, 5/06, p. 45-62

Van Calster, P. (2005a) *Georganiseerde criminaliteit als Emergent Fenomeen van Complexe Wisselwerkingsprocessen*, Brussels, PhD thesis

Van Calster, P. (2005b) 'Een Pleidooi voor Wetenschappelijk-Criminologisch Onderzoek naar Micro-Processen oftewel het Vragen van Aandacht voor het Besef dat Criminelen, Rechercheurs en Wetenschappers ook maar Mensen zijn', *Panopticon*, 26, 6, p. 1-8

Van Calster, P. (2005c) 'Georganiseerde Criminaliteit als Emergent Fenomeen van Complexe Wisselwerkingsprocessen', *Panopticon*, 26, 4, p. 83-89

Van Calster, P. & T. Vander Beken (2004) 'Denkers en Doeners. Onderzoekstradities inzake Georganiseerde Criminaliteit in België en Nederland', *Tijdschrift voor Criminologie*, edition '30 jaar NVK - 45 jaar TvC', p. 9-14

Van San, M., E. Snel & R. Boers (2002) *Woninginbrekers en Zware Jongens. Daders uit Voormalig Joegoslavië in Beeld*, Apeldoorn, Risbo, Rotterdam/Politie en Wetenschap

Wesselink, L., Schuilenburg, M. & P. Van Calster & (2009) 'De Collectieve Winkelontzegging in Den Haag', *Tijdschrift voor de Veiligheid* 8, 1, 6-19

Winlow, S. (2001) *Badfellas: Crime, Traditions and New Masculinities*, Oxford, New York: Berg

Assemblage Theory and the Future for Criminology

Don CREWE
Leeds Metropolitan University (UK)

Introduction

What I intend to do in this paper is illustrate some aspects of the utility of what has come to be known as "Assemblage Theory"[1] (Deleuze and Guattari 1987, DeLanda 2006) for considerations of the future for criminology, in particular for the identification of the proper target of criminological inquiry. In other words I will demonstrate that assemblage theory can show us what criminology should be about, or what is, or should be, criminology's object. Whatever the nature of our inquiry, whatever we wish to know, our investigation is possessed of some object: it is *about* something. A significant problem for criminology is that it supposes that its object is crime and events associated with it. The reason this is problematic is because crime is that very thing, the nature of which we *presuppose* our study should reveal. In other words we do not know what our object *is*; we only know what the *supposed* object is called. And here is a further profound problem; if we don't know what 'crime' *is*, we cannot know, indeed, if it is the nature of 'crime' that our inquiry is about: it is not at all clear that 'crime' is, or indeed should be the proper object of criminological study. Paradoxically, we appear not to be able to know what the object of criminological inquiry is until we have finished our inquiry. Some claim this problem is alleviated if we accept the position of commentators like Michael and Adler (1933) who suggest that crime is simply that which is defined as such by the law. Whilst this claim is essentially true at one level, it is problematic, because in the real world laws change and that means that this 'Black Letter Law' way of defining crime cannot account for any essential feature of the supposed criminological object, crime. In fact, it makes questions concerning the nature of crime redundant because all we would have to do is to look up what the law said on any particular topic. Of course, we are aware that other commentators have said that it is fallacious to attempt to identify the nature of crime or to try

1 This is not intended as a complete or definitive account of assemblage theory, but merely of some aspects as they may apply to the future for criminology. For an authoritative account readers should turn to DeLanda 2006. Some aspects of what I have to say indeed do not find expression in assemblage theory. I hope to point to the origins of those ideas as we meet them in the text.

to isolate any quality that is peculiar to criminal acts, because the fact that the law changes shows us that criminality does not inhere in any quality of an act. Labeling theorists take this view and suggest that criminality inheres in people's reactions to acts and putative offenders' reaction to *that* reaction. That is, the offender persists in acting in a particular way because he[2] internalizes the label given to him by people who have reacted to his earlier offending. It will be apparent that this view presents two problems. The view appears to suggest that there *is* a particular quality to criminal acts, namely that of deviance, however, this view does not tell us what kind of acts might be classed as deviant, or which forms of deviance come to be crystallized in law as crimes, or, indeed, how this happens. The second problem is that whilst this view tells us that crime is deviance, it cannot tell us why primary deviance occurs.

There is another major body of theory that sees the criminological object as deviance. This body of theory suggests that deviance occurs when controls are insufficient, deficient, or reacted against. These theories occupy a large proportion of criminological theorizing. They stretch from the Chicago school theories of Park and Burgess (1925), through strain theories and subculture theories to more contemporary rational actor and control theories. A significant problem is taken to exist with all theories that postulate deviance as the object of criminological study, and that is that not all harmful acts are deviant (or illegal) leaving us unable to talk about significant portions of what have come to be known as corporate, white collar, or organized crime.

More recently, some criminologists, most notably Henry and Milovanovic (1994) have suggested that the law, criminality and social structures are ineluctably intertwined. In this view, the law is not merely a set of over-arching rules, but a flexible structure that is bound up with the norms and cultures found in all walks of life. According to many postmodernists what constitutes the criminal, or what behaviours are deemed harmful is governed by discourse. Discourses are a facet of 'power/knowledge' that delimit what constitutes acceptable speech in a given matter. In *The Order of Things* Foucault (1970[1966]) tells us that discourses are made up of the statements of 'experts'. These experts are deemed such because they speak from within the discourse. They thus have the power to define the discourse, defining what lies within, and what without the discourse. This of course means they define who can count as an expert. The law (and thus what is criminal) is seen as resulting from the processes of discourse that create the criminal as subject of the law (see in particular Smart 1992). It should be clear, therefore that discourse and that which is subject to it is self defining. It is in this claim concerning the power of such discourses that much postmodernism is revealed as itself being the subject of its own discourse (Einstadter and Henry 1995), because if all such 'power/knowledge' is constituted in discourse, then postmodern criminology is

2 Throughout this paper I use the masculine neuter pronoun.

no less a discourse. In other words, where this view is concerned, criminology is seen to *create itself by creating itself as its own object.*

This, of course is very much an oversimplified view, but I hope to have suggested the scale of the difficulties, indeed the conventionally intractable nature of debates concerning the criminological object. Nonetheless each of these perspectives is 'criminological', they presuppose the ontological reality of some defined or definable criminological object: crime, criminal, or process of law, indeed, even Hulsman's (1986) statement that crime has no ontological reality suggests that such an object – criminalization – exists as the *product* of criminal policy. In order to provide criminology with an identifiable object that is not merely presupposed nor the creation of the inquiry itself, it is necessary to suggest the nature of the social processes within which that object would operate without recourse to that object. This is so because we don't know what that object is. Thus it is my intention to proceed along the following lines; I will outline the nature of social structures and processes as conceived of in assemblage theory and show that certain events occur in that model that in some ways resemble those entities that we have previously *presupposed* to be the object of criminology. However, it will become plain that in this view these events or entities do not have any essential properties, functions, or causes, but are events emergent from complex processes of assemblage and disassemblage.

Totalities and Assemblages: Interiority and Exteriority

Totalities and Interiority

It has long been the dominant view of social structure that it is a whole – a totality – made up of parts. Those parts have been taken to be its various institutions and other collections of individuals. On this view, societies are made up of government, police, army, health service, educational institutions, civil service, unions, clubs, families, companies and so on. The society thus formed is a whole. It is the sum of all its parts, and each of those parts has certain properties which delimit their function in maintaining the whole. Thus, on this view, if we take away one of these elements, the society is no longer whole. Each element in this kind of picture of society exists in a reciprocal relationship with its neighbours that is dependent upon the *properties* of each element. These relationships so conceived are referred to as "relations of interiority" (DeLanda 2006:9). This mode of description of societies has a long tradition, the height of which, it may be suggested is the work of Talcott Parsons[3]. In this view, the

3 Incidentally, this is still true of the work of Giddens (1979 & 1986 *inter alia*), agency and structure – routines and cultural resources – mutually instantiate one another dialectically, presenting a continuous flow of action which contributes to a social whole, each element having its

elements of a society exist because they serve a function in sustaining that society as a stable whole. This view prohibits any account of phenomena that are not reducible to those parts because the whole is *no more than* the sum of its parts. Why, you may ask, is this a problem? If we imagine our police force as being constituted by the *properties* (aligned with functions) of the individual policemen, how do we conceive of roles or functions or properties, or indeed a functioning whole in the absence of one of them through sickness let's say? First, we might suggest that the police force is no longer whole. This would mean that it was no longer fully functional. However, we know that the sick officer's colleagues will alter their properties (their function – what they do) to accommodate the absent officer. We would then have to say, one of two things; either the policeman was surplus to requirements – in other words he served no function and therefore was not a part of the functioning whole, or the force is not whole now: there is one policeman missing. Either this is the case or its function must have changed, and if that is the case, so must the function of all the reciprocal elements of the society of which it is a part. What this means is that views that reduce structures merely to the sum of their parts – that view societies as totalities – can have no account of change. Clearly the world is not fixed and does change and thus we need an account that permits change. We might say that the societies are not in a state of being but in a process of becoming.

Assemblages and Exteriority

The dominant challenge to this view of societies comes from assemblage theory. What have been conceived of as wholes are here conceived of as *assemblages* of entities. The relationships between entities are held to be products of their *capacities* (what they *can* do) and the relationships are referred to as "relationships of exteriority" (DeLanda 2006:10). Whereas in the old view the dominant metaphor invoked the various functions of the organs of the body, where the properties and functions (co-conceived) of each organ reciprocally contribute to the body as a whole (totality), Deleuze and Guattari (1988) conceive of assemblages of different species. Symbiotic relationships such as that between bees and plants are based upon the capacities of each. Whilst it is true that the relationship is functionally necessary to the well-being of plant and insect, it is merely contingently so: the bee and the plant have come to rely on one another's *capacities* through evolution, and at some point in the future this assemblage will cease to exist in its current form. Individual elements may be removed from one assemblage and inserted into another without changing their capacities, but whilst changing their properties. We can see that it is wit-

---

own function in generating or maintaining that whole. This whole is analyzable only as an aggregate of the properties or functions of its internal elements: that is, it is reducible to them.

hin the *capacities* of our absent policeman's colleagues to adapt and cover for his absence. Similarly, in assemblage theory, an ecosystem is not a finished, functional whole, but an assemblage of the thousands of different plant and animal species. A point to which I shall return, is that each of those species, and indeed each of the individuals within that species is also an assemblage. This view deprives conventional organismic theories of their primary metaphor, the whole, immutable organism, since the organism's boundaries are arbitrary and its constituents historically contingent. Furthermore, that contingency removes the possibility of essentialism, since all essences are seen in the historical long view to be contingent. We tend to think, for example, that the essence of all matter is that it is made of atoms. DeLanda (2006) points out that whilst today's chemist may reduce all atoms (and thus all matter) to collections of protons, neutrons, and electrons, such an essentialist (reductivist) view does not hold true immediately after the "big bang" when protons, neutrons, and electrons were yet to be formed. This particular essence is historically contingent. The phylum *chordata* consists only of creatures with backbones, not because backbones are the essence that makes these creatures what they are, but because only creatures with backbones have been included. This is called 'taxonomical essentialism'.

The view of assemblages as co-evolutionary relationships of historical contingency means that assemblage is always a process: a becoming. Furthermore, because elements can be removed as well as inserted into the assemblage, assemblages are always unbecomings too. These (dis)assembling processes are characterized by movements of intensification and homogenization, or of dissipation or heterogenization. These movements are respectively referred to as territorialization, and de-territorialization. Thus assemblages have qualities such as density, homogeneity, scale, or speed, for example.

Assemblages (or their elements, which are also assemblages) are also defined in terms of their position along two primary axes. One identifies an element according to its role in stabilizing or destabilizing this process of territorialization: sharpening or blurring the boundaries of the assemblage. The other stretches between the material and the expressive. Both identify roles that can be mixtures, an element may have various roles according to its various capacities. The picture here then is one where the concept of assemblage deconstructs the organismic whole as a reified structure with limited scope to describe the complexity of the fluid nature of the world of interrelationships between elements.

People as Assemblages

Having deconstructed the notion of societies as totalities, and suggested a way of conceiving of collective entities as assemblages, what I intend to do now is to address the internal elements of such assemblages. Above, I suggested that the constituent parts of an assemblage may be assemblages themselves, and, when we consider institutions or other social structures as assemblages, then, humans themselves, as *their* internal elements, may be considered simultaneously as assemblages and elements of assemblages. Deleuze and Guattari (1988) offer an image which brings us closer to this realization. Drawing upon an incident related in Freud they describe a child distressed by the sight of the driver of a carriage abusing his horse. The horse has collapsed and is dying, whilst the driver continues to whip it. For Deleuze and Guattari, the Horse-carriage-driver-whip is an assemblage, but so is the horse, and this is crucial.

> The horse is a list of active and passive affects in the context of the individuated assemblage it is a part of: having eyes blocked by blinders, having a bit and a bridle, being proud, having a big peepee-maker, pulling heavy loads, being whipped, making a din with its legs, biting, etc. These affects circulate and are transformed within the assemblage: what a horse 'can do'. (1987:257)

So, as the horse is an assemblage and the observing little boy, so are we also assemblages. But the strong insistence here is that we cannot know what any assemblage is until we know what it "'can do"'.

Human beings, however, have a special way of being[4], so they have a special way of being assemblages: that is, there is something special that humans can do. Husserl (1976 [1913]) tells us that rather than representing to ourselves some real object or other, we actively constitute that object. However, we can only constitute objects that are meaningful to us, and we can only constitute those objects that are coherent – 'compossible'. Thus, it is taken by many that humans have the *capacity* to engage with the world in a peculiar way in that, for them, there are two kinds of entity – objects and subjects: the latter representing to itself the former. This gives humans the capacity to see *themselves* as objects; moreover, it gives them the capacity to see themselves as objects of the future (see Heidegger 1996 [1926]). That is, they have the capacity to exercise will toward their imagined becoming. One element of humans as assemblages then, is the capacity to see themselves and others as beings, and to see themselves and others as beings of the past, but they can also see themselves and others as becomings. In order to move from the complete beings – of the infinitesimally temporal totality – of the present, it is axiomatic that they must adopt some currently un-possessed supplement to their existing selves to complete the being of the immediate future. This is because, as Bergson (1992) points out, no two states for humans are ever identical, therefore something new, something *additional* must have been added to the being of the present to make the being of the new present. We are assemblages of all of these supple-

4 This is not to suggest any essentialism but merely durability of this capacity.

ments[5] and we refer to our disposition to future additions or supplements as having will towards the assemblage that would be produced. We have the capacity to view ourselves as objects of the future. Thus we have will to complete ourselves, (I have spoken about this "will to self consummation" and expanded upon it at length elsewhere Crewe 2007 & Crewe 2009) and we do so by the constant adoption of new supplements to our existing assemblages. The problem in the social world, however, is that we are not free to choose to see ourselves in any way: merely in ways that we can imagine. Imagination, however, is not infinite; it is dependent upon our experience of others: it is conditioned by our experience of the world, by our background, by our ethnic heritage, by our socio-economic status, by our culture. Furthermore, we are not free to adopt any supplement that we choose from our imagination because there are processes at work that have the power to prohibit the adoption of certain supplements that we might choose (this is not necessarily the same as what are referred to in criminological theory as social controls). I shall return to this matter of constraint later. Nonetheless, we may summarize the nature of the human assemblage by saying that it is the product of constrained will, where each supplement adopted to satisfy our will, past present and future, is an element in that assemblage which is us.

People and Assemblages: When is a Culture?

Because as individuals we are assemblages of all the supplements that we have adopted to create new assemblages in our attempts to fulfill what I have termed our 'will to self consummation', and those supplements and the assemblages that we imagine them creating are drawn from our experience, the supplements and the resulting assemblages are similar in many ways. For example, it has taken people in the UK a long time to envisage themselves as the kind of people who eat garlic. This is in part because as individuals we may not have any acquaintances who eat garlic whom we should like to be like, or whom we wish to impress by being cosmopolitan enough to eat garlic. We may believe that the odour on our breath will cause people who don't eat garlic to shun our company. We may feel that it makes us appear 'French' and therefore unsavory in some 'foreign' way. These are forces of territorialization. They permit the establishment of an homogenizing group of people who don't eat garlic: they promote a non-garlic-eating culture. It is the contiguity of our experiences which provides the sense of coherence between each of our various perceptions of objects that must of necessity be otherwise entirely heterogenous. That is, the coherence of 'compossible' objects which Husserl (1977

5 Actor Network Theorists call these supplements extensions see for example Callon 1986, and Latour 1988 *inter alia*.

[1931]) explains through the 'transcendental subject', for example, far from being transcendent is immanent in our everyday association of one with the other. It is formed in the continuous association of ideas through relations of temporality and topicality, their association or negation through conceptions of similarity or alterity, our constant association of cause with effect. This provides an assemblage constructed of capacities, and capable of emergent properties and capacities, one of which is to make our communal objects comprehensible to one another (as subjects) and coherent in relation to one another (as objects). This is what we speak of when we speak of a culture: cultures are those assemblages of people (rather, since all assemblages are either becoming or un-becoming, collectivities that are in the *process* of being made up of people) that permit the coherence of the representation to themselves of objects or meanings. Cultures occur when the collectivities adopt assembling processes that permit the emergence of the capacity to make comprehensible; to promote the unification of sense making, and the homogenization of meanings, styles, representations, and other affects. The resultant consensus is a product of the sense making capacities emergent from that culture. The similarity of its products, affects and representations are emergent properties and capacities of that culture. It is an emergent property of the *capacity* of the culture to do that. That is what the culture does. When it does this, it is a culture

Scale: Friendships and Institutions

We have insisted above that assemblages have as one of their qualities temporality. All assemblages – which all cultures are, which all institutions are – are on their way somewhere, they are in the process of becoming and unbecoming, forming and dissolving, producing or destroying, appropriating or rejecting, often simultaneously. This temporality also means that assemblages or cultures have the property of durability or stickiness. This quality may be brought to mind when we look at the English aristocracy which has managed to perpetuate itself (with a few minor hiccups) for nigh-on ten centuries. The older and more stable an assemblage, the more *likely* it is to have the capacity to survive to get even older and more stable.

Assemblages have as another of their qualities density. The Anglican Communion is a religious culture that is noted for its heterogeneity, the Roman Catholic Church, less so: it is more homogenous. The "concentratedness" of belief in a belief system might be characterised in terms of the density of an assemblage. Moreover, the more dense an assemblage, the more dense it is *likely* to have the capacity to become.

There is one other quality of human assemblages that I should like to introduce, and that is a quality which I will call "practiced". The more ritualised (for example) a culture becomes, the more dense it is *likely* to have the capacity to become. The more a group of friends see each other, the more likely they are to have the capacity to see more of each other. Old university friendships have a tendency to fade away as the extensions that join the assemblage together get stretched and less practiced. The assemblage gets less dense, and thus less durable. The assemblage thus weakened is less capable of homogenizing meanings.

Cultures as assemblages also have, of course, the quality of scale. It is imperative that we note that they need not have any *particular* scale. They may possess any scale, but scale is a quality possessed by assemblages that is not to be ignored. That is, where two or more people interact to begin to homogenize or make comprehensible to one another (share) their meanings, we have a culture. We also have cultures that consist of many millions of people. Depending on which group of meanings we wish to select, we can talk about a Chinese culture, for example, and this, of course, involves a significant proportion of all living humans. In the realm of scales somewhere in between friends and humanity, we have assemblages of varying scales. These cultures –the Home Office, the Fire Brigade, Richmond Borough Council, the Boy Scouts – are relatively large, relatively dense, relatively slow, relatively practiced and not surprisingly, powerful. We tend to refer to such cultures, such assemblages, as institutions. In the next section we shall see why power is associated with these qualities of assemblages. Assemblages are made up of elements that are themselves assemblages and we should recall that one of the axes along which we may place an assemblage or internal element is the axis that distributes between elements that tend to territorialize and elements that tend to deterritorialize. Larger, denser, more practiced assemblages have the tendency to possess the capacity to increase their power to territorialize. Large assemblages *tend* to get larger.

Assemblages and Power: Power Equates to *Can*

Having very briefly sketched some of the qualities of assemblages that involve people and characterized them as what we mean when we speak of cultures or institutions, it is now incumbent upon me to show why this way of conceiving of culture is useful in our study of the nature of crime, transgression, and deviance. There is one other thing, however, that we need to do first. Earlier I suggested that human conduct can be summarized by saying that it is the product of constrained will. If we accept that we have will, divorced from arguments concerning freedom or determination[6], then we have to ask: What are the (social) mechanisms constraining that will? That is, if we have will and we cannot do everything that we will to do (i.e. have *free* will), someone or something has the *power* to stop us doing that thing. The concept 'power' has proven

6 See my 2007 & 2009 and Nagel 1987

to be amongst the most slippery concepts in the whole of the social sciences. Nonetheless, I shall attempt to show briefly how this concept is illuminated when social collectivities are viewed in terms of their capacities rather than their properties: that is, as assemblages.

We have stated that we can only know what an assemblage is when we know what it *can do*. What something can do is its capacity. Power is about what you can do. Assemblages are made of capacities; thus they are made of power in varying degrees, that is, "all reality is already a quantity of force" (Deleuze 1983:40). The point here is that power is emergent from assemblages. Deleuze and Guattari (1987:399) illustrate this notion of the emergence of power from processes of assemblage through the idea of the man-hammer. Neither the man nor the hammer has the capacity to knock in nails, but together this assemblage has this capacity. Thus we might suggest that power emerges from the assemblage. This shows how cultures can come to have capacities to affect the outcome of human will, when conceived of as assemblages. Supplements adopted into assemblages have the *disposition* (always, but to varying degrees) that they can imbue *capacities* upon those assemblages. They bring their own capacities and in so doing new capacities *emerge*. Power, we might say, is the property emergent from the *adoption* of extensions that imbues assemblages with the capacity to affect change. We must point out that this capacity is always in conflict (successful or otherwise) with the capacities of others – "[t]he essence of a force is its quantitative difference from other forces, and the quality of the force in question is constituted by this quantitative difference" (Deleuze 1983:50). When the policeman joins the police he creates a new assemblage, from which process of assembling his power emerges. Each day he goes to work he re-assembles that assemblage. That is why he still retains that power of arrest when having a cup of tea at work, but loses it when he goes home to his family. Moreover, he has significant power because the assemblage which he is involved in constituting is massive, dense, slow (old), practiced. It involves all the assemblages of the law, the police force, the judiciary the government and the state: their histories, presents and possible futures. Governments are more powerful than crowds of demonstrators, even in their millions. Power emerges from the formation of assemblages in proportion to their scale *and* durability – crowds of demonstrators dissipate relatively rapidly. Power is, as Morriss (2002) argues, a disposition, but it is also, as insisted upon by Hindess (1982), situated. Power is an emergent dispositional property of situated, territorializing processes of assemblage. What all this means is that power is self replicating and self defining: power merely equates to *can*.

The Normalizing Power of Cultures as Assemblages

Originating at least in part in the phenomenological account of humans' experience of the world of others alluded to above, what has come to be known as 'Symbolic Interactionism' tells us how social groups bring about the homogenization of meanings[7]. Following from our capacity to represent to ourselves both ourselves and others as objects, we become aware of differences and similarities between ourselves and others who are neither entirely similar nor entirely different. Crucially, because we can see similarities between ourselves and others, we can conceive of the way in which certain of our behaviours may be viewed by them. That is, we may wish to constitute ourselves in a particular way. We may wish to appear like a hip-hop star, for example. We can view ourselves as the object of the future created by the adoption of the supplements – behaviour, dress etc – that would effect this transformation. We can conceive of the reaction of others similar to ourselves and we *may* choose to alter our aspirations for ourselves. We may normalize ourselves, we may homogenize our behaviour with that of others (behave as territorializing assemblages) every bit as much as we may choose to be different (behave as *de*-territorializing assemblages). The expectation of what others are like and how they will behave is known as 'typification'. Altering our behaviour to fit in with these typifications is known as 'behaving to the generalized other'. However, neither the typifications nor the behaviour of those typified is fixed, they are negotiated in 'the situation' and what those typifications and behaviours are is altered by the 'definition of the situation'. A situation is 'defined' as one in which certain meanings are agreed upon, meaning that certain behaviours become normal or acceptable. The greater the power to define the situation, the greater the power to affect certain kinds of behaviour. The more people who internalize those norms, the greater the scale and therefore power of that cultural assemblage to cause others to internalize those norms. The single individual turning up at the Royal Opera House dressed as a gorilla will be made (at least) to feel most uncomfortable by a large assemblage of people exhibiting the cultural artefact that involves wearing a dinner jacket and black bow-tie to the opera. The larger, more durable assemblage is more able to define the situation as one where gorilla suits are not normal. The wearer of the gorilla suit's behaviour should undergo homogenization; he should go and change into his penguin suit! Various qualities of assemblages are involved in complex ways. However, by and large, scale, density, slowness, practicedness, all contribute to domination of the definition of the situation. Behaviour to the generalized other promotes normalization and homogenization of meanings, styles, representations, and behaviours. Definition of the situation defines which meanings, styles, representations, and behaviours are acceptable, or normal and therefore, by extension, those which are unacceptable. The power to normalize thus tends to be self-replicating, giving rise to the situation that the power to normalize tends to increase the density of the assemblage increasing the power to normalize.

---

7 A particularly clear account of Interactionism is to be found in Hewitt 1997 [1976], and, of course, in Blumer 1969.

I use the locution 'tends to' because there is of course a flip side to this. He who is deviant performs a deviant act. This act of deviance, particularly if it is transgressive, is a de-territorializing event. Broken free from the constraints of the merely normal, the deviant may continue constructing new meanings and new expressions of his view of himself as an object of the future. At some time, his path will intersect with others who will see in him desirable aspects for their future selves and thus a new seed of a new assemblage or culture is formed. It will be apparent that this de-territorializing and new territorializing process is consistent with the formation of sub cultures (we are currently very concerned about the sub cultures we call gangs). Cultures are *sub*-cultures while they remain relatively small, heterogenous, less dense, less practiced, short lived and so on.

Assemblage, Culture, Crime

What is different from the normal is deviant. People who fail to internalize the norms defined in any situation are classed as deviant people. People who *choose* to be deviant in the full knowledge of that deviance are transgressive. The *production* of any norm axiomatically makes a deviant of anyone who contravenes that norm. The choice of which supplements to adopt in the process of becoming is dependent upon the history, present and the imagination of each individual. Some will make choices that are made deviant because others have the capacity to – they *can* – define the situation as one where their norms are established over the choices of becoming of others. It is qualities belonging to the assemblage – culture, institution – such as scale, age, practicedness, density, and so on, that imbue that culture with the capacity to do this over others. The supplements that people choose in their acts of becoming – in their process of 'self consummation' – are not the product of *free* will but of will that must be conceived of outside notions of freedom or determination (see Crewe 2009a). Thus becoming deviant is not a matter of choice, nor of determination, it is a matter of the limits placed upon one's imagination in conceiving of oneself as an object of the future. It is furthermore a matter of the constraints placed upon choices – concerning style, behaviour, or meanings – thus made by those with the power to define those choices as acceptable or otherwise through definition of the situation. Larger, more durable assemblages have greater capacities to define the situation. They have greater capacities to define the situation as one whose norms require the creation of legal definitions should they be breached. These are the cultures or institutions with the power to – that *can* – criminalize. The complex, fluid nature of assemblages means that norms change. Each assemblage is an event with a certain duration. Each iteration of this event is different. The nature of criminalization is to ossify in law what would otherwise be a fluid transgression of complex, fluid norms. Thus the law is necessary to 'fix' the concept crime. Hence, the concept crime *creates* law. Crime in this view is the inevitable effluent of assembling processes of cultures and institutions.

Deterritorialization and Complexity: Will, Deviance, and Transgression

I have suggested elsewhere (Crewe 2009a & 2009b) most strongly that human behaviour should be viewed as the outcome of constrained will. What I have been talking about in much of the above, it will be apparent, involves aspects of the constraint of actors to conform in ways that homogenize meanings and have territorializing effects on collectivities. You will recall, that I pointed out above, that assemblages, and elements of assemblages (as assemblages themselves) may be placed upon an axis that represents their tendency to territorialize or to deterritorialize. I wish to talk now about the other side of the coin, deterritorialization, and I shall do so, relating this idea to will. Will is always bound up with possibilities. It is the recognition, according to Heidegger, that death is 'the possibility of the impossibility of every way of comporting oneself towards anything, of every way of existing' (1996:307) that makes us realize that our lives are full of possibility. Furthermore, those possibilities presented to us are always greater in number than one: we always have choice. This of course means that the territorializing forces referred to above can never be totalizing. If that were the case then, once again, as with functionalist accounts of societies, we should be left with an account that was unable to account for change in the world. What this means is that there must be at work events that tend to deterritorialize, and in assemblage theory these forces are related to ideas of complexity (dissipative systems, far from equilibrium systems, catastrophic systems, complex systems, systems exhibiting self-limiting criticality, self organizing systems and so on) and, whilst DeLanda doesn't use the term, to Deleuze and Guattari's notion of *lines of flight*. In criminological terms these deterritorializing events are often related to deviance. However, since deviance is not necessarily willful, it is the notion of transgression as presented to us in the work, most famously of Jack Katz (e.g. 1988) and of Jeff Ferrell (e.g. 2006) for example, that best captures the deterritorializing moment in criminological thinking.

Deterritorialization

Deleuze and Guattari describe deterritorialization as a 'coming undone' of an assemblage 'where the flows cross the threshold of deterritorialization and produce the new land ... where the person who escapes causes other escapes, and marks the land while deterritorializing himself' (Deleuze 1983:332). An 'assemblage has both *territorial* sides ... which stabilize it, and *cutting edges of deterritorialization*, which carry it away' (Deleuze and Guattari 1987:88). Furthermore these deterritorializations are 'not only physical and mental, but spiritual – not only relative but absolute' (Deleuze and Guattari 1994:68). Thus the thought or will that causes the deviant behaviour is a deterritorializing 'line of flight' as is the physical relocation of the behaviour to a place where it might begin reterritorializing. It is this concept that represents Deleuze and Guattari's account of freedom as a non-voluntaristic change of the state of an entity. Thus, deterritorialization represents the creative *capacities* of an assemblage, it frees a body from its fixed relations in an assemblage, and opens it up to reterritorialization and the possibility of new assemblages. It also represents the freedom of the actor to generate his own life project inasmuch as it is not constrained. It should be pointed out that deterritorialization and reterritorialization are simultaneous processes: in the very moment that I separate myself from the herd, I begin the formation of a new herd. In that moment that I deviate from the dominant culture I plant the seed of a new subculture. And a dominant culture might deterritorialize me, in that it might move to a place where I do not will myself to be.

Territorialization, Deterritorialization, and Complexity

Deterritorialization is bound up with complexity. That is, not that it is complex in that it is difficult to understand, but that it operates in ways that have been identified by the body of study known as 'Complexity Studies'. There are two kinds of complex behaviour that I wish to invoke here, namely 'self organizing systems' and the behaviour known as 'bifurcation' typical of the Lorenz attractor (Lorenz 1993).

It is taken by thermodynamics that all systems are leaky or 'dissipative'. They leak energy into and out of bordering systems and thus affect, and are affected by them. This increases the number of degrees of freedom in the system to an unknown degree. Some of these dissipative systems, when in far from equilibrium states, exhibit self organizing properties. This characteristic is illustrated by the appearance of the loops of convection known as Bérnard cells in liquids (see fig 1).

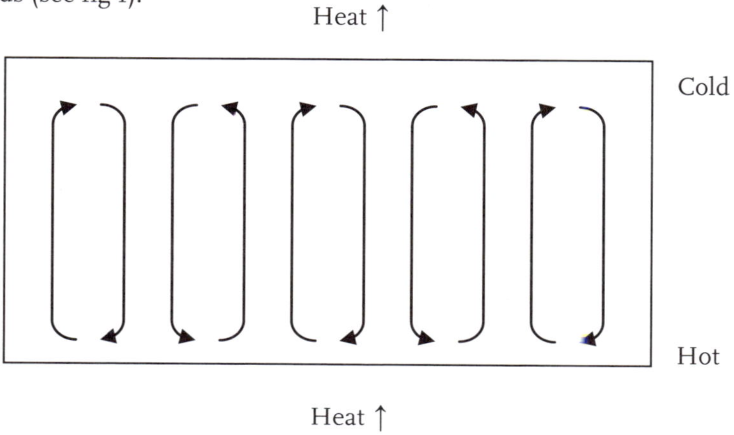

Fig 1. Bérnard Cells.

Energy in the form of heat is introduced to the system from the bottom and the system 'dissipates' energy from the top, producing the highly stable cells at far from entropic conditions. The point here is that nonequilibrium thermodynamics and the study of dissipative structures suggest that complex systems exhibit the capacity for self-organizing. Such self-organization is represented in assemblage theory by territorializing processes that tend to homogenize assemblages. A particularly important issue, however is that all systems are dissipative. No matter how clearly we define them for the purposes of experiment or explanation the *definitional* boundary is merely that. The actual boundary is porous, increasing the degrees of freedom to an unknowable degree. This makes all systems, in the nth degree, unpredictable at least on the micro scale. However, even if a virtual system can be defined in clearly delineated, mathematical terms with a relatively small number of degrees of freedom this problem of predictability will not go away. As Lorenz found (1993) relatively simple systems, given starting points that differ by microscopic amounts can exhibit behaviour where for a period the two systems will produce the same result, but after a time their behaviour diverges markedly in an entirely unpredictable way. This is known as bifurcation and is the reason for failures in predictions of weather systems amongst other things. What this observation contributes to the present discussion is this. Even in a highly homogenized assemblage where many of the people involved have highly similar pasts, highly similar views, highly similar behaviour, their future behaviour is likely to bifurcate unpredictably from the homogenous behaviour of the assemblage. This is true even of the simple, determined, and closed system of the Lorenz attractor, it is even more the case when the number of degrees of freedom of the system is great or unknown. Any system has embedded within it the seeds of deterritorialization.

Complexity and Will

The formation of will is complex. The behaviour of complex systems that I have spoken about above known as bifurcation shows us that people who, to all intents and purposes have the same background and experiences will always have sufficient difference, no matter how small, to produce markedly different outcomes. This comes about even where choices are severely restricted as we know to be the case in socioeconomically deprived backgrounds. What we choose for ourselves, even in restricted circumstances, will always differ in some respect from the choices of others, even among those who are considered conformists. This means non-conformity. Non-conformity is deterritorializing, it serves to heterogenize the assemblage. What I can will for myself as an object of the future, may be drawn from a very limited store of possibilities that are presented to me by my background and experiences – what Heidegger calls thrownness (criminologists should be in the business of investigating these limited stores, their contents, and the structure of this 'thrownness') but Lorenz's work shows us that the form of will generated in the face of such 'thrownness' will differ in every case. The outcome will always be unique and unpredictable: deterritorialization is always complex and unpredictable.

Will and Transgression (and Deviance)

Transgression is willful. Deviance merely deviates from norms, the transgressive deviates *knowingly*. The deviant or transgressive deterritorializes the normalizing process by doing something that is not normal. The transgressive actualizes his will towards himself as an object of the future, in the way that the bifurcatory capacities of the assembling processes permit these bifurcations are deterritorializing. This possibility produces deviance and some deviance is willful: it is transgressive. Thus, deviant behaviour constitutes a moving away from the norms of the assemblage. In the willful it constitutes transgression and authentic behaviour – it constitutes a moving away from the fixed or fixing qualities of the homogenizing assemblage. It represents for the transgressive a 'carrying away', a 'coming undone' of an assemblage 'where the flows cross the threshold of deterritorialization and produce the new land ... where the person who escapes causes other escapes, and marks the land while deterritorializing himself'. For the mere deviant it is an accident, for the transgressive, it is a life affirming *line of flight*, an expression of an authentic life project.

Conclusion: Assemblage Theory and the Future for Criminology

What this means for criminology is that there are no acts that are inevitably crimes, there are no people who are inevitably criminal. Thus we cannot speak of the causes of crime; we may only speak of events that are seen as deviant. Some of these events will be codified in law as criminal. These events are not to be identified by any quality of rightness or wrongness, or any kind of social or psychological pathology, but merely by the power of the group doing the criminalizing. The power of these groups is emergent from the territorializing processes that intensify the durability and scale of the assemblage. Some events that are harmful are normal and not criminalized (as in the case of Enron for example) for the same reason that the acting person belongs to an assemblage that is large enough, durable enough, practiced enough to establish that harmful behaviour as normal.

We may however, speak of circumstances that led to a particular event. We may rightly inquire into the background and current circumstances of the person involved in that event; that led him to choose a particular behaviour – to choose to attempt to adopt a particular supplement or extension to his existing self. We may ask, what in his circumstance or background made him want to be the kind of person who wears the gold chain which he stole. What constraints and encouragements were there or are there upon his imagination that limit or promote a particular view of himself as a particular object of the future. We can ask these questions of any event, not just criminal or harmful ones. This means that the kind of criminal or harmful events that can be inquired into is similarly unlimited. Assemblage theory permits us to look at harmful acts that are neither deviant nor criminal. Thus it is not restricted by its identification of deviance as an object from viewing what has loosely been called white-collar, corporate, or organizational crime. Indeed, assemblage theory tells us how it is that harmful behaviour can continue, indeed become perfectly normal, and thus avoid criminalization. What criminology should investigate in addition to those factors that contribute to the individual motivation to behave in a particular way is the collective processes that tend to homogenize behaviour such that norms are generated and thus breached, or that norms are generated and some harmful acts thus *not* criminalized. What are the actual mechanisms that individuals use to enable them to define the situation as one where certain norms apply? Thus the object of criminological study is the body of processes, individual and collective that produce normalizing effects on behaviour or which bring about choices that deviate from those norms and destabilize assemblages. It does not matter, in this view whether an event is harmful or not: this is the realm of ethics. It does not matter whether a particular behaviour is a crime, nor whether it is deviant. What matters are the processes that define it as deviant or normal, and assemblage theory gives us a framework within which to conceive of those processes.

Thus the question is not: What acts are criminal? But what processes lead to certain acts being codified as such? The question is not: Who can pin the label on whom? But how does the label come to have the meaning it does? The question is not: Why do certain people breach social controls? But what is the nature of those controls and what are the processes that establish them as such? The question is not: Why do some people accept or reject cultural goals? But what are the processes that mean that some aspirations become acceptable and others not? The question is not: What is the nature of discourses that construct people as certain kinds of subject, or criminology as a certain kind of study? But what processes permit certain discourses to dominate. The question is not: Who has power and how does he distribute it? But whence does his power arise? Because it is the origin of his power that governs the way he uses it. Power equates to *can*, and what he *can do* equates to the capacity of the assemblage from which his power emerges.

Crime and criminalization are not concepts that are isolable in any essential way from other social concepts. We know that criminalization is not distributed in any way differently to the distribution of any other kind of 'bads' in society. What this really means for criminology is that it has no future as a separate study because its proper object is simply that of all social study – the nature of social processes.

Acknowledgement

I should like to thank Ronnie Lippens for comments on earlier drafts of this paper.

References

Bergson, H. (1992) [1946] *The Creative Mind: An introduction to Metaphysics* trans. M. Andison, New York: The Citadel Press.

Blumer, H. (1969) *Symbolic Interactionism: Perspective and Method*. Englewood Cliffs: Prentice Hall.

Callon, M. (1986) The Sociology of an Actor-network: The case of the Electric Vehicle. In Callon.M., Law. J., & Rip, A. (eds.) 1986 *Mapping the Dynamics of Science and Technology*. London: Macmillan.

Crewe, D. (2007) *Will, Power, Constraint, and Change: Prolegomena to a Study of Self and the Emergence of Structure in Young Offender Institutions*. Unpublished PhD thesis, Keele: Keele University

Crewe, D. (2009a) Will to Self Consummation, and Will To Crime: A Study in Criminal Motivation. In Lippens, R., & Crewe, D. eds. *Existentialist Criminology*. London: GlassHouse

Crewe, D (2009b *forthcoming*) 'Beyond Agency and Structure: Methodological Considerations for Researching the Use of Restrictive Physical Intervention Against Children in Jail.' *Journal of Theoretical and Philosophical Criminology*. 1:2

DeLanda, M. (2006) *A New Philosophy of Society: Assemblage Theory and Social Complexity*, London: Continuum.

Deleuze, G. (1983) *Nietzsche and Philosophy*, trans. Tomlinson, H. Minneapolis: University of Minnesota Press.

Deleuze, G. & Guattari, F. (1987) *Thousand Plateaus: Capitalism and Schizophrenia*. Trans. Massumi, B. Minneapolis: University of Minnesota Press.

Deleuze, G. & Guattari, F. (1994) *What is Philosophy?* Trans Tomlinson, H and Burchell, G. New York: Columbia University Press.

Einstadter, W., and Henry, S. (1995) *Criminological Theory: An Analysis of its Underlying Assumptions*. Fort Worth: Harcourt and Brace.

Ferrell, J. (2006) *Empire of Scrounge*. New York: New York University Press.

Foucault, M. 1970 [1966] *The Order of Things: An Archaeology of the Human Sciences*. London. Tavistock. & New York. Pantheon.

Giddens, A. (1979) *Central Problems in Social Theory*, London, Macmillan Press,

Giddens, A. (1986) [1984] *The Constitution of Society: Outline of the Theory of Structuration*. Berkley CA: University of California Press.

Heidegger, M. (1996) [1926] *Being and Time*. Tr. J. Macquarrie, & E. Robinson. Oxford: Blackwell.

Henry, S., and Milovanovic, D. (1996) *Constitutive Criminology*, London: Sage.

Hewitt, J. P. (1997) [1976] *Self and Society: A Symbolic Interactionist Social Psychology*. 7th edn. Boston MA: Allyn and Bacon.

Hindess, B. (1982) Power, Interests and Outcomes of Struggles. *Sociology* 16/4:498-511)

Hulsman, L. (1986) Critical criminology and the concept of crime. *Contemporary crises*. 10/1:63-80

Husserl, E. (1977) [1931] *Cartesian Meditations*. The Hague: Martinus Nijhoff

Husserl, E. (1976) [1913] *Ideas, General Introduction to Pure Phenomenology*. London: Allen & Unwin.

Katz, J. (1988) *Seductions of Crime*. New York: Basic Books.

Latour, B. (1988) *The Pasteurisation of France*. Cambridge MA: Harvard.

Lorenz, E. 1993 *The Essence of Chaos*. Seattle. University of Washington Press.

Michael, J. and Adler, JM. (1933) *Crime, Law and Social Science*. Glen Ridge NJ: Patterson Smith.

Morriss, P. (2002) *Power: a Philosophical Analysis*. Second Edition. Manchester. Manchester University Press

Nagel, T. (1987) *What Does it all Mean? A Very Short Introduction to Philosophy*. Oxford: Oxford.

Park, R., and Burgess, E. (1925) *The City*. Chicago: Chicago UP.

Smart, C. (1992) The Women of Legal Discourse. *Social and Legal Studies: An International Journal* 1:29-44

Germinal Deviance: Deleuze & Guattari and Criminology

Jamie MURRAY
Liverpool John Moores University (UK)

Introduction

Deleuze & Guattari's theoretical work is complex and involving, and does not specifically address matters of crime in any depth. However, the question is nonetheless whether there is a possible cross over between the world of criminology and the world of Deleuze & Guattari (a transversal, as Guattari would theorise a cross over concept). In this paper the theory of Deleuze & Guattari will be introduced, largely by way of a number of primer sections, but within the framework of a cross over concept of *germinal deviance*, which it is hoped allows a productive cross over of the worlds of criminology and Deleuze & Guattari.

Germinal deviance is deviance in itself: it is not deviance in relation to a departing from or transgression of a norm. It is the swerve or clinamen, a deviance on a fractal attractor, which is creative in all processes in the cosmos, nature and social organisation. It is a concept that translates and connects up to so many of the key working concepts within the work of Deleuze & Guattari, and it is a concept designed to connect into criminology through the concept of deviance (at the risk of marshalling a monstrous, hybrid, cross over concept of deviance). It is in Deleuze's *Difference & Repetition* that a concept of germinal deviance is first most thoroughly worked through in terms of his discussion of difference and repetition. There Deleuze sets out, in explicit contrast to the dominant approach in Western thought, the thought of difference in itself as opposed to difference in identity, with difference in itself as pre-representational and pre-propositional singularity. Difference in itself operates in ontological processes of genesis that through repetitions on this difference in itself give rise to our extensive – i.e. physical, perceptible – world where difference in identity and representational thought tend to accumulate and obscure the more profound and germinal operations of a) difference in itself, b) repetition, and c) the eternal return. Alternatively, in the conceptual language of Deleuze & Guattari's *Anti-Oedipus* germinal deviance is desire, desiring production, the body-without-organs, a schizz, becoming, desiring machines. Or, in the terminology of *A Thousand Plateaus*, germinal deviance is the plane of immanence where cosmic processes machine self-organising assemblages in cosmic, natural, and social registers, moving through processes of deterritorialisation that prevail over territorialisation and reterritorialisation to work to create a new earth.

What could be the consequences of pouring all of this thinking into the concept of deviance for a thinking through of the concerns of criminology? I think the consequences would be that a Deleuze & Guattari approach to criminology would not ask a first question 'What are the causes of crime?', and not a first question 'What are the workings of the criminal justice system?', and not even a first abstract question of 'What is crime?'. Rather the starting point would be the further exploration of the profound and creative operation of germinal deviance in terms of the problematic of social organisation. On the basis that germinal deviance comes first, is primarily productive, and prevails, the problematic of social organisation for Deleuze & Guattari presents an inescapable and unresolvable tension between germinal deviance on the one hand and the constitution of sociality on the other (field of immanence of germinal deviance, field of transcendence for normative sociality). For any society to bring itself into being a portion of the germinal flow must be blocked in order to constitute extensive social structures. Societies take a portion of the germinal flow of deviance and code it as prohibited, and it is the prohibited that takes up the inescapable and unresolvable tension in sociality between the forces of immanence and the forces of transcendence. It is from the coding of the prohibited that a society would constitute its concept of crime, and it is this social coding, repression, and the regulation of the prohibited and allowed flow of germinal deviance that becomes a criminal code and criminal system (Deleuze & Guattari, 1984, 139-165).

Thus the starting point, the first question, for Deleuze & Guattari approach would be more abstract than even 'What is crime?'. Once the context of germinal deviance has been set out, one can then ask the question: 'What flow of germinal deviance needs to be blocked to constitute that society?'. Different social machines will address the tension between germinal flow and sociality differently, and so for a Deleuze & Guattari criminology the first task is to understand a) the *problem field* of social organisation that different social machines self-organise as answers to, and b) the concept of crime that this social organisation produces. It is in this setting that a next question about the nature and workings of any given criminal justice system could be considered. Here for Deleuze & Guattari I think the line of questioning would run, just as it did with Foucault, in the direction of how particular social machines and accompanying social assemblages *(dispositif)* operate through (both transcendent and immanent) power to produce crime – or 'deviance from norm' – as the capture and conversion of germinal deviance into normative deviance. Whereas germinal deviance is the operation of *creative* forces in *intensive* (i.e. virtual; see later in this chapter) organisation, the development of *extensive* (i.e. actual, located in time and space; see later) social institutions of power (e.g. systems of criminal law and crime control) lead to the production of deviance as 'deviance from norm'. It is then in the context of this criminological theorisation that questions could then be asked as to the causes of crime, but already here realising that the causes of crime would involve an investigation of a dynamic complex of germinal deviance, social machines, desiring production by subjects, the operation of power in social assemblages, and the production of 'deviance from norm'.

Thus, a Deleuze & Guattari approach to the concerns of criminology would go: 1. Germinal deviance and sociality 2. Abstract concepts of crime 3. Power assemblages (e.g. institutions of crime control) 4. Aetiology of crime in complexes 5. Ethical alternatives (on this point, see the Conclusion). However, before moving on to introduce the work of Deleuze & Guattari, one more consequence of the concept of germinal deviance needs to be pulled out in terms of thinking about crime and criminology, and it is precisely on the term of *thinking*. A great deal of effort goes into schooling and advanced education to ensure the production and policing of subjects that know how to think properly, to express common sense and good sense, to think in the identity of the same, of analogy, of representation, and of judgement. Deleuze & Guattari reject this image of thought on the basis that it cannot think deviance in itself, and then as such cannot think creation, and cannot grasp the full complexity of becoming. Deleuze & Guattari themselves practice a germinal deviating thought. In so far as any contribution of Deleuze & Guattari to criminology would be to the philosophy of criminology, the cross over concept of germinal deviance would not only be a cross over object of investigation but also a cross over practice of thought.

A first section, 'Capitalism & Schizophrenia', provides a general descriptive introduction to the collaborative work of Deleuze & Guattari, and does not presume any prior knowledge. In particular, there is a breakdown of the structure and content of their two key books *Anti-Oedipus* and *A Thousand Plateaus*. These two books make up the *Capitalism & Schizophrenia* project, and by way of a general introduction to Deleuze & Guattari the headline thesis of this project is explained.

'The Field of Immanence' section introduces the complex ontology that is so central to their work. This ontology is introduced in terms of the field of immanence as a univocal field of becoming and creation. Unfortunately, this discussion will be brief, but the reader will have at least the outlines of the ontological context of their work.

'War Machine Thought' introduces the philosophical method that Deleuze & Guattari develop in the light of their understanding of germinal deviance, and which they oppose to the form of thought exercised in State thought (the, no doubt, prevalent image of thought operative in criminal law and criminology).

'Schizoanalysis and Social Ontology' addresses selective aspects of their ontology of the social. 'Schiz' is the term Deleuze & Guattari develop to discuss what they theorise as the primary mode of how force and desire operate in social organisation. In the final chapter of *Anti-Oedipus* Deleuze & Guattari set out what they consider to be the two key tasks for a schizoanalysis of social organisation: the investigation of desiring production at the level of the subject; and the investigation of desiring production at the level of the full social field. This section also introduces the further development of schizoanalysis into rhizomatics in *A Thousand Plateaus* with a social ontology of abstract machines and assemblages. 'Rhizomatics' is the study of the field of immanence with the war machine image of thought. Here some of Deleuze & Guattari's technical tools for theorising the operation of social machines of repression and control are brought forward.

In reading these sections within the framework of the cross over concept of germinal deviance, the thesis from *Capitalism & Schizophrenia* can be read as a criminological thesis on the relation between germinal deviance and capitalism, the discussion of the field of immanence as the field of germinal deviance with becoming and creation as germinal deviance, the discussion of war machine thought as germinal deviance thought, and the discussion of social ontology as the ontology of the tension between germinal deviance and sociality. Desire, desiring production, and schizzing can all be read as conceptual variations on germinal deviance, and the discussion of rhizomatics, social machines and assemblages as the complex of germinal deviance, social machines, power, and social assemblages producing law and 'deviance from norm'.

Capitalism & Schizophrenia

The collaborative work of Deleuze & Guattari comprises four co-authored books: *Anti-Oedipus* (1972); *Kafka: Towards a Minor Literature* (1975); *A Thousand Plateaus* (1980); and *What is Philosophy?* (1991). *Anti-Oedipus* and *A Thousand Plateaus* form the two volumes of *Capitalism & Schizophrenia* project. Before addressing *Capitalism & Schizophrenia* directly, the books *Kafka* and *What is Philosophy?* will be briefly introduced.

The *Kafka* book is a short study, and in many respects a bridge text between *Anti-Oedipus* and *A Thousand Plateaus*. Whilst *Anti-Oedipus* primarily works with desiring production and desiring machines in a still psychoanalytical theory milieu, Kafka presents the first working out of the broadened social ontology of abstract machines and assemblages. This rhizomatics is used to explore the different ways assemblages appear and work in the novels, short stories and letters of Kafka. Deleuze & Guattari do so to produce a characterisation of Kafka as on a creative *line of flight* away from transcendence, guilt and subjectivity, and an example of a writer of a *minor literature* that is political in nature and concerned with the relation between desire, law, power, and revolution. *What is Philosophy?* is their last collaborative work, somewhat at a distance from the concerns of the problematic of social organisation that were so central to *Capitalism & Schizophrenia*. The book devotes a number of chapters to the nature of thought and philosophy (what we are terming in this chapter war machine thought), and on the relationship between thought and processes of territorialisation. A topology of the relations between philosophy, art, and science is developed, and their status as the only disciplines that think by "casting a plane over the chaos", rather than just purveying opinion, is celebrated.

However, the core of Deleuze & Guattari's collaborative work is clearly the two volume *Capitalism & Schizophrenia*, and this is certainly the case with the problematic of social organisation. There are undeniable challenges for the willing reader to get to grips with *Capitalism & Schizophrenia*. The first challenge is the simple size of the books: *Anti-Oedipus* is just short of 400 pages, *A Thousand Plateaus* just short of 600 pages. The second challenge is the stylistic idiosyncrasies and complexities. *Anti-Oedipus* stylistically is theory set at volume 11. *A Thousand Plateaus* consists not of ordered chapters but of complexly linked 'plateaus of intensity'. The third challenge is that, across both stylistic approaches, there is a formidable breadth of material discussed and drawn upon. In *Anti-Oedipus* the breadth of material covers: the history of philosophy; Lacanian psychoanalysis; Marx; ethnology; and modern American and British literature. In *A Thousand Plateau* added to the existing breadth of materials are: linguistics; semiotics; ethology; mathematics; topology; physics; chemistry; biology; molecular biology; and (*avant la lettre*) what is now known as complexity theory. The final challenge to the potential reader is the complexity of Deleuze & Guattari's philosophical method of the creation and proliferation of concepts. For Deleuze & Guattari the task of philosophy (and so of a philosophy of the problematic of social organisation) is to ceaselessly create new concepts, and the neologisms that name these new concepts, with part of the practice of conceptual proliferation including a constant putting into variation of these new concepts and neologisms. Getting to grips with *Capitalism & Schizophrenia* is a labour of love, but it does reward with two stunningly complex and broad-ranging books.

The secondary literature on Deleuze & Guattari is very extensive, but someone interested in Deleuze & Guattari on social theory could turn to Patton's *Deleuze & the Political*, or Bonta & Protevi's *Deleuze & Geophilosophy*. It should also be noted that the field of Deleuze & Guattari studies is by no means a closed field of textual scholarship. In some respects we could now talk about the label 'Deleuze & Guattari' not merely designating two authors and four collaborative projects, but rather an active field of continuing conceptual creativity. Work from Alliez, Massumi, and DeLanda is certainly new conceptual work in the neighbourhood of the Deleuze & Guattari field, as can be viewed the work of Hardt & Negri (see Alliez, 1995 and 2004; Massumi, 1992 and 2002; Dean & Massumi, 1992; DeLanda, 1997, 2002 and 2006; and Hardt & Negri, 2000 and 2004).

A consideration of what Deleuze and Guattari were doing independently prior to their collaboration in 1969 can serve as a useful contextual background to further introducing their collaborative work (their collaboration was in many respects a response to the events of 1968).

Deleuze in 1969 was an accomplished philosopher both in terms of a deep grasp of the history of philosophy and in terms of his own novel philosophical production. Deleuze produced a series of studies of great philosophers: Hume, Kant, Spinoza, Bergson, and Nietzsche. For Deleuze the three names of Spinoza, Bergson and Nietzsche were the great line of a *minor philosophy* in western philosophy and a counter-trend to what Deleuze saw as the hegemonic trend of dogmatic totalising thought exemplified by Hegel. In 1968 Deleuze produced his own summative work, *Difference & Repetition*, which developed a sophisticated ontology and practice of philosophical thought drawing on and adding upon the work of Spinoza, Bergson and Nietzsche. To some degree this philosophy remained a transcendental expressionism, though Deleuze developed a strong theory of difference in terms of multiplicity, repetition as the eternal return, and a practice of philosophy opposed to the dogmatic image of thought of dominant philosophy. It is this latter ontology and practice of philosophical thought that we will see developed further and in different terms in the collaborative work.

In 1969 Guattari had pursued an altogether different career than the academic philosopher he would collaborate with. From the start of his career he had been working in psychiatry, and at the experimental La Borde psychiatric hospital he was working with institutional therapy of schizophrenic patients. It is from the practice of the institutional analysis of schizophrenics that Guattari derives many of his insights into what he theorises as the schizophrenic process, at least initially through the language of Lacanian psychoanalysis, but later through his own schizo theoretical framework of desiring production and desiring machines. Desiring production and desiring machines provided Guattari with ways to think subjectivities beyond psychoanalysis as the full desiring investment of the social field and the self-organising novel machining of heterogeneous elements into novel formations. In addition, Guattari had a life long commitment to militant politics – often communist (Guattari had already developed a theorisation of capital in terms of schizo flows) but soon to be ecological also. His involvement in political activism and groups also significantly contributed towards his writing on groups, desire and politics.

The collaboration between Deleuze & Guattari connects these two lines of thought together into a machinic ontology in which the philosopher becomes politicised and in which the political activist and psychiatrist becomes also a philosopher. Deleuze's ontology from *Difference & Repetition* is crossed with Guattari's theorisation of schizo processes of desiring, as both thinkers see in each other's work the same machinic ontological processes. Guattari's understanding of the processes of schizo machining in thought is crossed with Deleuze's counter-trend image of thought, as both thinkers realise they think the same way and can think between them. They conceptualise what they are doing together by very many different terms: schizoanalysis, rhizomatics, stratoanalysis, nomadology, pragmatics, the science of multiplicities. What is common in their practice however termed is their non-totalisable ontology of the processes that run through the non-organic, organic, and social, and of the entities that these processes give rise to. The particular concern that appears to animate and drive their project is that of theorising the problematic of social organisation, and the attempt to theorise an ethical mode of social organisation for a 'people yet to come'.

Anti-Oedipus is the book of concentrated schizoanalysis, in which the development of the concepts of schizo desiring production and the critique of psychoanalysis are the key concerns. The book is structured into four substantial chapters. First, a chapter 'The Desiring Machines' introduces the key terms of desiring production, the body-without-organs, the unconscious as process of production, and desiring machines. The second chapter is 'Psychoanalysis and Familialism: The Holy Family', in which the critique of psychoanalysis is pursued in greatest depth, and building upon the conceptual work of the first chapter the alternative account of subjectivisation is developed in the substantive principles of schizoanalysis. The third chapter 'Savages, Barbarians, Civilised Men' is the startling chapter on ethnology and social machines, in which the social machines of primitive societies, State societies, and capitalism are theorised by schizoanalysis in terms of processes of territorialisation and deterritorialisation. The final chapter 'Introduction to Schizoanalysis' presses the theorisation of the relationship between schizo processes, psychoanalysis, and capitalism, and also sets out the first two positive tasks of schizoanalysis: discovering desiring production at work in subjects; discovering desiring production at work in the social field.

A Thousand Plateaus is the book of concentrated rhizomatics. *Anti-Oedipus* is focused around the subject, and the subject's relationship with the social. *A Thousand Plateaus* is a more open book, theorising the machinic ontological connections between processes and entities from non-organic, organic and social registers. The chapters are conceived as 'plateaus' where an intensive consistency of conceptual connections adhere between heterogeneous elements, and are dated where the conceptual connection under consideration was actualised most intensely. Each plateau also is provided with a signature image. As a result, the book cannot be read in a conventional linear manner. Some of the plateaus collect in the neighbourhood of concerns of rhizomatic connections and consistency in modes of (social) organisation ('Introduction: Rhizome'; '1440: The Smooth and the Striated'; '1874: Three Novellas, or "What Happened"'). Some plateaus appear to address concerns of subjectivity and desiring production that relate to the terms of *Anti-Oedipus* (November 28, 1947: How Do You Make Yourself a Body Without Organs?'; 'Year Zero: Faciality'; '1730: Becoming- Intense, Becoming-Animal, Becoming-Imperceptible...), though doing so in new remarkable ways (the sorcery of '1730: Becoming-Intense, Becoming-Animal, Becoming-Imperceptible'). Some other plateaus also reprise from *Anti-Oedipus* themes of group organisation, desire and politics ('1914: One or Several Wolves?'; '1933: Micropolitics and Segmentarity'). Several plateaus clearly collect around the concerns of chapter 3 from *Anti-*

Oedipus, considerably deepening the prior discussion of social machines ('7000B.C.: Apparatus of Capture'), and also considerably extending the Deleuze & Guattari theorisation of sociality and modes of social organisation ('1837: Of the Refrain'; '1227: Treatise on Nomadology: - The War Machine'). A new area of development for *A Thousand Plateaus* is the very largely extended consideration of the semiotic dimension to social machines, and a couple of plateaus work through the new conceptualisation of semiotics as regimes of signs ('November 20, 1923: Postulates of Linguistics'; '587B C.-A.D. 70: On Several Regimes of Signs'). One plateau has a picture of a giant lobster on the front, and it is pretty fair to say this is the best way to summarise what the plateau is about ('10,000B.C.: The Geology of Morals:-Who Does the Earth Think It Is?' – it is probably philosophy of nature).

The volume title *Capitalism & Schizophrenia* thus masks two rather different books. However, by drawing out what is common to both books we can perhaps progress one more layer into the complexity of Deleuze & Guattari.

Taken across *Capitalism & Schizophrenia* there is the central argument of Deleuze & Guattari's work and their headline thesis: that there is a relationship between schizophrenia and capitalism. The schizophrenia Deleuze & Guattari refer to is not the institutionalised or socially cast-adrift ill schizophrenic. They are referring to processes of organisation that are evident as operative in the schizo unconscious before the social field collapses these processes into schizophrenia as state. The capitalism that they diagnose as our contemporary social machine is theorised after Marx as a system for the full decoding and deterritorialising of social codes and social territories of previous social machines into pure flows of capital and desiring production. Within this capitalist system, psychoanalysis is one of the great supporters of capitalism, since psychoanalysis through the Oedipus complex introduces desire as lack into subjectivity and so facilitates the seductions of capital. Psychoanalysis also ties the operation of the Oedipus complex into the delegated private sphere of the nuclear family. In addition, psychoanalysis has both missed and suppressed the schizo unconscious, thus obscuring positive schizo desiring production and its machining of assemblages of desire in play with all elements of the social field. Worse, psychoanalysis mangles the productive schizo unconscious in a neurotic frame of representation and repression. However, since the latter half of the twentieth century capitalism has developed processes of decoding and deterritorialising pure flows of capital and desiring production to such an extent that it comes out itself as exhibiting the schizo processes in these flows of capital and desiring production. The issue, though, with capitalism operating with schizo processes and modes of organisation, is that this really is crazy because it can do so only within the constraints of the ever expanding accumulation of capital and the reproduction of the system. For Deleuze & Guattari, therefore, schizo desiring production is thus the general operative mode of organisation and investment of the social field that comes at the end of capital. This mode of organisation and social investment is facilitated in subjects and brought into the social field by capital itself through its general decoding and deterritorialisation of all flows. At the final limit of capital we are at the cusp of creating an ethical mode of social organisation through freeing schizo modes of organisation and investment from the structures and operation of Oedipus and capital.

To progress further in introducing Deleuze & Guattari's thought on desire, law, power and social organisation, the chapter will now break off to introduce, first, their ontology, then second, their concept of images of thought.

The Field of Immanence

In Deleuze & Guattari everything is created from chaos: cosmos, nature, thought, subjectivity, social organisation, language. In their ontology cosmos and chaos are one: *chaosmos*. The field of immanence is this field of chaosmos, and is the ontological modality of the virtual. The ontological modality of the virtual is prior to, creative of, and subsisting alongside the actual ontological modality of extensive time and space. Creation in the field of immanence taps forces and processes of emergence and self-organisation available in the field of immanence to organise matter-energy flows. These forces and processes of emergence and self-organisation are theorised to be *virtual* and *intensive* modes of organisation that occur in far-from-equilibrium conditions, and to operate through molecular and supra-molecular processes of organisation that machine dynamic consistencies between heterogeneous elements. The field of immanence can be characterised in the following ways:

Philosophically – the field of immanence is the discovery of the quest for the transcendental conditions of real experience, and is the key philosophical element in a univocal ontology of becoming. The field of immanence has been the concern of a number of philosophers before Deleuze & Guattari: Spinoza's total plane of nature; Bergson's virtual movement as duration; and Nietzsche's theory of force as will to power and the eternal return. With Deleuze & Guattari the field of immanence becomes the virtual realm of all becoming in emergent and self-organising dynamic heterogeneous consistencies.

Psychoanalytically – the field of immanence is the chaos of the perceptions, intensities, affects, and desire that play across a body, and is the *virtual* and *intensive* realm of potentiality of what that body can do in terms of affecting and being affected. The field of immanence of a body can be theorised as a body-without-organs. This body-without organs exists *virtually* alongside the *actual* body, and it is where the desiring production of the schizo unconscious takes place. The organisation of the body-without organs is through dynamic processes of heterogeneous consistencies of flows of perceptions, intensities, affects and desire.

Scientifically – Chaos and Complexity Theory – Chaos is not the absence of order, but rather it is found to be characterised by incredibly complex fractalised orderings on all scales, and populated by strange attractors that can effect movements and produce creative non-linear effects (as argued and demonstrated by Mandelbrot, Lorenz). Emergent self-organisation is found to develop out of chaos in what are termed dissipative structures and self-organising criticality systems (see the work of Prigogine, Bak). The field of immanence is the field of chaos as movement and self-organisation of emergent structures, and of organisation on attractors. The field of immanence is the field of creation and the co-existence of cosmos and chaos.

Emerging from the field of immanence is the field of transcendence. The field of transcendence is the *actual* ontological modality and organisation of *extensive* time and space. The transcendent mode of organisation is theorised as *molar* and operates near-to-equilibrium by making a distinction (molar fold), closing sets and statistical aggregation.

Ontological becoming and being is the relationship between these two fields. In the field of immanence *virtual* processes of machining self-organise into *intensive* arrangements in matter-energy that then give rise to the *actual* and *extensive* organisation and structures of the field of transcendence. On the field of transcendence actual and extensive organisation and structures are broken up by intensive forces into free matter–energy, which in turn gives rise to intensive and virtual interactions which alter the field of immanence and provoke changes in the ever renewed creation of existence.

Thus, following this ontology, Deleuze & Guattari theorise desire, law, power and problematics of social organisation as having processes of virtual organisation in the field of immanence, or, in other words, having intensive arrangement processes in assemblages of far-from-equilibrium consistencies of matter-energy, and having actual and extensive organisation in embodied, habitualised, and institutionalised structures on the field of transcendence. Their theory of social machines, abstract machines and machinic assemblages is how they develop their social ontology of the processes that operate *between* the field of immanence, intensive creation, and actual transcendent structures.

War Machine Thought

Deleuze & Guattari operate a particular philosophical method. In *Anti-Oedipus* they term it 'schizo thought', and in *A Thousand Plateaus* it becomes 'war machine thought'. They contrast their philosophical method with what they term 'State thought'. Therefore, in order to understand what Deleuze & Guattari are doing in their schizoanalysis and social ontology, it is crucial to appreciate the difference between war machine thought and State thought. This is particularly the case since the philosophical method of State thought will usually be the implicit philosophical method of new readers of Deleuze & Guattari (State thought is taught in schools).

The discussion will examine how each philosophical method relates to the field of immanence, how the respective planes of thought they each draw are characterised, how thought on each respective plane of thought is characterised, how the concepts each creates are characterised, and how they differently conceive of the point of thought.

In State thought the field of immanence is closed off by the operation of constructing a plane of transcendence. A plane of transcendence is made of the field of transcendence, so that this plane can serve to *represent* the field of transcendence. This operation of constructing a plane of transcendence is the *molar* fold. The molar fold is where a multiplicity of differences is turned into a totalised unity through a master distinction of an identity assumed on the basis of a difference conceptualised as negative difference from the identity. The molar fold operates with language to make the distinction, and thereby ties language to the field of transcendence as the representational medium. Language itself is then also organised as a totalised unity. The representational molar fold constitutes the fundamental inside-outside distinction, which facilitates the conceptualisation of thought in terms of subject-object.

The plane of transcendence is a representational schema operated by consciousness. It is a closed set where component representational units are constituted and organised by the relation they have with other representational units by virtue of the totalising unity of the plane. The plane organises the representation of the properties of things through a generalised development of the logic of the molar fold in a mapping of the field of transcendence through negative differentiation into closed sets and closed sub-sets, and through the differentiation of hierarchies of these sets.

On the plane of transcendence thought is conceptualised as the harmonious accord of the faculties in the correct identification of identities, the making of analytical distinctions, the legislation of rules to thought, and of making correct logical judgements of the application of these analytical categories and normative requirements to the field of transcendence. Thought takes place in language, and so thought and thinking are propositional. Thought represents the outside to the interiority of the consciousness of a subject.

Within the representational schema, thought operates with concepts that are organised on the model of the molar fold. Identity is in the concept, and concepts organise the field of transcendence into categories based on the identity as essence of the thing, defined as a totalising unity of identity based on negative difference. Concepts are representative, and concepts are of necessity formulated propositionally in language.

The point of State thought is the discovery of the true and the application of the plane of transcendence to states of affairs. Thought aims at the true as the one correct answer and solution to any confusion or problem on the plane of transcendence. What is important is to remove errors from thought, and to correctly identify, analyse and apply the plane of transcendence to the field of transcendence (given that the field of transcendence issues from the plane of immanence and is perpetually subject to the forces of immanence).

War machine thought draws a plane of immanence across the field of immanence as 'a sieve across chaos'. Thought inhabits the field of immanence with no transcendence.

The plane of immanence is a section of the field of immanence, and as a plane for thought is characterised in the same manner as the field of immanence. What the plane of immanence does bring is that it sections the field of immanence as a problem field. The plane of immanence is not limited to the extensive existence of the field of the plane of transcendence, and is not limited to the properties of a thing. Rather, the plane of immanence sections the intensive and virtual becoming of the world, and is concerned with the *becoming* of things, with the exteriority of relations, and with the *potentials* of the *capacities* of things to a) affect and be affected by each other, and b) to bring the creation of novel and new solutions to encounters. This becoming in the field of immanence is problem solving, and the plane of immanence is the plane of problematics of organisation.

On the plane of immanence thought proceeds by exploring the virtual and intensive problem space of that plane. Thought involves a going beyond of the faculties, where thought is the *sensing* of the *intensities* and *affects* of the plane of immanence. Thought proceeds as the sensation of the sense of the problematic field. Thought becomes engendered in thinking through an intensive encounter with an event in the problem field, and moves to explore this problem field with the event catalysing emergent and self-organising processes within thought. Thought operates in intensities that are pre-representational and pre-propositional, and is the self-organising synthesis of consistencies of sensations, intensities, and affects.

Thought on the plane of immanence creates concepts, but war machine thought has a very different conceptualisation of the concept than State thought. Concepts are created in response to a problematic and to encounters as self-organising syntheses of thought. Concepts here are virtual and intensive dynamic consistencies of pure differences, sensations, intensities and affects. A concept here is not representational, but is creation of a new virtual and intensive entity that responds to a particular problem field. Such a concept does not disclose an essence, but rather a dynamic topological *diagram* of the problem field. It does not close a set in a totalising unity, it rather machines consistencies between virtual and intensive sensations and intensities that are singular attractors within the problem field understood as positive and pure differences.

The point of war machine thought is to experiment and explore problem spaces and problematics. It is to explore the potential of this problem space, to create new concepts in response to the problematic understood virtually and intensively (as well as extensively), and to create potential change in the virtual and intensive sphere (and ultimately also in the actual sphere). Particularly in terms of the problematic of social organisation, the aim of war machine thought is to challenge State thought, and to create new concepts of social organisation to displace dominant State concepts of social organisation. The aim is to connect to new vectors of emergent social organisation that are more ethical than State (and other) organisation.

Schizoanalysis & Social Ontology

Having now established that Deleuze & Guattari work on problematics of social organisation, needs to be set within the context of an immanent ontology, and that this work is pursued through a particular philosophical method, it is now possible to turn to examine the schizoanalysis and rhizomatic social ontology that they develop to pursue their overall thesis in *Capitalism & Schizophrenia*. The key tasks of schizoanalysis according to the concluding chapter of *Anti-Oedipus* are the exploration of desiring production at the level of the subject, and the exploration of desiring production at the level of the social field.

Ethical Social Organisation at the Level of Subject

Anti-Oedipus is the book where the schizoanalysis of desiring production at the level of the subject is most clearly developed, and this book will be the clear interest of any researcher interested in addressing the problematic at the level of the subject (only chapter 3 'Savages, Barbarians, Civilised Men' has the clear focus on the social field). From *A Thousand Plateaus* only a few of the plateaus focus on desiring production at the level of the subject: 'November 28, 1947: How Do You Make Yourself a Body Without Organs?'; 'Year Zero: Faciality'; '1730: Becoming- Intense, Becoming-Animal, Becoming-Imperceptible'.

Schizoanalysis is an alternative to psychoanalysis and to phenomenology generally, and has interesting implications for biopower and biopolitics (see also Lobo-Guerrero's contribution to this volume), and for theorising group politics. The key concept here is *desiring production*. Desire, in contrast to psychoanalysis, is seen as a positive immanent and productive force that is operative in nature as it is in humans. Everything flows and is produced from desiring production, with desire as the *creative* excess forces of existence. For Deleuze & Guattari this desire operates in *desiring machines* which operate in desiring production by connecting up and breaking apart flows of desire matter-energy. This machining of desiring production operates on what Deleuze & Guattari term the *body-without-organs* (field of immanence). A subject will have an extensive (i.e. physical, located in time and space) body with organs and ways of connecting this body up with flows of desire (its organisation as organism), but the subject will *also* have a *virtual* and *intensive* body-without-organs where flows of desiring production can be machined and intensities experienced in a virtual and intensive register of emergence and self-organisation. On this body-without-organs, the subject now becomes a nomadic subject moving about the body-without-organs, experimenting with desiring machines and experiencing intensities and intensive becomings as it connects to new intensities and affects (in processes of e.g. becoming animal, becoming imperceptible, ...). The task of schizoanalysis at the level of the subject is to break from and move beyond the practices of the extensively organised body-with-organs (this body is captured by power) and to allow a body-without-organs to emerge, for desiring production to take place there in desiring machines of connections and cuts of flows of desire. In other words: to affect, and to be affected by other desiring machines. The task is then for an *intensive* nomadic subject to arise, capable of experiencing new intensities and affects, and capable of creating new desiring machines, and of connecting with other desiring machines. The task is to produce new forms of social organisation and becomings beyond the extensive, organismic human.

A very significant feature of the schizoanalytical view of the subject (and this feature is present again at the level of social ontology) is that the force of desiring production is taken by Deleuze & Guattari to be primary to the operation of power. The schizo subject can be captured by power in transcendent overcoding or immanent axiomatisation of flows. Indeed, the subject will be caught within power in a massive way in a social machine in multiple ways: as an organism, as subject of the statement and addressee of law, as an axiomatic set of desire flows within biopower regimes. However, for Deleuze & Guattari the problem of being caught within such power and being subjectively constructed by this power is secondary to the immanent emergence and self-organisation of forces of desire and *lines of flight* and escape from power.

Desiring production is, however, always related to groups (even within an individual) and to the desiring investment of the social field. In terms of the social field, for Deleuze & Guattari there are two key aspects of the social investment of desire: a) that there are two poles to desiring production and how it can invest the social field; and b) that there are two forms of social groups that may arise from this investment of the social field.

The social field is made up of desiring machines and nothing but desiring machines, and subjects invest these flows at the level of their own desiring production, which will operate unconsciously but in primacy to any (pre) conscious registering of their objective interests. In desiring production and the investment of the social field there are two poles to desire: the schizo-revolutionary pole, and the paranoid fascist pole. The schizo-anarchic pole desires with all the forces of the field of immanence, taking up residence on the body-without-organs, exploring desire as pure affirmation and production, making intensive connections that produce intensities and affects that increase the ability to experience and think intensities, and finding strength in the flux of continuous variation of individual and social circumstances. By contrast, the paranoid fascist pole of desire is in love with power and the field of transcendence, and flees the plane of immanence. The paranoid power of desire is desire captured by power, and operates the way psychoanalysis says it does. The desire here is to repel the body-without-organs by fully investing the *extensive* body and the wholes that power imposes on anarchic free desiring production: organism, subjective consciousness, identity, rules, law, regimes of discipline and self-surveillance. What is valued above all in paranoid desire is that desire derives from an operation of power over the subject, which is invested in so far as it rigidifies flows of desire and enforces stability to that organisation of flows of desire. When faced with generalised decoding of flows of desire this paranoid pole has the potential to turn fascist, demanding a totalising State to enforce the law of an absolute coding of the social field. It will demand an attack upon any traces of desiring production in the territories that threaten to escape this absolute coding.

This theorisation of the two poles of desire in schizoanalysis further leads to the analysis of two different poles of social group formation: subject groups and subjugated groups. Subject groups are organised immanently and intensively amongst a multiplicity of heterogeneous singularities that nonetheless maintain their singularity at all times. The group being immanent and intensive does not have boundaries of inside/out, only intensive thresholds of dynamic consistency which it can as a group cross or not cross. Without bounded identity, and without specified long term goals (other than an increasing of experienced intensities and the increase of capability to affect and be affected in becomings) the group explores intensively its own potential as a group, tapping the forces and thought of the plane of immanence. By contrast a subjugated group is organised around a totalising operation of transcendence, through which the individual elements of the group give up their singularity in order to accede to a perceived greater collective and individual identity. The group is captured by power, rather than being the open self-organisation of forces. The group, as well as supplying an identity, operates with a defining inside/outside boundary that is closely policed. It also includes a progressively detailed internal differentiation whereby the operation of power on itself is in the form of hierarchised bureaucracy. The subjugated group pursues the implications of the transcendent *molar* closure of power in producing law and regulation to be applied to itself, and there will arise detailed procedures for which other groups the group may interact with, and if so, how. The subjugated group is always a group of managers, bureaucrats and policemen.

Ethical Social Organisation at the Social Level

A Thousand Plateaus, drawing on and considerably developing the social field chapter 3 from *Anti-Oedipus,* pursues a significantly broader approach, developing a social ontology that embeds the ontology of subjective desiring production with a social ontology, and embedding this social ontology within a general ontology of nature. There is considerable conceptual development in *A Thousand Plateaus* although it does remain a clear philosophical partner to *Anti-Oedipus.* In *A Thousand Plateaus* a new and extended conceptual language of social ontology of abstract machines and machinic assemblages, of territorialisation and re-rerritorialisation, first experimented with in the *Kafka* book, is fully developed. The clear continuation of chapter 3 of *Anti-Oedipus* is in the plateaus '7000B.C.: Apparatus of Capture', '1837: Of the Refrain', and '1227: Treatise on Nomadology: - The War Machine'. An additional feature in *A Thousand Plateaus* to the ontology of social machines is that the semiotic dimension to social machines is now extensively developed in terms of a theory of regimes of signs tied closely to the material dimension of social assemblages: see 'November 20, 1923: Postulates of Linguistics' and '587B.C.-A.D. 70: On Several Regimes of Signs'. Themes of groups and politics a pervasive concern in *Anti-Oedipus*, are also seen developed in the plateaus '1914: One or Several Wolves?' and '1933: Micropolitics and Segmentarity'. However, *A Thousand Plateaus* goes much further than its predecessor in developing a social and natural ontology in terms of rhizomatics: 'Introduction: Rhizome'; '1440:The Smooth and the Striated'; '1874: Three Novellas, or "What Happened"'. This ontology of nature is explored in, at times, a dizzying level of complexity and depth: '10,000B.C.: The Geology of Morals (Who Does the Earth Think It Is?').

In *A Thousand Plateaus*, schizoanalysis is broadened into a more ontologically ambitious and developed rhizomatics. Rhizomatics pursues a philosophical understanding of the rhizome as a primary and immanent mode of creation and organisation in existence, in contrast to an arborescent tree hierarchical structuring of existence. The rhizome is the immanent multiplicity network mode of organisation that we have seen as operating the field of immanence; as operating in the war machine practice of thought; as operating in schizo desiring production and thought; and as operating in subject groups. In *A Thousand Plateaus* this investigation of the rhizomatic mode of organisation is further extended across all non-organic-organic-social registers of existence. Again, this is developed in the constant play in Deleuze & Guattari's philosophy between the field and plane of immanence and the field and plane of transcendence, between rhizomatic organisation and hierarchical tree organisation, with the latter always theorised as a reduction and stratification of the former, but with a constant coming and going between the two. The primacy always is of the field and plane of immanence over those of transcendence, and of becoming over being.

Chapter 3 of *Anti-Oedipus* had already introduced in a quite well developed way Deleuze & Guattari's theorisation of social machines and their topology of them. The basic idea of social machines is that societies form and self-organise on the basis of virtual co-ordination and machining and on the basis of ongoing *intensive* (virtual) processes of change to then form *extensive* (i.e. actualized in time and space) structures and institutions of social life. This allowed Deleuze and Guattari to think of a virtual space for certain viable machines of social organisation, and thus the ability to topologically name and map viable social machines. Of these (in the chapter 'Savages, Barbarians, Civilised Men') they mapped primitive societies of the code, State societies of over-coding, and capitalist societies of decoding. In *Anti-Oedipus* they developed this topology in great depth, and the theory of social machines would clearly be of great theoretical relevance for very many social science problematics. As such, the further development and refinement of this theory of social machines in *A Thousand Plateaus* into a fully fledged social ontology is highly significant.

A Thousand Plateaus both increases the complexity of the treatment of social machines as well as increases the number of social machines. In addition to the State social machine which receives further theorisation in a dedicated lengthy plateau, and further reflection upon the capitalist axiomatic, the new social machines of monotheism (see '587 B.C.-A.D.70: On Several Regimes of Signs') and the nomad war machine are introduced ('1227: Treatise on Nomadology: The War Machine'). These developments greatly extend the scope of Deleuze & Guattari's topology of social machines and assemblages, and allow for continuing conceptual creativity in thinkers pursuing social science problematics. Perhaps, though, it is the development of the nomad war machine that has the profound theoretical consequences for the encompassing social ontology. The war machine, although it does organise examples of nomad social organisation, is further a mode of organisation that can structure small groups, an individual, practices of thought, and practices of creation. The war machine is developed as the mode of organisation on and of the field and plane of immanence (or at least drawing close to it). It taps the forces of emergence and self-organisation available on the field and plane of immanence. It is the social machine opposed to the State social machine. It organises social formations in the field and plane of immanence, with the result that the nomad machine – or war machine – and the State machine are enemies (the object of the nomad machine however is not war, except at its limits when it confronts the State social machine).

A Thousand Plateaus also fully develops the ontology of social machines in term of abstract machines, assemblages and stratification. Abstract machines are the proto-co-ordinators of the mode of organisation of the social machine at the level of the virtual and the field and plane of immanence. Some social abstract machines remain at the level of the field and plane of immanence, leading to a form of social organisation close to that field and plane, whilst other social abstract machines (State social machines) immediately rise up to compose a transcendent totalising social organisation and draw a plane of transcendence. Assemblages are the manner in which social organisations are *intensively* produced and organised. In an assemblage the co-ordination of the (virtual) abstract machine is developed in the (actual) material and processes of sociality. Deleuze & Guattari theorise social assemblages in terms of a semiotic regime, a material regime, and a territory. Every social machine first effectuates and draws a territory on the earth on which it establishes itself. Exactly how the territory is drawn will depend on the particular social abstract machine. On this territory the social assemblage will develop elements of expression, theorised in depth in *A Thousand Plateaus* as regimes of signs. Beside the regime of signs the assemblage will also collect together a material regime of technology, actions and passions. As the semiotic, material, and territorial intensive practices of the assemblage build up in extensive deposits (tools, buildings, etc.) and become habitual and institutionalised (settled language, social codes) the social machine sets down strata where the intensive processes of the assemblage give way to actual material entities and institutionalised social processes. Different social machines exhibit different levels of stratification: for example, the State social machine is social stratification as a process and goal; the nomad war machine sets down a minimal and variable stratification. In an assemblage, the relation between the intensive (virtual) processes of the assemblage and the extensive (actual) deposits of the strata is operated by the social *abstract machine* of the assemblage. The abstract machine releases the creative forces of the field of immanence into the assemblage both in its creation and its continuing processes and existence. Precisely how the abstract machine releases creative force on a continuing basis, of course, depends upon the precise social machine: some maximise it, some minimise it. However, either way, assemblages in addition to constituting a regime of signs, a material regime, and a territory are also run through with lines of deterritorialisation as a result of the abstract machine and the field of immanence. What this means is that the territory, the social codes, social technology, and all the strata are incessantly subject to forces of disruption, destruction, variation, innovation, revolution, deterritorialisation. Deleuze & Guattari take deterritorialisation to be primary in social machines as it is the operator of their creation and the operator of their intensive consistency as operative social machines. However, a near inseparable process of reterritorialisation accompanies actions of deterritorialisation, where the disruption or innovation is captured by the social machine and re-coded or reinserted back in the established territory of the social machine.

Social organisation is thus theorised by Deleuze & Guattari in an elaborate social ontology (increasingly now being referred to as 'assemblage theory'). Given that assemblage theory is created, formulated, and operative within the war machine practices of thought that Deleuze & Guattari themselves operate with, it is a theory of social organisation that may engage productively with many social science problematics. It should be noted that the assemblage theory operates at all levels of social organisation, and not only at the level of totalised societies (this is clearly the case with the nomad war machine). The productivity of assemblage theory also runs to thinking through bio-power practices and institutions (Deleuze, 1988). Deleuze employed assemblage theory to produce a theorisation of contemporary society with social assemblages beyond those of discipline but rather as assemblages of control and surveillance (see 'Control and Becoming' and 'Postscript on Control Societies' in Deleuze's *Negotiations*, at 169-182).

Conclusion

There are two aspects of deviance where concept of *germinal deviance* can operate as a cross over concept for criminology and Deleuze & Guattari. Firstly, touched upon in the last section, there is the theorisation of 'deviance from norm' as produced in social machines and social assemblages of power. In this discussion of social machines, assemblages and power Deleuze & Guattari are very close to the concerns and practices of Foucault, and their work could productively cross over into criminology as a return to and development along other lines of the influence of Foucault. However, in this introductory chapter I have developed germinal deviance as the privileged cross over concept that would deliver into criminology a 'monster' (i.e. cross over, hybrid) concept of germinal deviance, and bring concerns of criminology deep into the workings of the Deleuze & Guattari theoretical machine. On this point, there is an interesting footnote in *A Thousand Plateaus,* on their intellectual relation to Foucault. After a highly approving discussion of Foucault's work, Deleuze & Guattari comment:

> Our only points of disagreement with Foucault are the following: (1) to us the assemblages seem fundamentally to be assemblages not of power but of desire (desire is always assembled), and power seems to be a stratified dimension of the assemblage; (2) the diagram and abstract machine have lines of flight that are primary, which are not phenomena of resistance or counterattack in an assemblage, but cutting edges of creation and deterritorialisation. (Deleuze & Guattari, 1988, 531)

This quotation, as well as reiterating the concept of germinal deviance that has been used to frame discussion throughout, indicates the ethical and political implications of Deleuze & Guattari's thought, and gives some insight into the potential ethical and political implications of a cross over of the concepts of germinal deviance and war machine thought into criminology. In the struggle of forces between the plane of immanence and the plane of transcendence, in the struggle between desire and power, in the struggle between germinal deviance and criminalisation and normalisation, Deleuze & Guattari are ethically and politically on the side of germinal deviance. The forces of the plane of immanence - the forces of germinal deviance - are ethically superior to the powers of the State, criminal law systems, bio-power normalisation systems, and capital, and if the forces of the plane of immanence and germinal deviance are ceaselessly defeated by molar power they prevail defeated. The cross over of Deleuze & Guattari and criminology would presage not only deviating concepts of crime, but also deviating ethical and political becomings in strategic and tactical operations in both power social assemblages and deviating social assemblages of force.

References

Alliez, E. (1995) *De l'Impossibilité de la Phénomenology*. Paris: J. Vrin

Alliez, E. (2004) *The Signature of the World*. London: Continuum

Bonta, M. & Protevi, J. (2004) *Deleuze & Geophilosophy*. Edinburgh: Edinburgh University Press.

Dean, K. & Massumi, B. (1992) *First & Last Emperors*. New York: Autonomedia,

DeLanda, M. (1997) *A Thousand Years of Non-Linear History*. New York: Zone Books DeLanda, M. (2002) *Intensive Science & Virtual Philosophy*. London: Continuum

DeLanda, M. (2006) A *New Philosophy of Society*. London: Continuum

Deleuze, G. (1988) *Foucault*. London: Athlone.

Deleuze, G. (1995) *Negotiations*. New York: Columbia University Press.

Deleuze, G. & Guattari, F. (1984) [1972] *Anti-Oedipus*. London: Athlone.

Deleuze, G. & Guattari, F. (1986) [1975] *Kafka: Towards a Minor Literature*. Minneapolis: University of Minnesota Press

Deleuze, G. & Guattari, F. (1988) [1980] *A Thousand Plateaus*. London: Athlone.

Deleuze, G. & Guattari, F. (1994) [1991] *What is Philosophy?* London: Verso..

Hardt, M. & Negri, A. (2000) *Empire*. Cambridge: Harvard University Press

Hardt, M. & Negri, A. (2004) *Multitude*. London: Hamish Hamilton

Massumi, B. (1992) *A User's Guide to Capitalism & Schizophrenia*. Cambridge, Mass.: The MIT Press

Massumi, B. (2002) *Parables for the Virtual*. Durham: Duke University Press

Patton, P. (2000) *Deleuze & the Political*. London: Routledge

Paul Virilio:
A Logistic Perspective on Crime

Gijs VAN OENEN
Erasmus University Rotterdam (the Netherlands)

Introduction

The French theorist Paul Virilio (born Paris, 1932) is certainly one of the most incisive critical analysts of modernity. His work is however not easily situated within any tradition of thought, and not even within any particular discipline. He deals with media, architecture, war, and speed, effortlessly mixing themes and concepts from cultural theory, sociology, and philosophy. Although he published a large number of books and articles, none of these seem to discuss all these topics in a sustained systematic way. That is not to say that his thought does not make sense, on the contrary. But it does suggest that we do better to discuss Virilio's insights from his own, unique, and somewhat idiosyncratic vantage points. It also means that reconstructing his thought feels a bit like playing a classical game of Tetris, frantically trying to tilt and slide all the incoming pieces so that they interlock into some consistent and meaningful whole.

This contribution aims to assess how Virilio's work may provide new directions for criminology. I will start out with a discussion of some central lines and concepts in Virilio's work in general. Next, I will ask in what way(s) Virilio's work might be of interest to criminology. I will focus on three themes: the rise of nodal policing, the present concern with security, and the rise of Ambient Intelligence. All three themes will be closely related to Virilio's central interest in *logistics*, or *war*.

Understanding Virilio

During his whole professional life, Paul Virilio has been affiliated with an institution of architecture, the École Spéciale d'Architecture in Paris. First as a teacher, later as a professor and director. Architecture, in a very general sense, is about constructing dwellings, an art both technical and aesthetical. Such construction is necessarily implicated with space; a building exists as an unmovable object in space, 'real estate'. And indeed, Virilio says, this is how human beings for a long time have experienced the world and its architecture.

This 'architectural experience', however, has changed drastically in modern times.

The German idealist philosopher Immanuel Kant already showed, in what is known as the 'Copernican turn' in philosophy, that space and time are not external properties of a world independently existing outside of us, but rather ways in which our mind structures the world, ways in which we 'make sense' of it. The world is thus, in a way, dependent upon us, upon the structure of our mind. As a former student of the French phenomenologist Maurice Merleau-Ponty, however, Virilio would not so much emphasize the structure of the mind in this respect, but rather the way we experience the world in concrete terms, as human beings equipped with a body and with a specific sensory 'regime of perception'. It is thus, to summarize a long story, our bodily experience rather than our 'mindset' that structures the world for us. Accordingly, Virilio is above all interested in how the world appears to us; how we experience it in concrete, bodily terms.

The advent of *modernity*, around the beginning of the 19th century, implied a radical transformation of this experience. Although architecture is still concerned with putting together interlocking elements, like in the Tetris game, we now have to reckon with what for Virilio is the most incisive characteristic of modernity: velocity, or *speed*. In the Tetris game, as the game moves to higher levels, the building blocks fall towards us at ever increasing speed. Where others, most famously Karl Marx, interpret the changes in the modern world primarily in terms of the production and distribution of wealth, Virilio highlights the role of speed. Modernity has speeded both things and human beings up in a quite incredible way. What was once stationary, or moved with what Virilio calls 'metabolic speed' or what a human being can 'digest', now moves with 'technological speed', 'the speed of cars, telephones, the media, missiles' (2008, 150). And much of what used to be earth-bound is now 'airborn', and increasingly even 'virtual' – that is to say, projected with the speed of light. For Virilio, this means that 'architecture' has also changed dramatically. We no longer 'dwell', but move around in the world at an increasing speed, constructing and experiencing our world as a space of flows, rather than as a collection of fixed places.

From a more sociological perspective, we may take the example of capital. For Karl Marx, society revolved around capital; capital dictated our living conditions, our human relations, our working experience. Moreover, capital was essentially place-bound, e.g. by being 'invested' in a specific factory or firm. Nowadays, capital flows freely and abundantly around the world; mind-boggling amounts are transferred around the globe every split second. Value is no longer attached to concrete, material premises, but has become a function of (financial) expectations. Especially during the so-called dotcom bubble, stock markets often valued upstart internet enterprises higher than large, existing companies with extensive hardware possessions and millions of paying clients. The global financial crisis that broke out in October 2008 is even more the product of a financial 'wild-west': virtual money run amok, destroying the real economy in the process.

Still more relevant for Virilio is that the (electronic) media revolution has made the world 'shrink' in an experiential sense. The phrase 'global village' was coined back in 1962 by Canadian media theorist Marshall McLuhan, to indicate how mass media were smashing the barriers of time and space in human communication. Three important points of reference here are: the 1960 presidential election in America, the first election to be televised nationwide; the Vietnam war, the first war that was 'fought on television'; and the moon landing of Apollo 11, the first 'extraterrestrial' event broadcast 'live'. No longer did we have to wait for the morning paper to arrive – we were all 'there'. Since, media have only become faster, another important reference point being Ted Turner's 1980 decision to make CNN a 24/7 news station (Redhead 2004, 91) to be viewed everywhere and at all times. And nowadays, of course, we have the Internet and mobile phones, that continuously keep us 'updated', at our own discretion.

Well, perhaps not really at our own discretion, Virilio would argue. We simply live in a world of speed and acceleration, whether we like it or not. We are confronted with images, impressions, and stimuli, that follow each other at an ever increasing rate. One only has to watch a television show from twenty years ago to be amazed by the slow pace at which it all seems to move. In this respect, Virilio's work stands in a tradition that started with Charles Baudelaire, in the middle of the 19th century, and that was continued by Georg Simmel and Walter Benjamin in the early 20th century. These thinkers were all interested in how the hectic speed and the abundance of impressions characteristic of modern life influence our perception of the world. For instance, by becoming 'blasé' – 'seen this, done that' – while simultaneously craving new impressions. Or by transforming *Erfahrung* into *Erlebnis*, reflective experience into instantaneous satisfaction of superficial interests (e.g. Berman 1992) Thus, although we may feel that we have more choice and are better informed than ever, we simultaneously suffer from a kind of overload of choice and information. We can never get enough, and therefore we become in a way buried by choice and by information. In Virilio's plastic expression, derived from Albert Einstein, we get hit by an *information bomb* (2008, 198; Redhead 2004, 200).

This brings us to one more way in which the Tetris metaphor is apposite to introducing Virilio's philosophy. This concerns the place of *war* in his thinking. There are clear biographical (and thus experiential) grounds for Virilio's interest in war (Virilio 2008, 218; Armitage 1999). As a child during the Second World War, he was traumatized by the *Blitzkrieg* when he was evacuated to the port of Nantes. Later on, in adult life, Virilio was conscripted in the French colonial army during the Algerian war of independence – a war that, next to May 1968, was probably the most decisive, and divisive, experience for a whole generation of French intellectuals from Merleau-Ponty, Camus, and Sartre to Deleuze and Bourdieu.

In a way, for Virilio the *Blitzkrieg* stands for the organizing principle of modern society: a violent onslaught that has taken place almost before we realize it. It represents the transformation of experience that Benjamin was concerned about: a storm of impressions, stimuli, information, and images that hit us before we know it, and that we have no time to 'digest'. But although a metaphor, it is certainly meant to be militant. Modern life is about 'the conquest of time and space', and society is to be seen as an 'encounter of forces' (rather than more specifically classes, as in Marxism). War used to be static, but in the 20th century it is all about movement. And thus about detection, about finding out where the opponent is and how he is moving (what Virilio refers to as 'vectors'). The principle of war, and consequently of architecture, thus transforms from *fortification* – staying in one, unassailable place – to *logistics*: the translation of strategic space into logistic time. War is basically a matter of logistics, especially in a society that is not so much organized as a structure of fixed places and organizations, but rather as a system of flows, in which the (electronic) gathering of information on targets takes precedence over local, physical, face-to-face confrontation and contact. The prime modern example here is radar detection, invented during the Second World War, which enables one to establish both the presence and the movement of the enemy before actually seeing him. Just as with the Tetris game, it is of the essence to localize the bomb-like descending elements as early as possible. Time and information become of the essence.

Again, we should remember that what counts above all, for Virilio, is how all this affects our experience. In the form of architecture, it affects the way our habitat is shaped and organized. Architecture used to be about separation and fortification, but now it is about 'the arrangement of movement', about visibility and transparency. For instance, from the middle of the 19th century, large boulevards were created in many European cities (most famously Paris), enabling the movement of large numbers of people in order to go to work, or to go shopping. The invention of glass and steel building enabled large windows in office and commercial buildings, which destroyed the strict separation of public and private spaces, of inside and outside (e.g. Berman 1982). In general, the world becomes something that 'passes us by', simply when we walk on the street and observe the traffic, or when we use escalators and elevators. But most typically for modern life is that we observe it as a series of moving images. As Virilio puts it, the boulevards 'broke the ground for the film industry' (Redhead 2004, 97). 'Cinematic acceleration' is realized through the 'dismemberment' of space/time into isolated 'frames', or editorial 'cuts' (Wilson 2008). Real life becomes increasingly imbricated with life 'on screen': first in the cinema, later on television and on computer screens. But also, and perhaps even more typically, while *driving*.

Driving a car is a cinematic experience, Virilio says. Whilst driving, we 'conquer the world', and experience it as if it were projected on a screen, the car's windscreen (Virilio 2005, 105ff; see also Gane 1999, 94-95). In our computerized age, an increasing part of this 'screening' is electronically mediated. The dashboard becomes part of the 'display'. What we see on screen is increasingly an integration of projection and simulation of reality, as is vividly testified by the navigation screens now prominently attached to our windscreens. Some more expensive cars indeed project the dashboard and navigation information directly onto the windscreen. 'Tomorrow's transport machine', Virilio (1999, 69) writes, 'will first of all be a "driving-computer" in which the audiovisual feats of the electronic dashboard will prevail over the optical qualities of the field beyond the windscreen'. This technique is derived from fighter jet technology, where the helmet display integrates all sorts of tactical information, direct vision being of minor importance. Of supreme importance is informational speed and accuracy. Early detection, and pro-active intervention are of the essence. In modern logistics, 'to see is to shoot'; delay means defeat. Conversely, the best military defence is to prevent being detected – hence the importance of *stealth*.

Virilio's thought thus concerns the way the world gets 'constructed', the world's 'architecture' one might say, and more specifically how the modern architecture of speed affects our perception. The study of this reality is what Virilio calls *dromology*, the way we perceive our environment whilst being in motion (or perhaps better: whilst 'under speed'). In other words, this is a 'political economy of speed' (Armitage 1999, 35). The cinematic experience of driving a car is a 'dromoscopic simulation' (Virilio 2005, 107). In fact, Virilio claims, there was no 'industrial revolution', but only a 'dromocratic revolution'. In the same way, there is no democracy, only dromocracy; and no strategy, only dromology (Virilio 2006, 69). That is to say, there are 'classes of speed like there are classes of wealth', and the logic of such a speed-ridden society is, indeed, *logistics*.

Virilio is sometimes accused of being a mere aestheticist who lacks sufficient interest in concrete social and political problems (Leach 1999, 80-81). However this may be, it does take considerable interpretative effort to find out how his insights may translate into concrete practices. With regard to crime or criminology, few such efforts have yet been undertaken. I will briefly mention two of them, before providing my own analysis.

The British legal scholars Anne Bottomley and Nathan Moore (2007, 176-178) pick up on Virilio's idea that the architecture, and more especially the modern city, is basically a 'fortress': a construction of obstacles to block enemy movement. Developing this thought further, they propose that 'although the development of the fortress begins with a concern to protect those inside against the external forces of an attacking enemy, these developments impact upon the regulation of those inside'. Guided further by the work of Manuel DeLanda (another architect-philosopher!) rather than that of Virilio, Bottomley and Moore conclude that logistics inevitably becomes tied to 'total control' because, or once, there is no longer a distinction between 'the enemy without' and 'the people within'.

Australian criminologist Eric Wilson (2007) argues that speed creates the condition for what he calls 'power crime': 'fraud and corruption by elites that have substantial governmental or economic power'. Speed somehow produces a 'criminogenic environment' in which power crimes become 'invisible', undetected. After these sketchy introductory remarks, however, Wilson focusses exclusively on U.S. military strategy and praxis, and the relation to crime or legality becomes hazy at best. In what follows, I will develop my own ideas about how to make Virilio's work productive for criminological thought. As mentioned, I will focus on three themes connected by the principle of logistics: the rise of nodal policing, the present concern with security in relation to logistics, and the rise of Ambient Intelligence.

The speed of light and the rise of nodal policing

Virilio is not unique in noticing, or emphasising, that modernity is to be associated with speed, velocity, or acceleration. In their *Communist Manifesto* of 1848, Karl Marx and Friedrich Engels already painted modern life as being characterized by 'revolution', by continuous and restless change, both technological and social. All that was stationary is now set in motion, and transforms beyond recognition. 'Marx is not only describing but evoking and enacting the desperate pace and frantic rhythm (...) of modern life. He makes us feel that we are part of the action, drawn into the stream, hurtled along, out of control, at once dazzled and menaced by the onward rush', as Marshall Berman points out in his 1982 book *All that is solid melts into air*, the title itself a quotation from the *Communist Manifesto*. Later, the American journalist Henry Adams, the sociologist Georg Simmel, the futurist Filippo Tommaso Marinetti, the philosopher John Dewey, and the jurist Carl Schmitt all commented upon the relation between modernity and speed, or acceleration (Rosa & Scheuerman 2009, 33-74). German sociologist Ulrich Beck (1986) famously argued some 25 years ago that the growth of technological-economic power is structurally being 'outspeeded' by the *risks* entailed by this growth. Risk refers to the likeliness that a certain accident will be produced by a certain technology, or combination of technologies and circumstances. Thus the rise of *risk society*, in which an ever larger amount of power is consumed by assessing, containing, and countering possible accidents.

Virilio is unique, however, in declaring speed or acceleration to be the fundamental developmental principle of modernity. Technology and speed, which are basically the same since technology is what makes processes speed up, produce not risk but real accidents. With the invention of the railway, the railway accident was 'invented' as well; with the locomotive, derailments; with the highway, the car collision; with the airplane, the plane crash (2008, 46; 2003, 24). Where Beck would see these merely as unforeseen and unintended consequences that may or may not be contained, Virilio considers them to be dialectically implicated in the inventions themselves. That is to say, technology and speed imply and need accidents, which in a way is what *makes* them progress, because they call for modification, revision, and renewal. Dromology thus literally implies 'accidents waiting to happen'. Just as Ulrich Beck argues that risks overshadow the technology that produced them, Virilio maintains that accidents are now more important than the substance, or process, that caused them.

The limit to this development is the limit of speed itself: the speed of light. When speed is relative, accidents are local (as in a train or plane crash). But now that technology works with 'absolute speed', that is to say the speed of light, as is the case with electronic systems, accidents tend to become 'general'; their impact will be felt everywhere, and at the same time. Typical examples are in fact well-known: the explosion of nuclear weapons, and the collapse of financial markets (Virilio 2008, 41).

From the perspective of criminology, these extreme cases constitute what we might call the 'limit of crime'. They can be triggered by extremely small, almost unnoticeable causes, while their effects are immediate, encompassing, omnipresent, and far-reaching. It may not be easy to draw the line between widely accepted business practices and 'white collar crime', but it is certainly not far-fetched to say that in the years preceding the crash of October 2008 the financial markets were ever-more resembling a collection of 'Ponzi schemes', also called 'pyramid schemes', i.e. operations that pay returns to investors out of the money paid by subsequent investors, rather than out of real profits. But sometimes the line can indeed be drawn, as in the case of the Barings Bank that was broken by its employee Nick Leeson, and with Enron, an energy company proclaimed America's 'most innovative company' for six consecutive years by *Fortune* magazine, but whose CEO Kenneth Lay got convicted for securities fraud.

From Virilio's perspective, one might say that these dramatic consequences reflect the 'general' character of the 'accidents' involved. Space and time have all but been vanquished by the lightning speed of financial transactions. This causes the accident, and makes it happen at no particular place, that is to say, everywhere. While it would take months, or years, to scale up a normal manufacturing enterprise to double, or triple, its output, financial operations can be scaled up tenfold, or hundredfold, through the mere click of a button. The gains can be huge, the losses literally immeasurable, and omnipresent.

In the attack of September 11, 2001, the combination of airplane hijacking, suicide attack and instant, 'live' media coverage made this 'local' criminal act into an event that was instantly felt worldwide (Virilio 2003, 40-47). And of course the idea was also to not just physically, but also symbolically 'crash' the Twin Towers, so as to make 'Wall Street' implode. Ironically, that part of the mission was accomplished to much greater effect by America's own bankers and stock brokers in 2008, confirming the view of e.g. media sociologist Jean

Baudrillard that 'terrorists' are only those who light the fuse of a bomb that we have constructed ourselves.

Among the most noticeable effects of the attacks of 9/11 are the radical security measures that have been taken, especially at 'nodal' points where streams of goods or people are being recombined, such as seaports and airports. This points to another criminologically relevant aspect of Virilio's work. We now live in a 'nomadic' world that is better described in terms of movement, speed, and flux – or in Virilio's preferred term, logistics – than in terms of permanent dwellings. Think for example of telephone connections: previously making a telephone call meant being at home, or at the office; nowadays, parties can be anywhere, at home or abroad, and more likely than not they will be 'on the move'.

This does not accord well with traditional policing. Police, and more generally the criminal justice system, typically used to be, what one might call, post-active, or reactive. That is to say, suspects were only apprehended 'after the fact'; intervention 'before the fact' being proscribed by criminal law. But the fear of terrorist attacks, and especially suicide attacks, has made this principle increasingly problematic. It makes no sense to apprehend suicide bombers after the fact. Accordingly, police and other investigative agencies no longer wait with their investigation, and prosecution, until laws have actually been broken. They become 'pro-active', not only trying to prevent crime from happening –which of course police has always done– but more controversially they actively seek out 'the limits of the law', asking 'what they can get away with' rather than what is legally, or customarily, acceptable. For instance, they arrest potential troublemakers before a demonstration will actually take place, to release them only afterwards. Or they hinder, disturb, or hassle known criminals, follow them around ostentatiously, or ticket them for minor infractions, just to let them know "we're onto you".

Of no less interest here is the way police know that such 'usual suspects' are in town. This is a side-effect, almost, of the increasingly popular *nodal approach* to policing. Traditionally, police would do 'rounds': surveillance traditionally consists of police patrolling the area on foot, or by car. Additionally, of course, they respond to distress calls. But with the increasing mobility in and of society, the rise of the 'network society', 'policing' such a society increasingly requires a nodal approach. As Amsterdam police chief Bernard Welten recently confirmed: in the information and network society, *streams* increasingly determine social processes. This applies to all social processes, most obviously to the economy with its streams of capital, but it certainly also applies to criminology and criminal investigation. As David Garland (2001, 129) puts it, this new type of criminology 'aims to embed controls in the fabric of normal interaction, rather than suspend them above it in the form of a sovereign command'.

On the nodal points of real and virtual infrastructure, police must be able to monitor and control the streams of people, goods, money, and information. Almost all the highways leading into the city of Amsterdam, for example, are now in fact 'guarded' by radar- and camera-systems, primarily to check for speeding. But these systems can also provide police with almost real time information about all those who enter or leave the city. The arrival of a known criminal, or mere suspect, is immediately noted, and appropriate (or not so appropriate) 'counter-measures' can be taken.

The speeding surveillance technology example is not an accidental one, from Virilio's point of view, as in a society of speed the *control of speed*, in the broadest sense, must be the essence of 'policing' (2006, 39-40, 51). Nowadays, politics and policing are both about extending the possibilities of control beyond the mere 'guarding of a fortress', such as the city. Especially virtual streams and networks, and other forms of electronic information processing make this possible – but also *im*possible as, according to Virilio, the attainment of 'lightning speed', the speed at which electronics operate, will lead to a standstill, a virtual impasse. The example of highway speed control is indeed illuminating here.

First, we should remember that electronic means of highway surveillance and speed control came into being only with, and because of, the higher speeds and the denser volumes of traffic on the roads. It is much too cumbersome, and costly, to physically track down, and 'arrest', all speed offenders. The fact that people speed easily could, by the way, be tied to the phenomenological given that people typically assess danger and risk, in relation to speed, inaccurately. The relationship between kinetic energy and velocity is exponential, which means that as you increase your speed, you dramatically increase kinetic energy, and thereby potential collision damage. Almost no driver fully realizes this, and almost no modern car helps remind us. Speed limits do remind us, but few drivers appreciate the help.

A solution of a limited kind is provided by seat belts, and air bags, that protect the driver somewhat against the impact of a crash. Seat belts are, from Virilio's perspective, just as inevitable a product of speed as the crashes they anticipate. In most countries, wearing a seatbelts is compulsory, so that the seat belt becomes a prime object of 'policing'. But enforcing this obligation is difficult; police cannot visually check every car all the time.

Ticketing drivers for speeding is a more practical form of policing, because it can be automated, for instance by using radar equipment combined with camera surveillance. This only provides a partial solution, however, because drivers can take electronic countermeasures. Collective countermeasures include radio stations that broadcast the location of (mobile) surveillance equipment, updated by drivers themselves, who can 'phone in' any locations they spot. For individual countermeasures we have so-called anti-radar detectors that detect radar detection and give drivers timely notice. In turn, police have equipped patrol cars with anti-anti-radar detectors that detect anti-radar detectors. Anti-radar detectors may be declared illegal, and often are, but we can easily imagine other electronic countermeasures, for instance based on by now widespread GPS-systems. There is thus a race going on between detection and evasion, with each side 'speeding up' their information gathering in such a way that they will soon both reach a near 'real time' capability. That is to say, both detect each other at about the same moment. The speed race will then come to an abrupt standstill, an impasse. Ultimate speed has produced ultimate immobility – just as the automobile has always 'produced' the immobile driver, and the speed and density of motor traffic has 'produced' the motionlessness of the traffic jam (e.g. Redhead 2004, 109-120).

Virilio's model for such escalating developments, as we saw, is that of war and armament. There are two relevant connections here. First, military and civilian implementations of technology converge. Take for instance two systems of control that are being developed for highway surveillance and for military battleground intelligence, respectively. The Intelligent Vehicle Highway System is a step towards the goal of the 'fully automatic automobile', or driverless car, based on a total integration of automobile movement and highway surveillance into an encompassing cybernetic system. The Combat Zones That See (CTS) is a program of the U.S. military which develops technology that can 'identify and track all movement' in a battle zone through a massive network of surveillance camera's linked to a central computer. As Jeremy Packer (2006) argues, both systems increasingly overlap. Especially since the advent of the 'war on terror', it is likely that CTS will be applied in the 'battlefield' of society itself, thus making control of auto-mobility the model for the extending technological capabilities for the policing of society in general.

The second connection is the arms race. As the number of weapons and their sophistication grew, the response time for all parties decreased. Countries such as the United States and the Soviet Union once had several hours at their disposal to decide on a counter move, in case the other side fired a missile. In 1961 this was down to half an hour, according to Virilio's calculations in *Pure War*, and in 1983 the delay was down to fifteen minutes for intercontinental missiles, and two to five minutes for submarines. Virilio quotes naval officers in the Falkland war, in the early eighties, as saying that 'in this war, everything happens in a few seconds (...) the missiles go by themselves. We are finished...' (2008, 35). Laser weapons, Virilio surmises, will reduce the delay to milliseconds. When we thus no longer have any time for reflection, the rule of speed or 'dromocracy' will become the rule of computerized instruments (2008, 71-72). Split second decisions will instantaneously produce either triumph or disaster. Or more likely, what will arise is an instable stand off, a 'draw' that is ceaselessly being recalculated. Or, as Virilio prefers to call it, 'polar inertia', i.e. sedentariness replacing pure speed (2008, 79).

The demands of logistics and the claims of security

We saw how in Virilio's work, speed is directly connected to war or, logistics. Modern society, one might say, with Virilio, is ever more dependent on finely tuned systems of logistics. In the world of goods, and other shipped material items, implementation of economic principles such as 'just in time' and 'same day delivery' require highly sophisticated, and thus also highly vulnerable, logistical processes. Goods must be moving as soon, and as quickly as possible; inertia and delay cost money. But logistics are just as important in the virtual world. Both the Internet and more specialized, proprietary information systems depend upon complex protocols for authentication, transport, interaction, and conversion. This is true even down to the design of microprocessors themselves: shorter connections and more efficient working protocols enable higher processor speed.

Given the interrelation between speed, war, logistics, and technology, it is no wonder that western societies are increasingly preoccupied with *security concerns*. Technology that is claimed to enhance 'security' is rapidly becoming integrated, most of the time imperceptibly so, into almost everything around us. This enables 'a shift from reactive authorities, collecting information and evidence to be used on purpose, towards a proactive government, using technology to anticipate on and prevent crime', as a recent report on *Security Applications for Converging Technologies* states (Teeuw & Vedder 2008, 118). This is possible only when there is a shared belief, by government and citizens alike, that technology can positively affect security concerns. According to this report, this shared belief, together with the increased willingness of citizens to trade their privacy for security, 'induces the government and security organizations to invest heavily in the development and deployment of ambient security technology like for instance intelligent surveillance cameras and body scan devices' (id.).

Let us discuss some examples of how the present concern with security, or logistics, may make our daily life into something like the object of a criminal investigation. Something we are by now all familiar with is airport security measures. We all stand in line, shoes in hand, ready to have our bodies searched, our luggage X-rayed, our handbags inspected, with our carefully repacked liquids in a few 100 ml containers, holding chip-passports that electronically contain our facial scan and our fingerprints. Although these are pretty invasive measures, there is little or no protest from the general public, presumably because airlines, airports, and passengers are all more concerned with (presumed) security and logistic synergy than with matters of privacy or other limits on pro-active investigation and control. Logistical integrity, one might say, trumps personal integrity.

Not only people, but also goods travel around the world, at an ever increasing speed, answering to the logic of economic and financial pressures. Less visible to the public eye but certainly not less invasive than airport surveillance are the security measures that are implemented in and around seaports. In the wake of the 9/11 attacks, massive and wide-ranging measures were put in effect at seaports in the United States and Canada, as well as elsewhere in the world, to secure the complex logistical chain of cargo being imported, stored, and transported out. Here the people adversely affected are not the general public, but those who handle the cargo, the port workers. Access to restricted areas in Canada, sociologist Deborah Cowen notes, would be granted only following extensive background checks and demands for personal information on 'spouses, parents, and spouses' parents, details about postsecondary institutions attended, credit history, criminal history, personal details including skin colour, and five years of residential, employment, and international travel history'. The workers' union ILWU charged that 'the sweeping and subjective nature of "reasonable suspicion" as grounds for denying clearance meant that members could potentially lose their employment "on the basis of concerns that go well beyond those of preventing terrorist acts".' (Cowen 2007, 33-34)

Port workers thus transform from employees into potential security risks. Securing the logistical chain simply requires securing the human chain. The port workers' civil rights and their employment status threaten to become secondary to the logistical concerns of the ports. Not complying with the demands of logistics, which in this case became near synonymous with the demands of security and of economy, easily gets translated into something like a criminal act. Prevention of such 'criminal' acts in turn justifies the kind of investigation into one's personal life that would normally befit only a criminal investigation.

A final example concerns an item that has become, almost overnight, one of the most personal belongings of almost every person: the mobile phone. Many people would nowadays rather lose their wallet than their mobile phone. Because it is not just a phone, but a true database, a mobile 'server' that almost permanently exchanges information through an incredibly extensive and complicated phone and computer network. Many perceive this physical item, the particular brand and model of mobile phone they carry, as something very personal. Not merely because it has an increasing amount of personal data stored in its memory banks. Many also cherish their mobile phone affectively, as one would a piece of jewellery, or a diary. However, our 'handy' is merely one small (SIM-)chip in an enormous wireless computer system. Just as our mobile phone enables us to 'network', it is our phone that 'networks us'. While we use it to actively 'keep track' of friends, acquaintances, and business relations, it is now equally actively tracking *us*. For instance, railway companies use data from cell phone providers to compile precise estimates of how many people travel at a certain stretch at a given time. Because cell phones every few minutes emit signals to let the network know where they are, it is easy to establish how many cell phones there are on a train; one then only needs to know the provider's market share, the percentage of people carrying cell phones, and the percentage of cell phones switched off while travelling. The more mobile we become, the more exactly we can be pinpointed.

Moreover, mobile phones provide us with another example of a speed chase that ends in a kind of stand-off. Those who do not want their phone communication to be eavesdropped on by the police – presumably those with criminal intentions – can take countermeasures, such as switching cell phones often (to the point of using every phone just once), frequently changing the SIM-card, or both. Together with regular authentification procedures used by the cell phone, this might seem to make unauthorized eavesdropping impossible or extremely difficult. However, a device called an IMSI-catcher (IMSI stands for International Mobile Subscriber Identity) is able to identify and intercept mobile phone communications between multiple users, even when they regularly change phones and/or SIM-cards. What's more, they won't even know what happened to them. Needless to say the IMSI-catcher is a favourite of police investigators in several European countries (e.g. Haubrich 2003). And no doubt the parties they want to eavesdrop on will resort to more advanced methods of evasion, and police will try to pre-empt this once more. Eventually, this will also result in a nervous stand off, in which any move of one of the parties will immediately be detected, and countered, by the other.

The rise of Ambient Intelligence and how it may pre-empt crime

From this stand-off one might conclude, with Virilio, that the difference between detection and evasion has now basically disappeared. The car driver and the phone user can no longer be distinguished from the system that detects them, and vice versa. We are embedded in 'real time' in an encompassing electronic environment; or to put it the other way, the electronic environment has embedded itself in us. In its initial stages in the nineties, this interpenetration of man and technology was referred to as 'cyborg' culture. Now we would perhaps do better to situate it within the conceptual space of *Ambient Intelligence*, or that of ubiquitous computing.

The terms Ambient Intelligence and ubiquitous computing both refer to the state of affairs in which our environment, basically in any place and at any time, is able to adapt to our personal state, or identity (e.g. Aarts & Marzano 2003). Simple forms of this process are the ways in which we can 'personalize' the screen of our computer, or our mobile phone. In a way, pages on websites like Facebook could also be included, because they make the computer environment more 'homely'. Conversely, or simultaneously, they make our personal profile visible to the whole 'network'. This double-sidedness is characteristic for the whole development of Ambient Intelligence and ubiquitous computing. On the one hand, electronic mediation 'personalizes' our environment, adapting it to our preferences and needs in 'real time'; we might call this a permanently pro-active technology. But precisely because it is permanently pro-active, it needs to monitor our every move, and be aware of every preference and every connection we entertain.

Up to a point, we see this happening already in any Web 2.0-style environment such as, for instance, Amazon.com's website. There we get 'personal recommendations' every time we search for a title – recommendations that often fit our actual preferences surprisingly well. But more often than not, things happen without us being aware of them, as for instance with supermarket customer cards that tell the retailer all about our shopping preferences. Or chip-cards that detect our movements through the public transport system. Our chip-card controls our environment, for instance by opening the gate, just as much as the card controls us. To give just one more example: why shouldn't a subway AI-system alert me, for instance by sending me a text message, when my stop is coming up next? At larger stations, it might even give me personalized directions to the proper exit, or adapt advertisement screens on this route to show products that I happen to like.

My point here is not so much that all this is happening, or could be about to happen, because this in itself is already known –stronger still, many people do not yet seem to realize that technologies which they consider 'futuristic' are in fact already operational (Teeuw & Vedder 2008, 98). I do want to stress three specific points, though, that are of interest to criminologists. First, as we already saw with the IMSI-catcher, Ambient Intelligence and ubiquitous computer technologies offer untold possibilities to prevent and detect crime, or mere nuisance. Let me give just one example that extends the possibilities of common camera surveillance as it is already operational in many public places. In some of those places, loitering youths are experienced as a structural nuisance, or even a threat. 'Intelligent' cameras and microphones that can automatically detect cases of misbehaviour, could be coupled with so-called mosquito's (i.e. an already (in)famous ultrasound device that deter troublesome youths) while leaving everyone over the age of 25 unaffected. Perhaps just for a minute or so, as a kind of warning. Or perhaps even pro-actively, when the approaching youths are recognized through facial scanning or through their mobile phone signals, so that the mosquito can pre-emptively deter them.

Second, the spread and speeding-up of Ambient Intelligence and ubiquitous computer technologies may equally well produce new forms of crime, and instantaneously so. People's whereabouts may (illegally) be traced through their mobile phone signals, computers may be 'hacked' by spammers in order to use them to diffuse email advertisements. More generally, any personalized electronic environment may be taken advantage of by third parties, who can steal or misuse the personalized data involved in the creation of such environments. Ambient Intelligence may become particularly prone to phenomena such as data theft, (illegal forms of) data mining, and forms of fraud, in case financial transactions are also involved.

Third, Ambient Intelligence as a form of Virtual Reality may also be used for purposes of rehabilitation. Ambient intelligence is here able to realize what sociologist Manuel Castells (1996, 373) has called 'real virtuality': 'a system in which reality itself is entirely captured, fully immersed in a virtual image setting, in the world of make-believe, in which appearances are not just on the screen through which experience is communicated, but they become the experience'. In the Innovation Lab of the Dutch Dienst Justitiële Inrichtingen (part of the Justice Department), the possible uses of electronic equipment for the rehabilitation and reintegration of convicts are being investigated, including Virtual Reality applications. 'Concepts like gaming and simulation are being used to measure and register unconscious reactions of inmates' (Second Society 2007, 13). Also, simulations and Virtual Reality environments are used to 'train and experiment in a controlled environment'. A very convincing Virtual Reality is created through advanced systems of image projection and computer processing, making the environment 'react naturally' to any movement or action the tested subject performs. Such virtual environments make it possible, for instance, to confront people convicted of serious sex crimes, or violence, with a variety of 'challenging situations' – virtually simulated. In such cases, the 'real time' speed on which such technologies are based, is really used to (re)create, enable, or support personal experiences, which accords perfectly with Virilio's main philosophical interest: how does the increasing speed of modern societies affect the way we experience the world around us? (Redhead 2004, 149-150).

This seems more generally to be the kind of society toward which we are heading: increasingly, our environment will be able (and 'willing') to adapt to our personal preferences, either through instructions by us, or through interaction with some personal identification device we carry with us (most likely ever more sophisticated kinds of mobile phones). Inevitably, this will have the dual consequence of both enabling us to 'control', or personalize, our environment, and of letting our environment 'control' us – or enabling those who can tap into the relevant computer systems to monitor and affect us. An increased 'view', and control, of our own environment (whether it be through GPS, internet-searches, webcams, or Google-Earth) goes hand in hand with an increased view, and control, over our environment by others. A seemingly innocuous example is an internet service recently introduced by the Dutch police. A special website is created where speeders who have been photographed and ticketed by police cameras can now view the actual photographs of their transgressing vehicle. These show the precise date, time, and location of their transgression, including a Google map, and even details of the qualifications of both the equipment used and the police officers who processed the data. In order to log in one's 'citizen service number' is required, i.e. the personal code that gives access to a kind of 'my government' portal which provides all sorts of data that concern one's relation with government.

The combination of being photographed while speeding, and being enabled by the internet to view these photographs instantly to verify this fact, perhaps constitutes the best possible illustration of the narrow relation between (physical and electronic) speed, and how it is being 'policed'. It illustrates what Virilio meant when he worried about the 'collateral damage done [by virtual reality] to the ethos of reality, the highly vulnerable public space where individuals responsively interact' (Der Derian 1999, 224), and when he wrote that 'the banalization or popularization of global surveillance, or to put it another way the

DEMOCRATIZATION OF VOYEURISM on a planetary scale, has overexposed even our most private activities. (...) In the best case, only marketing specialists can gauge the amplitude of this risk; in the worst, the military, investigators charged with tracking unlawful activities, political police, and automatized systems of information collection.' (2002, 109)

And this may well be how our future looks like: intelligent cameras in public space, or even at home, that automatically film any transgression and deliver this footage to us in real time, so that our awareness of our transgression becomes fully mediated. Indeed, the car dashboard and windscreen may transform into a kind of computer server which picks up police signals and perhaps automatically initiates counter-measures, exchanges legal notices, negotiates solutions, and proposes settlements. Not unlike the stock market, and possibly in for a similar crash. A crash that will be more like an 'electronic traffic jam', keeping us 'on hold' while computers frantically work out their negotiating strategies and submit these to us for our approval. This may perhaps sound weird, but aren't we already being bogged down by our bulging e-mail inbox, the electronic messages gobbling up an ever increasing amount of our time? And aren't we waiting endlessly while being 'put through' by automated voicemail systems? This would be the final Virilian irony: despite there being sufficient space in physical reality, we are brought to a halt by a jam on the electronic super highway that lands us in 'polar inertia'.

Conclusion

What new ways for criminology does Virilio's work point to? Let me summarize my findings in a few salient propositions, related to the three points discussed above. First, ciminology will move in the direction of something like 'systems analysis', as policing itself is becoming ever more 'nodal' in nature. Both crime and its detection will more and more take place within a context of flows, networks, gateways, 'firewalls', gatekeepers, and such. In a way, crime will therefore also become more of a 'white collar' affair. The major criminals, both quantitavely and qualitatively, are now ever more those who are able to control these flows and manipulate them, to their own advantage, in illegal ways. Or more precisely, practices will develop in which it is ever more difficult to distinguish between breaking the law and circumventing it. Accordingly, criminology will have to become more concerned with this 'border issue' as well. For instance, returning to an issue discussed above: at what point, according to which characteristics and definitions, does a financial operation start to resemble a Ponzi scheme, and is thus something criminally liable? After the financial and economic crash that started to manifest itself in october 2008, stricter laws and regulations will certainly be enacted in this area. But just as certainly, in a (global) society of flows with nodal structures, new methods – or perhaps rather: algorithms – will be constructed to machinate, jockey, and engineer the flows and control its junctions; ways that will seem both profitable and legitimate at first, but may prove disingenuous and even fraudulent later. In this sense, criminology may also become more *political*, as it may have to join the debate on what distinguishes legal from illegal manipulations of flows.

Second, criminology might become more concerned with the exclusionary effects of the measures taken to protect the complex and vulnerable logistic processes against 'security risks'. Of course, as shown most prominently by the work of David Garland (2001), criminologists are already aware of, and engaged with, this 'Foucaultian' dimension of both the creation and the maintenance of social norms and processes. In at least two respects, however, these exclusionary effects take on a new dimension, or a new relevance. In the first place, the continued fear of terrorism tends to decrease the sensitivity for, and the importance attached to, exclusionary and discriminatory effects of 'security measures'. And additionally, such measures may be introduced under the guise of concern for terrorism, while in fact other goals and effects are being pursued, of a social or economic nature -goals and effects that may not have been deemed legal without an appeal to security considerations. In the second place, the security measures deemed necessary to protect contemporary logistic processes will adversely affect not only employees directly or indirectly involved with them, but also a great many 'ordinary', normal people in the course of their daily activities. Especially of course when they make use of airports, or other 'security sensitive' places. Many public, or semi-public, buildings and spaces around the world, especially in large cities, such as hotels, schools, and other educational or cultural institutions, nowadays employ metal detectors, security guards, and other more or less invasive measures. The possible exclusionary and discriminatory effects of these measures will also increasingly become an area of interest for criminologists.

And third, criminology will become ever more involved with Ambient Intelligence, or ubiquitous computing. The 'control' of crime, that is to say both its prevention and its detection, will become more related to features of the built environment. The 'shaping' of environments, both through physical and electronic means, will become an ever more important factor in crime control. In order to serve their wishes or steer their behaviour, Ambient Intelligence needs to know many things about its inhabitants – knowledge that it collects through a variety of means and from a great many sources. Such data collection in itself may be of interest to criminologists, as the collection of data raises ever more legal (and ethical) questions. Think only of 'data mining': the indiscriminate collection of data that are processed later using elaborate algorithms, so as to discover statistical relations and patterns that are commercially relevant, or of interest to criminal investigations. But more generally, the shaping of environments so as to prevent or control crime will become a major area of interest for criminologists, both theoretically and empirically, as the pilot projects by the Dutch ministry of Justice show.

Finally, Ambient Intelligence is not only relevant for the prevention and detection of crime, but also for the ways in which crimes that have already occurred can be investigated. Crime scenes have of course always contained traces of the crime committed, in the form of fingerprints, hairs, odour, DNA, or other body matter. But crime scenes that possess Ambient Intelligence features will retain many more traces, mostly through electronic means. Already, quite a few crimes are solved nowadays by watching footage from surveillance cameras. Ambient Intelligence environments will keep much more complex and diverse records of what is going on, and offer much more elaborate possibilities of analysing the data collected. Ambient Intelligence will no doubt thus push the already hugely popular notion of 'Crime scene investigation' to a new level. Ambient Intelligence may turn public spaces into potential crime scenes, offering almost unlimited possibilities for the reconstruction of past events, criminal or otherwise. Ambient Intelligence environments may even embody automated 'crime analysis' hardware and software so as to enable 'on the spot' or 'real time' automatic policing. That also would be something entirely in line with Paul Virilio's hypotheses and predictions.

References

Aarts, E., & Marzano, S. (2003) *The new everyday. Views on Ambient Intelligence*. Rotterdam: 010 publishers

Armitage, J. (1999) From modernism to hypermodernism and beyond: an interview with Paul Virilio. In J. Armitage & M. Featherstone (eds.) (1999) *Paul Virilio. From modernism to hypermodernism and beyond* (p. 26-55). London & New York: Sage

Beck, U. (1986) *Risikogesellschaft. Auf dem Weg in eine andere Moderne*. Frankfurt: Suhrkamp

Berman, M. (1982) *All that is solid melts into air. The experience of modernity*. New York: Schuster & Schuster

Bottomley, A. & Moore, N. (2007) From walls to membranes: fortress polis and the governance of urban public space in 21st century Britain. *Law & Critique*, 18, 171-206

Castells, M. (1996) *The rise of the network society*. Oxford: Blackwell

Cowen, D. (2007) Struggling with 'security': national security and labour in the ports. *Just labour: A Canadian Journal of Work and Society* 10, spring 2007, 30-44

Der Derian, James (1999) The conceptual cosmology of Paul Virilio. In J. Armitage & M. Featherstone (eds.) (1999) *Paul Virilio. From modernism to hypermodernism and beyond* (p. 215-227). London & New York: Sage

Gane, M. (1999) Paul Virilio's bunker theorizing. In J. Armitage & M. Featherstone (eds.) (1999) *Paul Virilio. From modernism to hypermodernism and beyond* (p. 85-102). London & New York: Sage

Garland, D. (2001) *The culture of control. Crime and social order in contemporary society*. Oxford: Oxford university press

Haubrich, D. (2003) September 11, Anti-Terror Laws and Civil Liberties: Britain, France and Germany Compared. *Government & Opposition*, 38/1, 3-28

Leach, Neil (1999) Virilio and architecture. In J. Armitage & M. Featherstone (eds.) (1999) Paul Virilio. From modernism to hypermodernism and beyond (p. 71-84). London & New York: Sage.

McLuhan, M. (1962) *The Gutenberg galaxy*. Toronto: University of Toronto press

Packer, J. (2006) Becoming bombs. Mobilizing mobility in the war of terror. *Cultural Studies*, 20/4, 378-399

Redhead, S. (ed.) (2004) *The Paul Virilio reader*. New York: Columbia university press

Rosa, H. & Scheuerman, W. (2009) *High-Speed Society: Social Acceleration, Power, and Modernity*. Pennsylvania State university press

Second Society. Over vernieuwing in de straat, de stad en de staat (2008). Rotterdam: CPI. Available from: www.publicinnovation.nl/downloads/congres 2007.pdf

Teeuw, W.B. & A.H. Vedder (eds.) (2008) *Security applications for converging technologies. Impact on the constitutional state and the legal order*. The Hague: BJu and WODC

Virilio, P. (2008) *Pure war. Twenty-five years later*. Los Angeles: Semiotext(e) (with S. Lotringer) (first ed. 1983)

Virilio, P. (2006) *Speed and politics. An essay on dromology*. Los Angeles: Semiotext(e) (Originally published as *Vitesse et politique*. Paris: Éditions Galilée 1977)

Virilio, P. (2005) *Negative horizon. An essay in dromoscopy*. London: Continuum (originally published as *L'horizon négatif*. Paris: Éditions Galilée 1984)

Virilio, P. (2003) *Unknown Quantity*. London: Thames & Hudson

Virilio, P. (2002) The visual crash. In Th. Y. Levin and P. Weibel (eds.), *Ctrl [Space]. Rhetorics of surveillance from Bentham to Big* Brother (pp. 108-113). Cambridge, Mass.: MIT press

Virilio, P. (1999) Indirect light. Extracted from Polar Inertia. In J. Armitage & M. Featherstone (eds.) (1999) *Paul Virilio. From modernism to hypermodernism and beyond* (p. 57-70). London & New York: Sage

Wilson, E. (2008) Speed/pure war/power crime: Paul Virilio on the criminogenic accident and the virtual disappearance of the state. *Crime, law, and social change*, 21 november 2008 'online first'.

Reading Criminology with Psychoanalysis: the Case for Singularity

Véronique VORUZ
University of Leicester (UK)

Introduction

The English-speaking world prides itself on a pragmatism supposedly free of ideology (for a counter-argument see Neocleous, 2008) and the ultra-modernity of its governmental techniques modelled on scientific processes (for a critique of predictive methods in the field of criminology see Harcourt, 2001, 2007; Hayward, 2007). Yet laws, norms and regulations have failed to produce 'well-adjusted' beings, and the messy business of being human endures. Criminology, enjoying an unprecedented expansion, has become the discipline of predilection to deal with the foretold residues (Foucault, 2003) of diagrammatic modalities of power destined to discipline bodies and souls (Foucault, 1977), and to govern populations (Foucault, 1978; 2004). Prisons multiply, while diverse apparatuses of power/knowledge reach ever further inside the private sphere in the name of prevention: mere incivilities are punished, biometric data is gathered, registers are kept, predictions of future behaviour are made, all in the hallowed name of the security of the majority. For "security", in the fitting words of David Fisher, undertaker extraordinaire in the American series *Six Feet Under*, "is the new freedom".

In the self-proclaimed age of ultra-modernity, psychoanalysis could seem woefully inadequate to the present. Freud's discovery of the unconscious, his once-scandalous claim that desire is born as transgression of the law, has lost its appeal at a time where law-breaking is no longer dignified with the subjective value of transgression,[1] but reduced to cognitive dysfunction, behavioural disorder, or in the worst cases of serial killing and paedophilia, the opaque psychopathy of the perverse monster. Psychical causality, the mysteries of subjective choice, no longer excite our imagination. This loss of fascination for the psychic, twice demystified by the normalising forces of psychology and the classificatory impetus of the DSM-IV, has reduced psychoanalysis to a curious avatar of the 20th century, effecting the rocky transition between the collapse of religion, as "mode of structuration of human communities, a global way of being of the social-human establishment" (Gauchet, 2002, xvi), and its suppo-

1 Cultural criminology is a notable exception in that it recognises the symbolic value of 'crime'. See Ferrell *et al.* (2008).

sedly advantageous replacement by the much neater discourse of science. Where the signifier fails to plumb the unfathomable depths of subjective choices, the number comes to the rescue, as with the paradigmatic example of Hare's Psychopathy Checklist-Revised (PCL-R), a clinical rating scale to verify the 'diagnosis' of psychopathy.[2] The scores are then used as predictors of the risk of re-offending and the probability of rehabilitation.

If 'forgetting Freud' is often justified because he is deemed to be of the past, by contrast Lacan, the French psychiatrist and psychoanalyst who taught under the auspices of a 'return to Freud', tends to be associated with the worst excesses of post-modernism: obscurity, wilful complexity, unintelligibility, arrogance and self-indulgence. And to be fair, a lot of secondary writing in the English-speaking world does substantiate this view, as Lacan's profuse inventiveness and cryptic style do lend themselves to the enjoyment of ciphering. So here, I will strive for clarity.

Going against the perceived decline of psychoanalysis as an interpretative framework relevant to our times, this chapter will stress the heightened pertinence of psychoanalytic theory for the challenges that face criminology. To my mind, it provides at least four distinct lines of enquiry, which I will only sketch out here in a preliminary manner, as befits the remit of this book. These four possible approaches can themselves be apportioned into two distinct series of questions: the first series starts from the perspective of the subject and emphasises the importance of psychical causality, while the second series takes the social bond as its vantage point to circumscribe the specificities of the present. I will draw on the current writings of the French-speaking Lacanian community, where Lacan's work is actively supplemented to keep up with the transformation of our civilisations.[3] I apologise for the fact that most of the books and articles I will quote from are not translated.

Crime is more than a social fact

For this section I will draw on Lacan's essay "A Theoretical Introduction to the Functions of Psychoanalysis in Criminology" (2006, 102-122) and the

2 Each of the items in the PCL-R is scored on a three-point scale according to specific criteria through file information and a semi-structured interview. In addition to lifestyle and criminal behaviour the checklist assesses glib and superficial charm, grandiosity, need for stimulation, pathological lying, cunning and manipulating, lack of remorse, callousness, poor behavioural controls, impulsivity, irresponsibility, failure to accept responsibility for one's own actions and so forth.

3 Note in this respect that in recent years, the psychoanalytic communities of France, Italy, Spain and many South American countries have started to engage with 'the social', providing free or low-cost treatment, working in prisons, in various institutional settings, delivering psychiatric opinions etc. See for further information http://www.wapol.org http://www.causefreudienne.net/

companion piece "Prémisses à tout développement possible de la criminologie" (2001, 121-125). They are of their time: the first was delivered at the 13th conference of French-speaking psychoanalysts in May 1950, and the second summarises the ensuing discussion. They precede Lacan's 'structuralist' period and are influenced by his reading of the sociological luminaries of the time: Mauss, Levi-Strauss, Durkheim and Tarde. These two texts have recently been commented by psychoanalyst Serge Cottet in his excellent article "Criminologie lacanienne" (2008), which I will also draw on here.

The question of subjective responsibility

In these articles Lacan speaks, unusually, from a humanist perspective, and still very much reasons within the parameters of the Oedipus complex, building on his 1938 observation that the "social decline of the paternal imago" is responsible for much of the "psychologies" of his time (2001, 60). His working hypothesis is that delinquency has to do with a partial failure of the Oedipus complex to fully bring about the socialisation of the subject, producing, instead of a sublimating superego, one that pushes the subject to crime.

> The superego must, in our view, be taken as an individual manifestation that is tied to the social conditions of Oedipalism. This is why the criminal tensions included in the family situation become pathogenic only in societies in which the family situation is disintegrating. In this sense, the superego reveals tension, just as illness sometimes sheds light on a physiological function. (2006, 111)

We can isolate two precious indications from the above quotation: first, criminal passages to the act unveil the "criminogenic function" of society. To say it otherwise, the forms of delinquency, the types of crime that prevail at a given time cast light on the nature of the tension between the subject and the social. And Lacan supplies a number of indications that could be useful to "statisticians", as he puts it:

> The following are objects of study regarding which the analytical theory can offer statisticians the correct coordinates on the basis of which to begin measuring things: a complete separation between the vital group, constituted by the subject and his family, and the functional group in which the vital group's means of subsistence must be found (a fact that we can sufficiently illustrate by saying that it makes Monsieur Verdoux seem plausible); an anarchy of desire-eliciting images that is all the greater as they seem to gravitate ever more around scopophilic satisfactions that are homogenised in the social mass; and an ever greater involvement of the fundamental passions for power, possession, and prestige in social ideals. (2006, 119)

Second, the signification of the crime pertains to an "individual manifestation" of the superego: "thus, no form of the superego can be inferred from the individual to a given society. And the only form of collective superego that one can conceive of would require a complete molecular disintegration of society" (2006, 112). There is, then, a complementarity between the social order and the criminality it produces – for "crime takes its symbolic coordinates from society" (Cottet, 2008, 25) –, and yet the personal signification of a crime endures.

This is why, having paid his dues to sociological readings of crime, Lacan asserts that criminology should not give in to "the dream of an entirely objective treatment of the criminal phenomenon" (2001, 123). It is because crime is more than a social fact, because it also harbours a signification personal to the subject that Lacan insists on subjective responsibility *beyond* legal responsibility, which is a social construction contingent upon the cultural values inherent in a legal order. Put simply, the criminal should be afforded the opportunity of subjectifying his acts, as responsibility is the pre-condition to integrating the community of men. In so doing Lacan goes against "the very tendency of criminology ... which, if it tends to humanise the treatment of the criminal, may only do so at the expense of his humanity insofar as a man is recognised by his fellow men through the acts for which he takes *responsibility*" (2001, 121, original emphasis).

Lacan's intervention is situated as counterpoint to the demise of "the expiatory signification of punishment" he ascribes to utilitarian values:

> A civilisation whose ideals are ever more utilitarian, since it is caught up in the accelerated movement of production, can no longer understand anything about the expiatory signification of punishment. While it may consider punishment useful as a warning to others, it tends to assimilate it into its correctional goal. And this goal imperceptibly changes objects. The ideals of humanism dissolve into the utilitarianism of the group. (2006, 112)

To the utilitarianism of the group, he opposes the humane value of psychoanalysis:

> The concrete action of psychoanalysis is truly welcome in a harsh order. The significations it reveals in a guilty subject do not exclude him from the human community. It enables a treatment in which the subject is not himself alienated, and the responsibility which it restores in him responds to the hope, which palpitates in any hated being, to take his place within an experienced sense. (2001, 125)

Lacan's respectful approach of the criminal's subjectivity does certainly not imply that we should not hold criminals responsible before the law, as he had clearly stated in his earlier analysis of the famous case of the Papin sisters:

> But we note, for those who are frightened by the psychological path which we shall follow in order to study the issue of responsibility, that the saying "to understand is to forgive" is subject to the limits of each human community, and that, beyond these limits, to understand (or to believe one understands) is to condemn. (1995, 569)

It is in this sense that Roudinesco, the French historian of psychoanalysis, can assert that Lacan is offering a third way to criminology:

> [T]he originality of a position tending to forge a new conception of the relations between psychiatry, criminology, and penal justice may be seen to emerge. Faced with the partisans of dynamic psychiatry attempting to save the insane from the guillotine as well as with the official experts who had become the executioner's accomplices, Lacan emitted, for the first time, the hypothesis of a third path... For him to explain a crime was neither to forgive nor condemn it, neither to punish nor accept it. It was, on the contrary, to 'derealise' it, that is, to restore to it its imaginary, then symbolic dimension. In that perspective, if the criminal is mad, he is not for all that a monster reduced to his murderous instincts... Lacan thus *de-realised the crime without dehumanising the criminal...* [He] emphasised that psychoanalysis resolved the principal enigma of criminology, which remained stymied by the dilemma of a symmetry endlessly pitting reason and madness, man and beast, God and Satan against each other. (Roudinesco, 1990, 128)

The universe of the fault

How does psychoanalysis propose to humanise the criminal? Through "the integration of the subject in the universe of the fault" (Cottet, 2008, 23): "humanisation [...] implies responsibility. This is not to say that irresponsibility is necessarily de-humanising [...] Punishment aims for the assumption of responsibility: the irresponsible [criminal] can become responsible. The implication of the subject in his act remains for Lacan an essential element of penology" (*ibid*, 32).

How does this position translate in practice, in terms of sentencing? Lacan is against both a systematic finding of irresponsibility by reason of insanity in cases where there is an averred mental 'disorder', *and* an ideological meting out of punishment disregarding the psychical causality of the criminal act. Psychoanalysis can make two valuable contributions here: first, by evaluating the dangerousness of the criminal in terms of the subject's own logic, in other ways than through statistical predictors. Second, because psychoanalysis can offer a differential typology of fault according to the subjective reality of the criminal, it can also offer its expert opinion on whether there is a possibility, for a given criminal, of a "subjective assent" (2006, 126) to punishment. This involves determining whether a given subject is amenable to responsibility, is able to answer for his acts.[4] In Miller's terms,

> Responsibility is the possibility of answering for oneself [....] The subject of law, in so far as he is to answer for his actions, is the subject of enunciation – we use a linguistic term. It is the subject who answers for what he articulates at the level of the statement, and this is why it is necessary that he should not confuse himself with his statements. [...] Criminology is of interest to psychoanalysis insofar as it poses the problem of knowing whether mental illnesses should lead to the suspension of the subject of law. (Miller, 1997, 17-19)

When the criminal is *identified* with his acts, with his statements, when he has nothing to say *about* them, then we can say that there is no 'subject' of the unconscious: for psychoanalysis, "our work, deals with the mental illnesses ... in which there is a legal subject, a subject who answers for what he does and says, to the extent that we know that if he can't, things are not going well" (Miller, 1997, 19). When a criminal feels no guilt for his crime, does not perceive it as a fault, is unable to take responsibility, then the verdict of not guilty by reason of insanity may well be the only appropriate option. For such criminals are impervious to the "expiatory signification of punishment".

Without responsibility then, or "the possibility of answering for oneself", there is no sense of fault. And culpability is necessary for punishment to effect the re-integration of the criminal in the community of men. To understand this proposition fully, we must recall that for psychoanalysis it is culpability that founds the social bond. The social bond is an effect of the renunciation to satisfaction that obtains as a consequence of repression. This is what Freud effectively said when he posed the foundational value of incest prohibition in his *Civilisation and Its Discontents* and other writings, such as *Totem and Taboo* or again *Moses and Monotheism*. Yet repression always fails – this is what Lacan meant with his famous aphorism that the repressed was the same thing as the return of the repressed (1988). For both Freud and Lacan, the psychical apparatus is designed to provide satisfactions that substitute for the repressed ones: fantasies and dreams are examples of 'hallucinated satisfaction'. But the superego 'knows' that these formations of the unconscious are ways to enjoy despite prohibition, and this produces the affect of guilt. This affect is, in turn, displaced onto the law as a substitute object of desire: "Law is a reactional formation which follows on from the evil present in each and everyone" (Miller, 2008,

4 On this point, see Biagi-Chai's remarkable book (2007), soon to be published in English under the title *Serial Killers: Criminology, Psychiatry, Responsibility*, with an introduction by Drs Suzanne Yang and Véronique Voruz (Routledge: forthcoming). See also Voruz (2000) for an elucidation of the idea of responsibility in terms of the ability of responding for one's statements at the level of enunciation.

10). And the quality we refer to as 'humanity' is perhaps "precisely the conflict between the two sides of Law and jouissance" (*ibid*).

To summarise the Freudian position: human desire emerges as a desire for transgression – we all know that prohibition's main effect is to render the forbidden object enticing. People for whom the Oedipus complex fully functions repress such desires, feel guilty for having them, and to alleviate this guilt, they invest the energy inhibited from discharge (by repression) in the law itself, as substitute for the prohibited object. The law then acquires a certain libidinal consistency, and feels real for the subject. By contrast, people for whom the Oedipus complex does not function do not experience culpability in this way, and for them the law, though they know it exists, has no libidinal consistency. It has no weight, and they feel no guilt for violating it. This is why psychoanalysts can say that culpability founds the social bond: it makes law exist as a "reactional formation" that substitutes for the solipsistic satisfaction of the drive.

What is the subject of the unconscious?

In this second section I would like to address two frequent, and related, confusions regarding the application of psychoanalysis to criminality. The first stems from a forced reading of Lacan's conception of the law, a misconception that is most evident in the work of French legal historian Legendre, for example in his analysis of the crime of Corporal Lortie (1989). The second has to do with the reduction of psychoanalytic concepts to psychology.

The subject of the unconscious is not the legal subject

Lortie was a young corporal in the Canadian army who, on 8 May 1984, entered the Quebec National Assembly with the intention of "killing the government", firing his automatic weapon in the halls leading to the Chamber (that day, the Assembly was not sitting), killing 3 and wounding 8. Legendre's analysis of this crime is premised upon the idea that the rules of subjective construction (or genealogy, filiation) intermesh with social prohibitions. Lortie's act was thus to be read as an attack against the order of filiation, an acting out his own faulty inscription in the genealogical order organised by the "Paternal Reference".

This interpretation arises out of an antiquated, formulaic reading of psychoanalysis that bears little relation to Lacan's own, far more subtle work: Legendre equates law with the symbolic order said to institute the subject. So for him, the subject of the unconscious is a product of the social order, the current dereliction of which he tirelessly deplores (2000): "on the subjective side, and on the institutional side, the thousand-year old constructions of the genealogical principle are attacked. There are no more fathers, nor mothers. The general, narcissistic mess of the new little familial hells...” (2009, 87; for a further critique of Legendre, see Voruz, 2008).

Yet for psychoanalysis there is no such thing as an *instituted* subject. The symbolic order – linguistic structures into which human subjects are born – produces *effects of subject*, but the unconscious is a *principle of interpretation*, not the internal replication of an external text. This point is well made by psychiatrist Chaumon (2004) in his introductory book *Lacan: la Loi, le Sujet, la Jouissance* (see Voruz: forthcoming, for a review):

> There is no text followed by the coming into play of the subject, but a knowledge that can be said in such a way that a subject is deduced as an after-effect. If language and symbolic laws do precede the subject in his concrete existence, it is false to say that they ‘institute’ him, as for example Pierre Legendre claims. Psychoanalysis teaches us, on the contrary, that there is an act of the subject which is irreducible to any institution. (Chaumon, 2004, 90)

Following Legendre, many commentators rely on the equation symbolic law/legal order in order to legitimise the *forced* imposition of responsibility. Criminals are defined as subjects that have failed, for one reason or another, to internalise the symbolic law. For the proponents of this autocratic version of psychoanalysis, if the law has failed in its institution of a ‘normal’ subject, then the legal order can be used remedially, through an imposition of the law from outside, as it were (Masson, 2006). In this, at best, naïve reading, the legal order can act as a supplementation of the law of the father. We can only imagine the perverse satisfactions such a position provides for those that feel authorized to occupy what, in Freudian terms, would be the position of the Father of the primal horde, the one who is not subjected to the Law.

The subject of psychoanalysis is not the subject of psychology

The second issue has to do with the assimilation of psychoanalytic concepts such as the drive, the unconscious, by psychology, usually when the act remains impervious to ‘objective’ interpretation. Yet psychoanalysis differs crucially from psychology, which tends to interpret the criminal act in a teleological manner, reconstructing the life of the criminal from the endpoint of the passage to the act – *as if* the passage to the act was the only logical outcome. On the contrary, from a psychoanalytic perspective, we try to resituate the criminal act within the logic of the criminal for sure, but not from the outside as it were, as if the criminal were an objective phenomenon that could be deciphered according to ready-made interpretative grids. For “... the subject is a discontinuity in objective causality, and the objective causality of a subjective act can never be fully reconstituted. There is something which is unfathomable in the subjective decision of the delinquent and the criminal” (Miller, 2008, 13).

It is because the subject is always a "discontinuity in objective causality" (Miller, 2008, 13) that the absolute singularity of each and every being is central to psychoanalytic ethics. Unlike psychology, a discipline often subservient to the objectives of the discourse of the master,[5] psychoanalysis cannot treat the individual as an object of knowledge to be apprehended, controlled, and regulated through pre-existing categories.

For psychoanalysis, every subject is an *exception*. The subject's acts are not reduced to the common sense peddled by psychology. Against sense, above all against common sense, psychoanalysis targets what is nonsensical for a subject, and seeks instead to interpret the subject's act as a *response*, an attempted *solution*,[6] to the haunting perplexity of life which for some cannot be reabsorbed into the ready-made world of meaning in which most of us find ourselves more or less comfortably at home. So a passage to the act is to be read as a forced attempt of the subject to re-integrate nonsense, the outside sense, into the realm of signification. For, and this is amazingly clear in the late Lacan, the function of language is above all to act as a barrier against the influx of excessive jouissance (or the *body's* demand for satisfaction, which takes place at the expense of the *subject*) to which each subject is confronted. And when language fails in its function as "apparatus of jouissance" (Lacan, 1998), then passing to the act may well be the subject's last resort against the invasion of jouissance his body is the unfortunate host to (for more precise indications see Maleval, 2000; Miller, 2006).

In order to produce a cogent psychoanalytic reading of the act, one that would yield useful coordinates for an informed strategy of prevention, but also provide a reliable estimation of the possibility of responsibility for a given being, there must be extreme attentiveness to the *words* of the subject, to what he can say of his act – if anything. Psychiatrist Biagi-Chai (2007) has recently carried out such work in her remarkable analysis of the case of Landru, the first French serial killer, who inspired his *Monsieur Verdoux* to Chaplin. She also applied her reading method to Foucault's cause célèbre Pierre Rivière (Foucault, 1982), the young peasant who murdered his whole family (except for his

---

5 Lacan's concept of the discourse of the master (2008) refers to the dominant discourse in a given civilisation. The primary aim of this discourse is to organise the circulation of jouissance (another Lacanian concept that refers to drive-satisfaction, or the quantum of satisfaction that every *body* demands of the *subject* irrespective of the forms this satisfaction takes) in civilisation by means of a few shared signifiers that are at the commands of this discourse. Today for example the common discourse governs the living in the name of risk-prevention, security, precaution. When successful, the discourse of the master imposes the semblance of order on the heterogeneous subjectivities that make up society. The price to pay for the dubious comforts of common, ready-made sense can be singularity when this singularity fails to find ways of articulating itself with the common discourse.

6 Thus Mme Lefebvre, a woman who murdered her pregnant daughter-in-law in 1925, and whose case was made notorious by Marie Bonaparte's commentary, stated after her act that it was "a cure through crime": "I have no worries now" (Lacan, 2006, 107; Naveau, 2006, 175-182, Cottet, 2008, 23).

father) in the early 19th century. The unprecedented value in Biagi-Chai's book resides in the uncompromising sourcing of her interpretations the writings of her subjects, court transcripts, witness accounts. For only the text of a subject may cast light on his motivations.

The subjective signification of the criminal act

This section will sketch out some of the ways in which psychoanalysis can elucidate otherwise enigmatic criminal acts. My focus will be on the subjective structure of psychosis, first on passages to the act and second on crimes whose coordinates are to be found in a subject's personal law.

Passage to the act as forced extraction of jouissance

In today's Lacanian orientation it is accepted that the Oedipal coordinates of subjectivity no longer function as a universal norm. Lacan's concept of the object a, which he invented in the face of the decline of paternal signification, is now configured as the key operator in subjective structures: it 'replaces' the Oedipus as a reading device. The object a has multiple meanings, but basically it refers to the necessary portion of satisfaction that a subject must give up in order to sufficiently des-invest his reality from jouissance. It is an avatar of the Freudian lost object, and often also designates objects of the body that are nonetheless detachable (or *extractable*) from it. Paramount amongst these, are the gaze and the voice, whose failed extraction accounts for visual and auditory hallucinations. In Lacanian theory, "in psychosis the object a is not extracted from the field of reality" (Naveau, 2006, 75). Thus it is frequent for psychotic subjects to hear *voices* or feel they are being *watched*. These hallucinations, referred to as *elementary phenomena*, can easily end up being persecutory – this is what happens when a subject's reality is too full of jouissance, too 'alive'. The 'alive' character of psychotic reality is depicted with astonishing insight in Polanski's *Repulsion* (1965), in which Carol, the main character (beautifully acted by a young Catherine Deneuve) is left alone in the flat she shares with her sister. The flat, objects within it, come to life, the walls fondle her, leading Carol to murder Colin, her would-be suitor, then her landlord.

In psychosis, "this non-extraction of the object a calls for the passage to the act so that a kind of forced extraction may be realised in this way" (Naveau, 2006, 75). Talking about the object-gaze for instance, psychology professor and psychoanalyst Maleval says the following:

> It is often the case that some psychotic passages to the act are linked to the emergence of the object-gaze, which regularly appears in the guise of the evil eye. The subject suddenly feels that the eyes of the devil are

> incarnated in those of his interlocutor, and that he has no other option but to extract them. [...] (2005, 68)

The classic case of the Papin sisters is a telling illustration of passage to the act as a last-ditch attempt at negativating the object. The story is famous – it is the inspiration for Jean Genet's play "The Maids". In 1933 provincial France, two maids savagely murdered their mistress and her daughter, gouging their eyes out, incising their buttocks and thighs, searching for the response to "the mystery of life" in the blood of their victims (Lacan: 1995). For Maleval, in this instance it was the object-voice that was persecutory for Léa and Christine Papin:

> We know that a mere observation on an electric iron that had broken down initiated the unleashing of violence of the Papin sisters towards their mistresses. In fact, Christine and Léa could not bear observations, i.e. critical, threatening words. In October 1928, 4 and half years before the facts, Mme Lancelin, the mistress, had spotted a piece of paper on the floor that had fallen out of the wastebasket. She got annoyed. [...] From that moment on, to protect themselves from these observations, because they could not avail themselves of symbolic or even imaginary mediations, the Papin sisters put into place real, acted defences against the voice. It is known that they had fallen out with their mother about 3 years before the fact, and from that moment they had stopped talking to anyone [...] Additionally, Christine had put into place a system of communication restricting all exchanges with the Lancelin to a strict minimum – since only the mistress could still speak to her. (2005, 68)

Maleval then recounts how, on the evening of the crime, Mme Lancelin had raised her voice. The sisters thought their mistress was about to become violent, like on the occasion of the wastebasket incident, after which she had pinched Léa. For Maleval, these observations amounted to "a persecutory and inassimilable object for them [...] once confronted with it, they were led to answer by an act" (*ibid.*).

This interpretation of the crime of the Papin sisters, an otherwise enigmatic act that had been interpreted in terms of class struggle at the time, illustrates how a passage to the act amounts to the forced extraction of an object. The extraction in question aims to 'mortify' a reality that is too 'alive', and therefore threatening, for the subject that passes to the act.[7]

---

7 Most frequently psychotic passages to the act take the form of suicide, not murder. In this configuration the subject is himself identified with the object and seeks to get rid of it by *leaving the scene*. I am in no way implying that all psychotic subjects are dangerous. On the contrary, a psychoanalytic understanding of the problematic of the object in psychosis offers an incredible potential for prevention both of suicides and violent acts.

Delusional Constructions

Not all acts of violence can be accounted for in terms of the forced extraction of an object. Thus sometimes a crime, or series of crimes, is the logical outcome of a subject's delusion. In *Le Cas Landru* (2007), a book that has all the halting suspense of a detective story, Biagi-Chai reconstructs this logic piece by piece for Henri-Désiré Landru and, with less detail, for Pierre Rivière. Her precise reading of Landru's case highlights the importance of paying close attention to the biographical details of the criminal, and of being mindful of the language in each of his statements as well as of the paradoxical tensions in the criminal's worldview. This attention is essential to understanding the psychopathology of the killer, and the motives of his crimes. Doing so allows one to account for a particular subject's specific acts instead of simply assuming that there is a generic causality, which has no explanatory power in relation to the specific facts of the case. Her close reading also allows her to show that the delusional constructions of psychotic subjects are built around the master-signifiers of their time. But these words take on a *neologistic* signification: to say it otherwise, they harbour a signification which is personal to them, though they are lifted from the common discourse.

Landru was a man who by all accounts led a perfectly normal existence. He was married, had four children, and was even in love with his mistress. Yet he killed 10 women and a man over a period of four years (which coincided with the first World War), after conning them out of their money. He used this money to support his family (or he thought he did, for in all truth it was his wife that kept the household going). It is well known that Landru disposed of the bodies by burning them in the cooker of his country house, which he had rented out for the sole purpose of discharging his gruesome duty. Biagi-Chai reads Landru's actions in the light of his delusional interpretation of the spirit of the time – that a man ought to be "doing everything for his family". But for Landru, this axiom was divorced from the signification which common sense, the sense common to all, gave this duty. Instead, it occupied the place of the law for the subject, albeit a truly personal one. It legitimised every one of his actions, and he showed no remorse.

> The key word 'family' defined a duty for Landru, but a strangely singular one, for it was a duty with a private signification. Because 'duty', this other word, was for him just as neologistic as 'family', and all his illicit activity converged toward a *raison d'être* which inscribed him, not in the Other of the pact, among others, but alone next to others. [...] The signifier 'duty' held singular echoes for Landru, and not the common sense that psychiatrists, police officers and judges conferred upon it during the trial, in recognizing that Landru had 'a sense of the family'. In the absence of the symbolic law that would define the ethical and moral coordinates [of this sense of the family], Henri-Désiré Landru took the

> principle 'to do everything for one's family' to the letter. 'To do everything for one's family' was therefore an absolute postulate and as such nothing stopped him. [...] The personal law, which organized the whole of the subject's conducts, can be said to be delusional. (Biagi-Chai, 2007, 49)

In the book's final chapter Biagi-Chai applies the same method to Pierre Rivière, the young man who "slaughtered his mother, his sister and his brother" in 1835 before wandering off into the wild for a month (Foucault, 1982). She reads Rivière's writings, in which he meticulously listed all the torments his mother inflicted upon his father as a justification for his murderous act. For Biagi-Chai, Rivière's world revolved around the idea of saving his father. She links his delusion with the emergence of the Father as a master-signifier of the time. After the Napoleonic period, which had already magnified the figure of the great man, "whose authority stems from his individual merit" (2007, 201), Louis-Philippe was chosen by the deputies to rule over France: "the image of a father, a man and not a living god, entered the historical landscape with the figure of the king and his government. It entered the social landscape with the growing importance of the *paterfamilias*" (ibid, 201-202).

I cannot do justice to her precise argumentation here. But her elaboration opens another theoretical avenue for the elucidation of otherwise enigmatic crimes, crimes that were once interpreted as reactions to the social context of the criminals. For although these criminals borrow their key words from the discourse of their times, these words do not function as symbolic coordinates lending themselves to the play of desire, but rather as injunctions, imperatives that target them personally, and which they feel compelled to act upon.

There are of course other types of criminals, other motivations for criminal actions that do not fit with the two interpretations outlined here. And for sure there are cases, such as perhaps that of the Columbine shootings, where the criminals may just be acting out of the jouissance of a destruction that includes them. But even then, instead of giving in to the temptation of seeing these criminals as monsters, or even as victims of their circumstances, as sociology is wont to do, we may instead choose to glimpse the desperation of subjects for whom life feels utterly factitious, their murderous acts a desperate attempt at a forced inscription in the real.

There is much more to be written on this particular topic, and this section merely indicates the wealth of potential avenues for future, collaborative work between forensic psychiatry, law, criminology and psychoanalysis. Let us just say for now that the psychical causality of a given crime should never be taken for read, that the appropriate punishment should be decided on a case by case basis, and not through the use of seemingly sophisticated predictive tools that foreclose the singular signification the criminal act may hold for a subject.

The Complementarity between Social Bond and Symptoms

At the beginning of this chapter I said that although the signification a subject gave to his actions was always singular, there was a complementarity between a given modality of the social bond and the symptoms that it produces. I would like, here, to elicit the logic of this complementarity.

What is the social bond for psychoanalysis?

In his 17th seminar Lacan (2008) developed a psychoanalytic theory of discourse, identifying what he thought were the four main discursive dispositifs at play in our civilisation. He named them the discourses of the master, analyst, hysteric and university. I won't go into detail here: suffice it to note, for our present purpose, that the great novelty of his theory resided in the assertion that a discourse was a social bond, and that it was primarily a *mode of jouissance*. To say it otherwise, a discourse's function in making sense is secondary to the satisfaction that it produces. More simply, sense is above all a vector of satisfaction, a mode of organising satisfaction in civilisation. This is perhaps clearer than ever today, when so many discourses endure in the face of their refutation (see Harcourt's disproving of the broken window theory, or of the reliability of crime-prediction tools, 2001; 2007). They endure, not because they are true or even effective, but because they provide ways for a given civilisation to curb the jouissance of its subjects, to channel it through the networks of signification they generate.

By envisaging a discourse as a modality of jouissance, we can see why symptoms are historically determined:

> As the discourse of the master changes in the course of history – which is a way of saying that the social bond changes – the world that 'speaks us' and of which we speak, also changes. The big symbolic roads change. Consequently, symptoms, which, in a certain way, complete discourse, symptoms, which reveal the power of what we call jouissance, corresponding to each discourse, also change. (Brousse, 2009, 11)

Symptoms are responses to the discourses within which they arise in two ways: as subjective modalities of jouissance, and as nominations from the social. For example we can think of the clinic of addictions, which is fairly recent. This is not to say that there were no addicts before the 1960s, but that the symptom of addiction as the social nomination of a modality of jouissance is relatively new. It is the same with eating disorders. They complete a discourse in which, according to Miller's hypothesis, the drive-object (providing surplus-jouissance) is at the commands of civilisation (2005a, 11), with ravaging effects for contemporary subjects.

> The dictatorship of surplus-jouissance is devastating nature; it is fragmenting marriage, dispersing the family and remodelling the body. This remodelling does not only concern plastic surgery or dieting [...] it can go further still, to more important surgery and other operations on the body. Now that the genome has been deciphered, decrypted, it is really going to be possible to advance towards what some authors have called posthumanity. [...T]he relation between the two sexes is going to become more and more impossible, so that, to put it this way, the one-all-alone will be the posthuman standard, the one-all-alone, all alone to fill out questionnaires in order to receive his or her evaluation, and the one-all-alone commanded by a surplus-jouissance presenting itself under its most anxiety-generating guise. (*ibid*, 19)

Here, Miller is pointing to the growing solitude of the modern subject, whose life is no longer sufficiently structured by the traditional symbolic values of work, sexual difference, the family. All that is left for the posthuman subject is to enjoy him- or herself all alone, without limits. Over-eating, oniomania (the 'medical' term for a 'shopaholic'), binge drinking and drug-addiction are symptomatic of a deregulated relation to the object, an all-devouring orality that can never be sated. These symptoms complete the 'all-alone' modality of contemporary subjectivity: subjects who cannot gain a sense of being through their ideal identifications strive to do so through their relation to objects of consumption. As these objects provide, at best, a temporary semblance of being (no sooner does one acquire a desired object that it transforms into a burdensome piece of waste), contemporary civilisation is marked by failure, compulsion, serialisation, and a never-ending push-to-consumption.

Governing by number

So what kind of discourse does give rise to such compulsive modalities of object-relation? Developing Miller's quotation, what specifies the social bond today is evidently its obsession with numbers: whether we are talking about breaking the code of human identity (biometrics), positioning ourselves in relation to the norm (questionnaires in magazines, self-evaluation practices, the RAE[8] process) or the practices of governing by number, it is clear that the current discourse of the master is not truly driven by an ideal to be achieved in a given society, such as justice, equality or democracy, but by the number. In a relatively recent lecture, entitled "The Era of the Man without Qualities" after Robert Musil's novel, Miller offered the following comments on the present:

8 Research Assessment Exercise (in the UK: periodic evaluation of academic research output).

> Becoming a countable and comparable unit is the effective translation to give of the contemporary domination of the master-signifier in its purest, most stupid form: the number 1... The man without qualities is the one whose destiny is to no longer possess any other quality except being marked by the 1 and, by virtue of this, to become part of the quantity.... The master-signifier as a countable unit is both the most stupid of master-signifiers to have appeared on the scene of History, the least poetic, but it is also ... the most elaborate, since it is precisely cleansed of any signification. It leads to what is apparently a necessity for contemporary societies, which is the establishment of lists. (2004, 75)

We no longer try to define reality through presupposed signifying categories, but by isolating regularities through empirical observation. Because nature is losing its credence as interpretative framework for human reality, we have lost the sense of who we are. So we seek to generate a representation of what it is to be human through statistical data. Because we fail to do so with any kind of consistency, the rapid consumption of objects presents itself as a 'solution' to the elusiveness of being.

According to psychoanalyst Brousse, it is with respect to the domination of the number that we can also understand another modality of completing the current discourse: it is the emergent subjective structure christened *ordinary psychosis* by Miller (2005b) during a clinical conversation held in Antibes in 1998. Ordinary psychosis, she argues, is the symptom that best responds to the contemporary discourse. Ordinary psychotic subjects evidence "super-social behaviour", they are subjected to a "statistical superego": "We are talking about an absolute submission, a metonymical one of course rather than a metaphorical one, to the common uses; to banality such as is defined by the average of the curve" (2009, 13).

This is the final way in which psychoanalysis can be of use to criminology: not only by diagnosing criminals, but also by 'diagnosing' ourselves, as subjects who complete the contemporary discourse, but who can also decide to decomplete it. The most difficult part is, as ever, to recognise the share we take in the ills we complain of.

Conclusion

Barely concealed beneath the wish to dispense with psychoanalysis, currently evident in the attempts to regulate the psy professions in many European countries, there is the desire to do away with the drive, with the "obscure share of ourselves" that makes us human. As Roudinesco (2007) reminded us recently,

> [Freud] conferred an essentially human dimension on the perverse structure – [as] jouissance in evil/suffering, the eroticisation of hatred, but not as a defect, degeneracy, an anomaly [...] This is how Freud introduced what one could call a universal of the perverse difference in the psyche: every human being is inhabited by crime, sex, transgression, madness, negativity, passion, *égarement*, inversion etc [...] By showing that the perverse disposition is specific to man, that each subject carries a potential for it within himself – and so that pathology clarifies the norm – Freud affirmed that the only limit to the abject deployment of perversion came from a sublimation incarnated in the values of love, education, Law and civilisation. (104-7)

Roudinesco's uncompromising assertion echoes with the title of one of Miller's recent articles: "Nothing is more human than crime" (2008). Psychoanalysis is not there to sustain the beautiful images we use to cloak the abject dimension of being. It offers no redemption, but merely the chance of humanising the radical solitude we experience at times when the cruel demand for satisfaction of the drive is most acute, and separates us from those we love. Through speech addressed to another, who knows how to receive it, the abjection of being can be taken up in the social bond that the analytic dispositif is. The same applies to criminals; they do not belong to another species, they are not monsters but subjects whose actions we can choose to read as *solutions* to their experience of the real, solutions that also *complete* the contemporary social bond. Psychoanalysis, itself a pragmatic discourse, makes no other promises than that of *respectfully* listening for the singularity of each and every subject.

References

Biagi-Chai, F. 2007. *Le Cas Landru: à la Lumière de la Psychanalyse*. Paris: Imago.

Brousse, M.-H. 2009. La Psychose Ordinaire à la Lumière de la Théorie Lacanienne du Discours. *Quarto*, 94-95, 10-15.

Chaumon, F. 2004. *Lacan: La loi, le Sujet et la Jouissance*. Paris: Michalon.

Cottet, S. 2008. Criminologie Lacanienne. *Mental: Revue Internationale de Santé Mentale et Psychanalyse Appliquée*, 21, 17-37.

Ferrell, J., Hayward, K., Young, J. 2008. *Cultural Criminology: an Invitation*. London: Sage.

Foucault, M. 1977. *Discipline and Punish: The Birth of the Prison*. London: Penguin.

Foucault, M. 1978. *The History of Sexuality vol. 1*. London: Penguin.

Foucault, M. Ed. 1982. *I, Pierre Rivière, Having Slaughtered my Mother, my Sister and my Brother... a Case of Parricide in the 19th Century*. University of Nebraska Press.

Foucault, M. 2003. *Le Pouvoir Psychiatrique*. Paris: Gallimard/Seuil.

Foucault, M. 2004. *Sécurité,Territoire, Population*. Paris: Gallimard/Seuil.

Freud, S. 1913.*Totem and Taboo*. PFL 13.

Freud, S. 1929. *Civilisation and its Discontents*. PFL 12.

Freud, S. 1939. *Moses and Monotheism*. PFL 13.

Gauchet, M. 2002. *La Démocratie contre Elle-Même*. Paris: Gallimard.

Harcourt, B. 2001. *Illusion of Order: The False Promise of Broken Windows Policing*. Harvard: Harvard UP.

Harcourt, B. 2007. *Against Prediction: Punishing and Policing in an Actuarial Age*. Chicago: University of Chicago Press.

Hayward. K. 2007. Situational Crime Prevention and its Discontents: Rational Choice Theory versus the 'Culture of Now'. *Social Policy and Administration*, 41-3, 232-250.

Lacan, J. 1988. *Freud's Papers on Technique 1953-1954*. New York & London: Norton.

Lacan, J. 1995. Motives of Paranoid Crime: the Crime of the Papin Sisters. *The Journal of Forensic Psychiatry*, 6-3, 564-575.

Lacan, J. 1998. *Encore: On Feminine Sexuality, Love and Knowledge 1972-1973*. New York & London: Norton.

Lacan, J. 2001. *Autres écrits*. Paris: Seuil.

Lacan, J. 2006. *Écrits. The First Complete Edition in English*. New York & London: W. W. Norton & Co.

Lacan, J. 2008. *The Other Side of Psychoanalysis*. New York & London: Norton.

Legendre, P. 1989/2000. *Le Crime du Caporal Lortie*. Paris: Flammarion, collection Champs.

Legendre, P. 2000. *La Fabrique de l'Homme Occidental*. Paris: Arte Editions & Fayard, Collection Mille et Une Nuits.

Legendre, P. 2009. *Vues Éparses: Entretiens Radiophoniques avec Philippe Petit*. Paris: Mille et Une Nuits.

Maleval, J.-C. 2000. *Logique du Délire*. Paris: Masson.

Maleval, J.-C. 2005. *Il n'y a pas d'Angoisse Psychotique*. Quarto, 85, 66-72.

Masson, A. 2006. Du Tomber en Responsabilité à l'Advenir Responsable. In T. Moreau and F. Digneffe (Ed.), *La Responsabilité et la Responsabilisation dans la Justice Pénale* (pp. 169-192). Louvain-la-Neuve: De Boeck&Larcier, Collection Perspectives Criminologiques.

Miller, J.-A. 1997. Santé Mentale et Ordre Public. *Mental. Revue Internationale de Santé Mentale et Psychanalyse Appliquée, 3*, 15-26.

Miller, J.-A. 2004. L'Ère de l'Homme Sans Qualités. *La Cause freudienne*, 57, 73-97.

Miller, J.-A. 2005a. Une Fantaisie. *Mental: Revue Internationale de Santé Mentale et Psychanalyse Appliquée*, 15, 9-27.

Miller, J.-A. ed. 2005b. *La Convention d'Antibes – La Psychose Ordinaire*. Paris: Agalma/Le Seuil.

Miller, J.-A. 2006. Jacques Lacan: Remarques sur son Concept de Passage à l'Acte. *Mental: Revue Internationale de Santé Mentale et Psychanalyse Appliquée, 17*, 17-28.

Miller, J.-A. 2008. Rien n'est Plus Humain que le Crime. *Mental: Revue Internationale de Santé Mentale et Psychanalyse Appliquée, 21*, 7-14.

Naveau, P. 2004. *Les Psychoses et le Lien Social: Le Nœud Défait*. Paris: Anthropos.

Naveau, P. 2006. L'Extraction de l'Objet a et le Passage à l'Acte. *La Cause Freudienne, 63*, 75-78.

Neocleous, M. 2008. *Critique of Security*. Edinburgh: Edinburgh UP.

Roudinesco E. 1990. *Jacques Lacan and Co. A History of Psychoanalysis in France 1925-1985*. Chicago: The University of Chicago Press.

Roudinesco. E. 2007. *La Part Obscure de Nous-Mêmes: une Histoire des Pervers*. Paris: Albin Michel.

Voruz, V. 2000. Psychosis and the Law: Legal Responsibility and Law of Symbolisation. *International Journal for the Semiotics of Law, 13-2*, 1-26.

Voruz, V. 2008. For the Love of the Law. *International Journal for the Semiotics of Law, 21-1*, 73-83.

Voruz, V. (forthcoming). Subjectivité Criminelle au-delà de la Dangerosité et du Psycho-Juridisme. *International Journal for the Semiotics of Law*.

Criminology and Forms of Life

Luis LOBO-GUERRERO
Keele University (UK)

Introduction

This chapter offers an introduction to the idea that criminalisation, crime, and crime control, as central concerns for the study of criminology, should be encompassed within a wider analysis of specific forms of life. Forms of life, seen here as a Nietzschean concept, do not operate in a vacuum of power. As explained below, they operate in relation to orders of governance and security discourses and practices. As such, forms of life constitute *an empirical space* from which to interrogate different forms of understanding the securing of a moral order. However, as criminologists very well know, it is not possible to speak of a moral order in general since moral orders reflect transformations in the understanding and the governance of what is understood 'to be alive'.

Within a broadly understood liberal way of governance, the form of life object of security is characterised by the celebration of difference and potentiality. Constituting a political economy of security, the liberal way of life depends on its capacity to promote and protect the heterogeneous and pluripotential character of individuals and populations. The question then is *how to understand criminalisation, crime, and crime control in such a way that heterogeneity and pluripotentiality be promoted and protected?* This chapter does not seek to answer this question but rather to provide some elements for the analysis of the problem it poses. In this spirit, the contribution does not seek to tell criminologists how to conduct their research but rather to contribute elements to fertilise their analyses.

The referent of security and the problem of collective protection

The concept of security has been a concern for social scientists since the very inceptions of disciplinary scholarship. Broadly understood, the security of individuals and societies has been analysed from the disciplines of Sociology, Anthropology, Psychology, and Criminology, while the study of the security between states has been a primordial concern for students of Politics and International Relations. However, when looked at in detail, the study of security always goes beyond disciplinary boundaries. The study of the drugs trade as a security issue is an example which cannot be accurately understood by focusing on one discipline in particular. In fact, security phenomena will always exceed the capacity of the disciplinary strategies devised to study it.

It is in principle possible of course to inform criminological approaches to security with security studies within International Relations. This would constitute an inter-disciplinary approach. Psychological dimensions could be added to the analysis as well as anthropological concerns with security and culture. However, the study of security phenomena will always go beyond interdisciplinarity, which, by definition, would entail negotiations between methodological and disciplinary perspectives. Whereas the traditional referent object of security for International Relations has been the national-state, and the principal security concern for criminology has been the theorisation and practice of crime prevention and control, both the state and ideas of crime relate to a common intellectual and practical problem: the protection of 'the human' (however this idea is understood) and the ways in which it lives. It makes sense in this regard to approach security not through the identification of objects of analysis and disciplined epistemologies and methods, but as a common knowledge 'problem space'.

The commonality of security as an intellectual problem is related to what in this chapter will be explained as the function of security practices and strategies, i.e. the promotion and protection of ways of being in the world. Not an easy problem since ways of being in the world are expressions of 'life' and of 'living', concepts which escape definition because they are always *in formation*. To complicate matters further, *forms* of life, or the ways in which individuals and collectivities live and interact with each other and with ideas of nature, are never homogeneous. Herein lies the problem of power understood as the exercise of influence of a way of being in the world over another. Analyses of security as well as analyses of power relations have to cope with the fact that there is no single understanding of life or being in the world. This is clear, for example, when looking at biological and social understandings of the concept.

Biologically speaking, accounts of life are constantly undergoing dramatic transformation. Take for example the history of the molecular revolution starting in the 1950s where a focus on the cell shifted to the gene, and now to the molecule (c.f. Neumann-Held and Rehmann-Sutter, 2006). Whereas the expectation for the last sixty years was that we would be able to reveal the genetic composition of life, as 'the book of life' (Kay, 2000), we have now discovered that the 'nature' of life rests on the capacity of molecules to recombine (Tyers and Mann, 2003). We also know that this is not a finalised process at birth but that vital activity continues throughout our lifetime and that 'death' is a human idea (Franklin and Lock, 2003). The promotion and protection of biological life through medicine and health care, for example, has had to account with these shifting imaginaries of vitality.

If life, on the other hand, is to be described through observations of the ways in which individuals, societies, and collectivities 'live', it is evident that there is no such thing as a single 'form of life'. Take any unit of analysis involving individuals and collectivities and you will find differences of vital expression. For example, and to take a case of International Relations, what can be understood as a liberal way of life cannot be generalised to the different countries that are meant to be characterised by it. If the defence policies of countries like Canada, the United States, and Sweden are compared, strong differences can be observed. When looking at their different approaches to health provision, the contrasts become even clearer. The same could be argued for members of a family and a given society. Careful observation of the ways in which individuals and collectivities coexist with each other indicates that forms of being in the world, if apparently in display of general features, are never unique and in fact exist in relation to each other. There is also an aspect of pluripotentiality and heterogeneity that will be explained later on. Diversity and heterogeneity in ways of being in the world are the rule and not the exception within societies.

If this is true, as this chapter assumes, and the function of security practices and strategies is to promote and protect ways of being in the world, 'forms of life', then, what are these and how do we as scholars go about researching security? In order to approach this question a second assumption must be made evident from the start. It has been traditionally assumed within the study of security, particularly within International Relations, that what constitutes the security of one produces the insecurity of the other. This has been referred to as a 'zero-sum game' (e.g. Booth and Wheeler, 2007). However, analysing security as the promotion and protection of forms of life makes it evident that if 'life' is meant to be the referent of analysis for security, different expressions of life do not fall within a zero-sum game rationale. That which promotes the existence of one does not necessarily have to operate against the existence of the other. The object of this chapter is to suggest that forms of life, their coexistence and mutual reinforcement, as well as their pluripotential and heterogeneous character, must be considered when approaching any scholarly study of security. To this end, the first section offers a discussion of the idea of forms of life, its emergence within the context of the modernity and its implications for the study of security. The second section offers a reflection of how forms of life can be used to analyse what Foucault referred to as *security dispositifs*, as will be explained then, in relation to criminological research. A final reflection is offered as conclusion

Forms of Life and 'ways of being in the world'

> As soon as any philosophy starts to believe in itself it always creates a world in its own image (Nietzsche, 2000a: 204).

Understanding life, not as a determined and unchangeable form, but in terms of the ways in which people live, is an idea that has been well-expressed in the development of what can be considered as a critique of modernity. Friedrich Nietzsche, for example, spoke of the idea that a form of life relates to the ways in which people have *fixed up* the world in which they live. This involves assuming 'bodies, lines, planes, causes and effects', understandings of 'motion and rest, and form and content' (2000b: section 121). These aspects entail a corporeality, a physicality, and an aesthetics that if unchallenged operate as 'articles of faith'. The ways in which a form of life is understood, and especially, the ways in which these 'articles of faith' are assumed (or rejected), become primordial aspects when understanding the ways in which forms of life are preserved, promoted, and protected. Any deviation from such assumed criteria (the norm), any act and doubtful practice, would be taken to exceed established or unwritten patterns of acceptability and would signify a performance of otherness that will in turn endanger the very coherence and stability of a form of life. Deviations, abnormalities and difference, operate as threats to that which has been classically accepted as 'desirable' and 'good' in the way that any attempt to 'be' outside the 'normal' patterns of existence is taken as a threat (danger) to the established order.

The idea of an established order that supports, or helps to express forms of life is operationalised around the concept of morality. Morality, although constituting a complex problem for modern philosophy, has been commonly understood in modernity, and following Immanuel Kant's idea of the 'categorical imperative', as a standard for rationality. For Kant, although this will not be a new idea for criminologists, a moral act would be one that could be used to exemplify the existence of a universal law ([1785] 1993: 30). A moral act would be a desirable rational act regardless of particular circumstances. One should only do to others what one would accept others doing upon oneself. Consequently, the idea of immorality involves a violation of the categorical imperative and is therefore considered as irrational.

A condition of possibility for this idea of morality, however, is the assumption that it is rationality which allows for the freedom of will. The possibility of exercising autonomous will, the possibility for a self-governing reason, in turn allows for the operation of a solid and moral society. However, this idea of a moral rational order is a secular construction that seeks to replace a Christian morality. Kantian moralism arises as a critique to the order of the Church and is traditionally presented as the emancipation from a Christian dogma premised on faith. In a Kantian world the operation of a new secular philosophy would establish the principles for order in society. Modern 'man' was to be rational in 'his' expectations of freedom. Kantian morality, nonetheless, sought to replace the old order of the Church by constituting new instruments of faith. The idea of the rational, for example, operated upon the possibility of a demonstrable logic. Truth had to be premised on causal and effectual evidence. Science resulted from the methodical and replicable analysis of nature and provided the basis for an accumulative knowledge that will help 'man' 'discover' the world, constituting an epistemology. A rational act was meant to replace one ruled by passions in which 'man' would obey 'his' instincts and barbaric desires (Hirschman, 1977). An education based on the new enlightened morality would provide secure foundations for knowledge and liberate 'man' from such enslavement making 'him' part of the civilised world. The history of such Enlightenment, however, and of the practices through which it proceeded, is the history of a complex political project that sought to transform the idea of the human into a form of life.

When analysed in detail, this modern form of life, to give it a label, appears to be not so universal. The scientific foundations of knowledge that supported it have become as relative as the dogma they sought to replace. The establishment of scientific truth, for example, can be challenged when analysing the practices of measurement and the politics of calculation involved in giving an account of reality (see Daston Lorraine and Galison, 2007). The history of the meter, as an illustration, is circumscribed within the power struggles related to the establishment of a centralised political economy in France (Daston Lorraine, 1994). And yet, a meter, and for that purpose any form of measurement, is used as a unit to 'objectively' determine a reality. Another case is Einstein's Law of Relativity which opened up the politicisation of matter introducing the variable of time and perspective into the analysis. When applied to Newton's Universal Law of Gravitation it became clear that the 'law-like' endeavour of scientific knowledge was not as objective as desired. This problem of 'objectivity' relates to a wider problematic of empiricism discussed by David Hume and recently represented and furthered by Gilles Deleuze (c.f., 2005, Deleuze, 2001).

Nonetheless, the political history of the twentieth century has shown how political projects radicalised the possibility of objective knowledge in the form of government and sought to frame 'life' within grand homogenising ideologies. Radically circumscribing the identity of individuals into the identity of the state through political regimes led to the systematic killing and exclusion of 'the other' with well known human consequences (e.g. the Holocaust). The problem, however, was that these radicalisations were extremely modern, extremely rational. They pushed their 'articles of faith' to their logical conclusion assuming them blindly as the foundations for the only possible 'form of life'. The radical exclusion of 'the other' within the Nazi regime was encompassed by the radical exclusion and encampment of the German 'citizen' in allied countries. A presumed 'race' or a nationality were taken to signify an enemy and according to their politics there was only one way of dealing with such forms of identification: concentration and subsequent annihilation. This radical homogenisation of life constitutes a crisis of the modern project and highlights the necessity to critically engage with the possibility of understanding life, not as homogeneous and actual, but as heterogeneous and pluripotential.

Radical politics aside, the problem of knowledge informing ways of being in the world, determining the validity of beliefs in what is to be taken as real, has been central to the concern of thinking the modern. The crisis of the governance of life in modernity has given rise to various critiques which can be explained as a centuries-old conflict between epistemological imaginaries. On the one hand there is a metaphysical tradition that seeks to support the idea that there is a divine benchmark for knowing the world. For example, Descartes's methodical discourse and Kant's categorical imperative imply that there is a subject/object distinction. For Descartes the subject seeks to identify the perfection of a divine order which is an object created by God. For Kant, the subject is a transcendental being that can uncover truth and truth is an objective matter that if rigorously researched can be acquired as knowledge. Objects are then a function of this form of knowledge that places the self at the centre, a centre which is metaphysical inasmuch as it derives its existence from a presupposed ethos. In both cases Truth presupposes the subject.

On the other hand we have the position championed by Nietzsche in the late nineteenth century. He argued that the subject and the object must not be understood separately since they are part of the same problematic. Knowledge of the world, he explained, cannot be objective since the subject that seeks to know is already a metaphysical category, a category that assumes its being on a divine origin. The self, he suggests, is instead part of a contingency that results from power practices. The self cannot be abstracted from all contingency (c.f. Owen, 1995: 27). The self as subject cannot be separated from the world as object because the self is constituted in the process of knowing. As put by Strong's interpretation of Nietzsche, 'the unity of the known and the unity of the knower are derived from the activity of knowing' (Strong, 1988: 301). For Nietzsche, it is the activity of knowing which deserves to be explored in order to understand the form of life constituted in the process. As put by Owen, 'ways of knowing the world are ways of being-in-the-world' (1995: 28).

If ways of being in the world are related to the ways in which we know the world, then life and forms of life are related to relations of power/knowledge. This was one of the conclusions of the work of French thinker Michel Foucault. Inspired and supported by the philosophy of Nietzsche and others he argued that ideas of 'power' and 'knowledge' were mutually implicated (Foucault and Faubion, 1997). In his later work he explained how the power/knowledge nexus materialised in ideas of 'subjectivity' and processes of 'subjectification'. In his analysis, the idea of forms of life was no longer an issue of measuring actions against the possibility of a categorical imperative but of analysing the power/knowledge nexus that materialised in the governance of individuals. Reason was no longer to be taken for granted, nor was logic. There was no logical conclusion to actions but complex ensembles of power, apparatuses as he called them, through which emerging forms of life were promoted and protected. Security was intrinsically related to the very processes through which subjectivity was constituted.

The idea of taking life as the referent of analysis led Foucault to focus on the possibility of thinking security, not in terms of killing and annihilating the other, but in terms of promoting and protecting existence itself (see Foucault,

2007). Instead of killing, the premise of this form of power was to 'make live', and in the process of doing so, promoting and protecting life as well as 'letting die'. Analysing power as agency and not as instrument led Foucault to suggest a philosophy of security expressed in the form of vital power. He called this form of power 'biopolitics' and explained it as the practices of 'making live and letting die', as the compound practices of promoting life. This understanding went beyond the microscopic justification of the logical conclusion of reason anchored on a Kantian morality. Biopower was to be analysed not through Kant's universal laws and imperatives, but in the detailed practices that enabled the grand political rationalities to take place. The analysis of the micro-practices of power, as he showed in his work, would help to prove that there is nothing necessary in political projects other than the practices through which they are actualised; that is, made material. For example, by looking at the micro-practices through which bodies were disciplined through sexual traditions he managed to dispel essentialist moralist assumptions that disciplined sexual behaviours in the West during the last three centuries. When these practices are analysed in terms of their conditions of possibility and operability, it is possible to observe that their ontological premises do not stand rigorous scrutiny.

By assuming that power is not a metaphysical category but a practice through which the conduct of individuals and collectivities is acted upon, Foucault conducted an interrogation of various practices of power through which subjectivity was constituted. For a criminological readership well exercised in Foucault's research on deviancy and abnormality this will not be a new idea. However, the main point of Foucault's work on this respect was that practices and traditions of disciplining and punishment were related to offences to established moral orders. Abnormal ways of being were dangerous for these orders. By taking the sites of the prison and the clinic, among others, he interrogated the conditions of possibility and operability of complex technologies of power that sought to promote and protect forms of life. But forms of life, as it becomes evident in his work, are intrinsically related to the ways the world is understood. Transformations in the forms of knowledge through which the world is known give rise to different understandings of life and forms of life. If disease, for example, is thought to be a form of divine punishment, then pagan beliefs and believers are to be identified and eliminated. If in contrast, disease was understood in relation to what we now know as hygienic practices, then a re-education of the self and a re-design of living spaces would help enhance and promote life. If this was so, as his researched detailed, there was no point in sacrificing 'life' to promote and protect a way of being in the world since forms of life undergo continuous transformation and change.

Moreover, and as a site for interrogating such transformations in the power/knowledge ensemble, he also showed that when traditions of knowledge change new forms of power are developed. A pastoral form of power, for example, serves the purpose of governing individuals through the administration of their souls. However, a pastor can only exercise power over his flock if souls exist. So a particular role of a pastoral form of power has been to ensure the existence of souls as a matter of faith. Scholastic debates in sixteenth century Spain in relation to the question of the non-slave character of 'Amerindians', as the new-found people in Spanish America were called, illustrate this point (Langholm, 1992). Francisco de Vittoria supported the idea that since Amerindians were soulful beings they could not be subjected to slavery. This case can be used to indicate that the ways in which identity is assumed determines the order to which it will be subjected. In this example, soulful Amerindians were to enjoy the benefits of God's universe governed through a pastoral form of power in constant negotiation with a temporal mercantilist order of the state.

A second form of power analysed by Foucault, sovereign power, relies on the sovereign's capacity to make decisions on life and death. Sovereign power is the exercise of power that can, in Foucault's words, 'take life'. The sovereign, however, is not restricted to Carl Schmitt's political theory of friend/enemy distinction. Nor is it solely circumscribed to the role of decision on the exception (Schmitt, 1976). For Foucault, a sovereign form of power governs on a general category of 'people' which is related to a political economy of the state, and although it encompasses a legal order, it also exceeds it. People, in Foucault's genealogical work, in the late seventeenth and early eighteenth centuries are understood as a resource of the state, as a resource that had to be controlled and enhanced. Police, or *polizeiwissenschaft* was developed for this purpose, not as it is currently known, but as a sovereign rationality of government developed for 'the internal refinement of 'reason of state'' (Foucault, Senellart, Ewald et al., 2008). The state, operating a very specific political economy known as mercantilism, had the role of promoting and protecting the life of people as an economic resource. For this reason the state was required to generate knowledge about its people in relation to their sex and age to assess availability of men for military purposes, for example. Occupations and levels of health and wealth were also important information. The exercise of sovereign power as police, however, was not without restraint. Sovereign power operated on its capacity to generate the knowledge of the state and the production of such knowledge was constrained by moral conditions enshrined in law. As noted by Michael Dillon, police 'was also subject to external restraint through the operation of public law; matters which included what Foucault aptly call[ed] "the royal questions" of state concerning constitutions, rights and legitimacy' (Dillon, 2006: 42). The identity of people was the identity of the state and the identity of the state was determined by the moral order of public law.

A third form of power identified by Foucault was that of biopower. Biopower was understood by him as the logic of political formation that takes 'species life' as its referent of governance (Foucault, 2003, Foucault, 2007). In contrast to the sovereign function of 'people' operating in relation to the state, biopolitics is a category of power concerned with 'populations'. Populations are a function of classification of the particularities and specificities of particular lives, *individuated* people. A population is not a subject, or a generality but already the result of processes of 'speciation' which are related to processes of classification (Dillon and Lobo-Guerrero, 2008). The term 'species' is not gratuitous. Species refers simultaneously to a form of classification (a class), a biological order, and also to a particular kind of coinage or money (Oxford English Dictionary). Species is an order of classification which is as much related to relations of power/knowledge, science and government, as it is to an economic ethic (Dillon and Lobo-Guerrero, 2009). Individuals as a function of species-life are not understood as part of a nation or a public, but in virtue of the observable specificities of their lives. Individuals are understood as objects and subjects of power through processes of subjectification. Individuals are understood as categories of government in terms of age groups, sex, occupation, level of education, levels of health, postcodes, risk groups, credit ratings, etc. The idea of biopower, as the form of power that takes species-life as its referent, arises in the late seventeenth early eighteenth-century in relation to an emerging liberal order of governance. The mercantile economic ethos slowly gives place to a form of governance premised on its capacity not to take life, but to 'make live' and 'let die'. This emerging biopolitical order seeks to enhance and promote the lives and forms of lives of populations under an economic ethos that profits from diversity and simultaneity in entrepreneurial and creative spirit. An acquisitive spirit of accumulation begins to give place to a spirit of economic circulation. A mercantilist economic order starts to give place to a liberal economics. New and reformed instruments of government such as probabilities applied to the practice of 'political arithmetic' (Petty, 1690) began to develop at this time as well as other sites of biopolitical practice, not necessarily related to the state, such as insurance (Lobo-Guerrero, 2008, Lobo-Guerrero, 2007, Ogborn, 1962). As a consequence, identity as a biopolitical category became a heterogeneous problem since the identity of individuals could no longer be circumscribed to the identity of the state but needed to be widened to encompass simultaneous identifications. Under this understanding an individual is now simultaneously identified as a subject and an object of power in its multiple capacities of citizen, student, mother, lawyer, patient-at-risk, client with a high risk rating, resident of a specific postcode, genius-to-be, etc. These simultaneous and numerous individual identities are the result of a mentality of government that has developed the technological capacity to know the world in multiple ways (Foucault, 1994). The effects of such a governmentality has been reflected in the capacity to conjugate different ways of being in the world while promoting and protecting the heterogeneity and pluripotentiality of forms of life.

Two final points must be made before advancing some reflections on the use of this analytic of power for criminological research. First, as reflected in Foucault's work and as he explicitly noted in his lectures, these forms of power do not operate independently from one another. It is not possible to analyse them as a historical continuum. Sovereign power interacts with biopower and pastoral power at any given time. Any security analysis should bear this in mind and any radicalisation of politics can fall into the mistake of privileging one form at the expense of the others. Second, the analysis of these forms of power has been developed by reflecting on the history of governance of the Western world. Modernity is a Western project that even if globalised is characteristic to specific economic, cultural, and political European circumstances. This is not to say that the value of Foucault's analytic of power is not useful for analysing security phenomena around the world. Even more so, because modernity is a globalising project, the categories here exposed become useful for understanding the ways in which a very general modern form of life has been exported to other cultures and human groups around the planet. As it might start to appear obvious to the reader, the idea of forms of life relates directly to the three main problems of criminology as dealt with in this book.

Criminology, forms of life, and the analysis of security apparatuses

> 'we need only look at the body of laws and the disciplinary obligations of modern mechanisms of security to see that there is not a succession of law, then discipline, then security, but that security is a way of making the old armatures of law and discipline function in addition to the specific mechanisms of security' (Foucault, 2007: 10).

As implied in the previous section there is a dynamic relationship between forms of life, orders of governance, and security practices. These relationships do not function as a closed system but operate as a complex emergent network where changes in one will affect the nature of the whole. Under such environment, understandings of crime will necessary operate in relation to ways of being in the world, the moral orders thereby instantiated, and the security practices used to promote and protect them. In this way, the analysis of criminalisation, crime, and crime control is intrinsically related to the analysis of the governance of the forms of life in which they take place. For the matter of this chapter, governance is here approached in relation to 'liberal' governance, however wide this category might appear. Liberal governance is here understood in its neoliberal form as described by Ericson, Doyle and Barry, as premised on the idea of a minimal state, stress over market fundamentalism, emphasis on risk-management and risk-taking, underscoring of individual responsibility, and the conception of inequality as a matter of choice (Ericson, Doyle, Barry et al., 2000). Neoliberalism, however arguable and detestable many of its characteristics might appear, has demanded from individuals an entrepreneurial behaviour that is constantly being monitored by 'fidelity techniques' such as audits, budgets, contracts, performance-related pay, competition, among others aimed at achieving an internalisation of 'techniques of self-government' (Rose, 2000). In this respect, the idea of neo-liberal governance as a political project provides a general frame from which to interrogate, and indeed challenge, key questions for criminological research. In what follows, I will explore some of the research opportunities arising from the analysis of criminology as a problem space related to an emergent liberal way of life and the forms of governance developed to govern and secure it.

Criminalisation and criminal accusations of behaviours and groups

The first suggestion, which will not be a novel one for criminologists, is that accusation relates to a process of rendering something within the terms of a criminal category. As a process, it always operates as a *relation* between those accusing those being accused and/or their behaviours, and the moral order that determines what is to be considered as criminal. Criminalisation refers to the actual production of criminal categories. The particular form of analysis expounded in the chapter at hand, then, leads to think about accusation and criminalisation as evolving processes, not essential ones for which fixed manuals and procedures can be established, but ones that demand a constant and careful circumstantial evaluation by those who accuse or criminalise. As typical of neoliberal governmentality, ways of governing an order of the real tend to fall within what Mitchell Dean has called 'technological rationality' (1996). A technological rationality is a technological standardisation of procedures and practices aimed at achieving efficiency and fairness in the system. However, as will appear obvious for anyone dealing with the minutiae of processes of accusation and criminalisation, it is the details of each particular case which make them an exception to the rule. If, for example, accusing actors operate a technological rationality by which they make 'technical' judgements as to how an individual, group, or behaviour fit within pre-established parameters (or 'criminal categories'), they will always be sacrificing valuable information that would allow for a different treatment of the case in point. If for example an accusing actor realises that what appears to be a racially-inspired crime is in fact related to socio-economical deprivation or professional frustration, and insists on presenting the case as one based on race, the case would likely fit the category but will not contribute towards an adequate treatment of the problem. This aside, the information that the accusing actor sacrifices for the sake of assigning the case to a well-known category for which a structured treatment exists (more often than not: punishment), is in fact alerting of the un-classifiable character of life. If we are to stretch this example it would be easy to realise that each particular case will necessarily exceed the category under which it is being treated, and yet, for the sake of efficiency and practicality criminal systems insist on accusing based on known systems of classification. The challenge is then to think of an alternative way of assessing an order of the real in which what appears to be a violation to an established moral order is in fact alerting of the unreasonable way of characterising morality. However, and in fairness with criminological research and other forms of security analysis, developing the capacity to govern without establishing fixed or semi-fixed categories of governance is a wider problem of liberal governance. It relates to the problem of what Foucault called 'economic governance' by which, and through which, efficiency of control over the conduct of individuals and populations can be achieved. Perhaps a way of rethinking accusation, or criminalisation, might be to challenge the idea that accusation and criminalisation are in fact a necessary practice within the promotion and protection of moral orders. Lots of thinking is required on these respects.

Crime causation or emergence and distribution of crime and criminal events

A second idea is related to the ways in which an action or behaviour is classified as crime or as a criminal 'event'. In this respect there is a useful discussion to be had in relation to what constitutes an event and particularly what the relationship of 'crime' as an event is with regards to temporalities (pasts, presents, futures). The philosophy of the event is quite wide and diverse. There is no single form of eventalness, as Deleuze has argued, but a complex reflection that foregrounds temporality. In this respect, temporality performs a role, not as a context that enframes an action or behaviour that has past, is happening, or will occur, but as an 'actant' (Deleuze, 2003). This is a very important aspect for criminological analysis because if temporality is assumed as an actant, then a future refers to a potential and not to a determined time to be. This goes in line with understanding forms of life as 'being-in-formation' and not as predetermined or predestined. In real terms it means that what appears to be is not necessarily what it really is; what a behaviour seems to indicate is not necessarily what will happen; and if a particular feature of behaviour or character is associated with a specific form of crime, it does not mean that the individual that displays it will necessarily commit such forbidden action. If to this line of thought is added the fact that one of the defining features of a liberal way of life is precisely its pluri-potentiality, it means that there would be no way to anticipate what that multiple potential could be. Within a context of neoliberal governance where individuals are expected to be entrepreneurs of their own life and embrace risks, it is expected that the liberal way of life will be pushing the frontiers of the permissible and acceptable all the time. The resulting moral order will therefore have to encompass such dynamism and adapt to the emerging circumstances. To complicate matters more, and to link this reflection with the previous one on accusation or criminalisation, liberal governance is therefore posed with the challenge of how to govern the conduct of individuals and populations under conditions of radical and *emerging* uncertainty. Of course there is no straight solution to this problem and any attempt to design a social science to forecast such pluri-potentiality will necessarily fail.

Emergence of forms and practices of crime control

Finally, the idea of emergence of forms and practices of crime control becomes absolutely relevant when looking at the way liberal life is currently governed. In the same manner in which the old management adage states that only that which can be measured can be managed, it can be argued that only that which is defined can be secured. It is known that the securing of a moral order is the challenge of governance; a challenge that, as everybody also knows, relates to the radical indeterminacy of the form of life that is sought to be promoted and protected. How can criminologists then analyse the emergence of forms and practices of crime control when what is to be defined as a crime escapes fixed definition? The answer is perhaps to be found in questioning the relevance and usefulness of the technological rationality referred to before. If each behaviour and action is unique, and if their uniqueness is to be assessed in actual life, then crime control would have to exceed traditional patterns of standardisation. What this means in real life is that 'one-size-fits-all' modular pre-determined off-the-shelf policies for crime control would simply not be effective regardless of the success rates and efficiency indicators that might be built to support them. Building on the two previous reflections, thinking crime control will necessarily entail thinking about the rationality that supports the idea of crime control as an economic form of governing crime. This, as already stated, is part of a wider liberal governance problematic which cannot be faced solely by criminologists. It constitutes a challenge to the whole idea of security as a modern political problem. For the time being, and as a contribution to reflection on this matter, it will be said that crime control must be thought of in relation to events that are by definition un-determined. Far from being able to operate a panoptic system in which 'big brother' observes, crime control will have to be thought of in terms of open ended promotion and protection of life rather than control. Maybe the way to proceed is not to police what seems to affect what is taken to be as 'good' life but, rather, to support and enhance such life and enable its resilience. Perhaps in such a way we would not have to understand security as an economy of protection in which the need to protect will always drive the offer of protection technologies, organisations, and materiel.

Conclusion

As argued in the chapter, security is not a disciplinary referent object but an intellectual problem that relates to the promotion and protection of ways of being in the world. The specifications of these forms of life are however the result of political and knowledge practices. Ways of knowing the world influence the ways in which forms of life are defined, promoted and protected. Traditions of knowledge are therefore implicated in forms of governance and security strategies. The way we know determine the way we operate in relation to the wider problem of security.

In line with this idea, understandings of security relevant to the study of criminology and other disciplined sciences are embedded within wider intellectual debates concerning the politics of knowing and the practices of power. The study of epistemologies and analytics of power are as pertinent to the study of security practices as they are to the philosophies that support them. In other words, whereas it might appear superfluous to engage with the analysis of philosophical debates underpinning the practices of security when one is concerned with the analysis of everyday security, not doing so makes us scholars hostages to fortune. In a non-objective world, descriptive and operational analyses of security would only reinforce the forms of violence that result from systematic and unreflective security operations.

In the specific case of criminology, definitions of crime and processes of accusation and criminalisation, the aetiology of crime, and crime control and reactions to crime, are all implicitly related to the forms of life they seek to secure. An intellectual engagement with these questions in relation to the heterogeneous and pluripotential character of contemporary liberal life, in the case of advanced liberal economies, will surely result in creative engagements with criminal law and the politics of security.

References

Booth, K. & Wheeler, N. (2007) *The Security Dilemma: Fear, Cooperation, and Trust in World Politics*, London, Palgrave Macmillan.

Daston Lorraine, J. (1994) *Enlightenment Calculations.* Critical Enquiry, 21, 182-202.

Daston Lorraine, J. & Galison, P. (2007) *Objectivity*, New York, Zone Books.

Dean, M. (1996) Putting the technological into government. *History of the Human Sciences,* 3, 9, 47-68.

Deleuze, G. (2001) *Empiricism and Subjectivity: An Essay on Hume's Theory of Human Nature,* Columbia University Press.

Deleuze, G. (2003) *The logic of sense,* London, Continuum.

Deleuze, G. (2005) *Hume. Pure Immanence: Essays on A Life.* New York, Zone Books

Dillon, M. (2006) Governing Through Contingency: The Security of Biopolitical Governance *Political Geography*, 26, 41-47.

Dillon, M. & Lobo-Guerrero, L. (2008) Biopolitics of Security in the 21st Century. *Review of International Studies*, 2, 34, 265-292.

Dillon, M. & Lobo-Guerrero, L. (2009) The Biopolitical Imaginary of Species Being. *Theory Culture Society*, 1, 26, 1-23.

Ericson, R. Doyle, A. & Barry, D. (2000) The moral hazards of neoliberalism: lessons from the private insurance industry. *Economy and Society*, 532-558.

Foucault, M. (1994) Governmentality. In FAUBION, J. (Ed.) *Michel Foucault: Power, the essential works 3*. London, Allen Lane -The Penguin Press.

Foucault, M. (2003) *Society must be defended : lectures at the College de France, 1975-76*, New York, Picador 2003.

Foucault, M. (2007) *Security, territory, population*, Basingstoke, Palgrave Macmillan.

Foucault, M. & Faubion, J. D. (Eds.) (1997) *Power: The essential works of Michel Foucault, 1954-1984*, London, Allen Lane.

Foucault, M., Senellart, M., Ewald, F. O., Fontana, A., Burchell, G. & Collège de France. (2008) *The birth of biopolitics : lectures at the College de France, 1978-1979*, Basingstoke, Palgrave Macmillan.

Franklin, S. & Lock, M. (2003) *Remaking Life and Death: toward an anthropology of the biosciences*, Oxford, Santa Fe: School of American Research Press.

Hirschman, A. O. (1977) *The Passions and the Interests: Political Arguments for Capitalism Before its Triumph*, Princeton, Princeton University Press.

Kant, I. ([1785] 1993) *Grounding for the Metaphysics of Morals* Hackett.

Kay, L. (2000) *Who Wrote the Book of Life: A History of the Genetic Code*, Stanford, Stanford University Press.

Langholm, O. (1992) *Economics in the Medieval Schools: Wealth, Exchange, Value, Money, and Usury, according to the Paris Theological Tradition 1200-1350*, Leiden, E.J. Brill.

Lobo-Guerrero, L. (2007) Biopolitics of specialised risk: An Analysis of Kidnap and Ransom Insurance, *Security Dialogue*, 38 (3): 315-334

Lobo-Guerrero, L. (2008) Pirates, stewards, and the securitisation of global circulation, *International Political Sociology*, 2, 3: 219-235

Neumann-Held, E. M. & Rehmann-Sutter, C. (2006) *Genes in development: re-reading the molecular paradigm*, Durham [N.C.], Duke University Press.

Nietzsche, F. (2000a) Beyond Good and Evil. in Nietzsche, F. (Ed.) *Basic Writings of Nietzsche*. New York, The Modern Library.

Nietzsche, F. (2000b) The Gay Science, in Seventy-Five Aphorisms from Five Volumes. in Nietzsche, F. (Ed.) *Basic Writings of Nietzsche*. New York, The Modern Library.

Owen, D. (1995) *Nietzsche, Politics and Modernity*, London, Sage.

Petty, W. (1690) *Political Arithmetick*, London Printed for Robert Clavel at the Peacock, and Hen.Mortlock at the Phoenix in St. Paul's Church-yard; available at:
http://socserv2.socsci.mcmaster.ca/~econ/ugcm/3ll3/petty/poliarith.html.

Rose, N. (2000) Governing Liberty. in Ericson, R. & Stehr, N. (Eds.) *Governing Modern Societies*. Toronto, University of Toronto Press.

Schmitt, C. (1976) *The Concept of the Political* New Jersey, Rutgers University Press.

Strong, T. B. (1988) *Friedrich Nietzsche and the Politics of the Soul,* Berkeley, University of California Press.

Tyers, M. & Mann, M. (2003) From genomics to proteomics (insight overview). *Nature,* 422, 193-197.

Crime, Crisis, Critique. On Dogmatic and Creative Use of Foundations

Claudius MESSNER
University of Salento (Italy)

Introduction

In discussing the functioning of foundations in the context of 'new directions for criminology', we must first clarify the topic. The words crime, crisis, and critique in my title evoke the image of a troika of ideas. In fact, in observations of crime they are inevitably tied together. But each of these notions stands for a knot of questions. The word 'crime' is derived from the Latin word *crimen*, which derives from the verb *cernere* (to decide, to judge) and refers to the sphere of judgment, accusation, offence. 'Crisis' derives from the Greek *krisis* which, while it literally means judgment, refers to a situation where things reach a decisive point, such as a turning point in a disease. It stems from the verb *krinein* (to separate, sieve, discriminate, discern, distinguish) which shares the same base as the Latin *cernere*. So both 'crime' as well as 'crisis' combine the level of facts and events with the level of distinction and decision. Calling something 'crime' implies a judgment which draws on its very own distinctions. The same is true for 'critique': it does not indicate first and foremost a negative valuation, a rejection or censure. It refers to the formation of a judgment, a consideration, or an examination which provides itself with the instruments needed in order to come to a judgment. Thus, the notion of critique includes both a decision and a question, i.e. the decision implied by the form of judgment, and the question of whether the judgment has legitimate foundations (Derrida 1990).

There is no doubt, then, that crime discourse cannot lack direction. It has, rather, a somewhat intrinsic sense of direction. But which is the particular course or 'line' pursued by criminology? To be clear, in so questioning criminology we are not interested in assessing the direction(s) criminology is moving in as either right or wrong, and we will ourselves not give directions. The subject matter of this chapter is not a new conception of crime or criminality, nor is it to suggest a new object for criminology or a new definition of criminology's scope. We are not concerned with what has happened, will happen, or should happen in crime discourses. Instead we will take a step back from criminology and test a form of questioning which does not merely question actions within the criminological field, but which also questions the way questions are asked in the field.

Our guide here will be Austrian writer Robert Musil (1953) who elaborated on the logic of the possible in his unfinished novel *The Man without Qualities*. Whereas realist narrative aims at explaining how things happen in such a way that a fictitious story appears likely, Musil tries to simply juxtapose many different interpretations of events and contexts, without a common thread or plot that produces coherence. By spreading out possible interpretations of events, possible contexts are opened up. Stable contexts become unhinged by reflexive framing. In a book that includes over one thousand pages, the paradoxes, points and counterpoints abound. The narrative develops and shows the contingency of all interpretations, including the one given by itself. This is an open-ended novel, and not even the author knows which interpretation ultimately prevails. Musil observes a variety of different, but complementary expectations of 'sense':

> If one wants to pass freely through open doors, one must bear in mind that they have a solid frame: this principle ... is simply a requirement of the sense of reality. But if there is such a thing as a sense - and no one will doubt that it has its *raison d'être* - then there must also be something that one can call a sense of possibility. Anyone possessing it does not say, for instance: Here this or that has happened, will happen, must happen. He uses his imagination and says: Here such and such might, should, or ought to happen. And if he is told that something *is* the way it is, then he thinks: Well, it could probably just as easily be some other way. So the sense of possibility might be defined outright as the capacity to think how everything could 'just as easily' be, and to attach no more importance to what is than to what is not (Musil 1953, 11-12).

Consider actuality and potentiality (e.g. in the phrase 'potentiality is actual'): the 'abnormal' use of the distinction 'being/not-being' here leads to the suspension of the formal-logical principle *tertium non datur*. The 'Law of the excluded third' observes events and things under the condition that all of them are what they are and are not what they are not. In contrast, the 'possibilist' reframing suggested by Musil not only allows us, but *compels* us to see things in a different light.

> Such possibilitarians live, it is said, within a fine web, a web of haze, imaginings, fantasy and the subjunctive mood. If children show this tendency it is vigorously driven out of them, and in their presence such people are referred to as crackbrains, dreamers, weaklings, know-alls, and carpers and cavillers. When one wants to praise these poor fools, one sometimes calls them idealists. ... A possible experience or a possible truth does not equate to real experience or truth minus the value 'real'; but, at least in the opinion of its devotees, it has in it something out-and-out divine, a fiery, soaring quality, a constructive will, a con-

> scious utopianism *that does not shrink from reality but treats it, on the contrary, as a mission and an invention.* ... It will be seen that the consequences of such a creative disposition can be remarkable, and unfortunately they do not infrequently make the things that other people admire appear wrong, and the things that other people prohibit permissible, or even make both appear a matter of indifference (Musil 1953, 12, my italics).

Obviously, this approach will produce neither theoretical nor empirical knowledge in the sense of science. However, Musil is engaged in a project of theoretical thinking that, if it does not pertain to the realm of science, should address precisely what science cannot observe. By 'trying out' distinctions which might or that could have oriented first-order observations (of what is 'out there'), observed events and actions are framed within other, i.e. second-order observations (that is: observations of observations as observations). In this way, the narrative is charged with contingency and, at the same time, sabotaged by it.

The consequences are remarkable indeed. The position of the ideal narrator/ observer is destroyed. Not only is the narrative not an image of reality; no narrative could guarantee the representation of reality. No observation could ever yield eternal scientific truth. No observation could ever pin down (biographical) identity, or moral or aesthetic norm. The text of the observer/narrator is inevitably self-referential. It observes itself as an attempt to perform the experience of the structural contingency that characterises modern society (Messner 2004a). The observer/narrator's objects are not realities, but discourses; not things, but signs; not experiences, but styles; not events but perspectives. The space wherein observer/narrator's text moves is the space of communication as opened up by different communicative forms and selective discursive practices. Communication refers to countless possibilities. Whoever wishes to say something will have to choose from these countless possibilities. Moreover, communication has become self-referential. Communication communicates by indicating its own practices of indicating.

This brings us back to our topic. As we have seen, our approach here is not based upon objects, but on *forms*, that is, on distinctions made and used by an observer. Form here is the form of a distinction, or the discerned unity of a discerned difference. Reality, for example, is the discerned unity of being/not-being. Sense, as we said, is the discerned unity of actuality/potentiality. An observation, then, is an indication within a frame of difference. A distinction (i.e. a distinction made in an observation by an observer) is a *choice* that requires certain other distinctions. As a choice, it excludes other possibilities. The point is to make observations (and their narratives) apparent as exclusionary distinctions: ' if you do that, if you choose that kind of take-off, you will have no room for manoeuvre, you will not be able to move in all directions'. In short, for the second-order observer (i.e. the observer who, reflexively and self-reflexively, observes observations), all observations are based on their particular guiding distinctions. Guiding distinctions divide the world and dictate how the world is observed. Having arrived so far, we may now be able to say that we are interested here in observing the distinctions made by criminology when it observes crime.

On the basis of some familiar definitions of crime and criminology, we will first outline the twofold problematic of what I would like to call ordinary crime discourse, i.e. the 'substance' question ('what is' crime) raised by the heterogeneity of discourses, and the 'frame' question evoked by the existence of naturalised, or hegemonic taken-for-granted frames. We will subsequently tackle the unspoken methodological premise of 'normal' discourse, i.e. the assumption that holds that disputes over framing can be resolved by the rigorous application of the 'scientific method'. We will take a step back and compare the fundamentalist model of scientific thinking with the contextual-interpretative one. In our final section we will take yet another step back and state the need for a different kind of theorising, i.e. the constructivist one, and illustrate this 'direction' with materials taken from *The Man without Qualities*.

Crime/ not-crime

The meaning of 'criminology' can be defined in various ways. One widespread definition seeks to explain the notion trough translation: criminology here is the 'science of crime', or the science, as a more detailed version adds, that studies the causes and manifestations of crime and criminality and that somehow engages with (or indeed *in*) the fight against crime and criminality. We learn that criminology is a discipline which combines empirical research and practical purpose. But what about crime and criminality? My dictionary explains *crime* as an objective fact defining it 'an act punishable by law, as being forbidden by statute or injurious to the public welfare'. Crime is an act that may prompt, as a consequence, legal punishment because it is forbidden by 'statute', i.e. the law, or because it inflicts injury. Accordingly, *criminality* is explained as the 'quality' of 'being criminal' of a person or act in relation 'to crime or its punishment'. The difficulties with this definition are evident. But more important is the fact that criminology seems (or seemed) to be interested only in acts of offending (or of attributing an offence) but not with any constitutive operation of judgment or decision. Crime –according to criminology- is either an il-legal or an un-just act. Legal/illegal, just/unjust: both paired sets are evoked here, with the sides 'law' and 'justice', in them functioning as unspoken premises of the process of making sense of crime.

Criminologists today, at least the 'critical' ones amongst them, are of course aware of the many questions raised by such a definition. Already Edwin Sutherland (1934), for instance, made a famous attempt to clarify the object of criminology and its status as a scientific discipline. Sutherland considers crime explicitly within the context of modern society:

> Criminology is the body of knowledge regarding crime as a social phenomenon. It includes within its scope the processes of making laws, of breaking laws, and of reacting toward the breaking of laws. These processes are three aspects of a somewhat unified sequence of interactions ... acts ... defined by the political society as crimes ... This sequence of interactions is the object-matter of criminology (...) The objective of criminology is the development of a body of general and verified principles and of other types of knowledge regarding this process of law, crime, and treatment (...) Crime is relative from the legal point of view and also from the social point of view. This should not only be acknowledged but emphasized. Crime and not-crime are not two distinct types of behaviour but constitute a continuum; the same is true of the criminal and non-criminal population (Sutherland 1934, 3, 18).

This definition is remarkable for several reasons. First, Sutherland regards crime as an outcome of 'interactions', that is, of social processes, rather than of single acts. At the beginning, there seems to be social order. In relation to it, crime is not a question, but a response. Second, the object of criminology is not the criminal person or act, but the interplay of making, breaking and reacting to the breaking of laws. Third, it is 'political society', that is, the State, who defines what 'crime' is. Fourth, all definitions of crime are relative to the particulars of State, law and society. Fifth, 'crime'/'criminal' (and their reverse others 'not-crime' and 'non-criminal') do not indicate discrete entities ('behaviour'), but refer to descriptive variables, that is, to categories of the observer. Sixth, crime relates to social (dis-)order. Note that Sutherland does not expect the discipline to only produce principled knowledge. He makes room for 'other types of knowledge' as well. Or so it seems.

To be sure, Sutherland heightens the awareness for the fact that crime is constituted in a broader social context which includes the law and the State. He was not a constructivist, though. He may have been prepared for the co-existence of a variety of definitions and perspectives on the object of criminology, but his frame of reference was still about focusing on action and on the empirical observation of actions, not on communication (that is, not on observing how communication communicates). What might appear as progress, though, in Sutherland's conceptualisation of crime, is his explicit acknowledgement of its relativity. However, his approach is quickly revealed to form a part of what I called 'ordinary crime discourse', where the grammar of crime and justice is relatively settled and, therefore, absolutely indifferent to questions of framing. Focused on what should count as an object of criminology, this discourse takes for granted the territorial State as the appropriate unit within which to pose and resolve disputes about crime and justice, and its citizens as the relevant subjects. Focused on what should count as the just ordering of social relations within a particular society, it presupposes and accepts what Nancy Fraser (2008), referring to the Treaty of 1648 as the basis of the modern international state system, calls the 'Westphalian mapping of political space'. 'Political society', in this imaginary, is represented as a geographically bounded unit, demarcated by sharply drawn borders, and arrayed side by side with others. This view invests the State with exclusive, undivided sovereignty over its own territory. There can be no 'external interference' in internal affairs'. The division between 'domestic space' and 'international space' is imagined to be of qualitative difference: here, the civil realm of the social contract, subject to law and obligations of justice; there, a state of nature, scene of the enacted *ragion di stato*. 'Before the law all citizens were equal, but not everyone, of course, was a citizen': Musil's ironical comment describes by no means a particular state; rather it is a summary of this whole political imaginary that, under conditions of what could be called 'world society', is now obsolete (Messner 2004a; 2000). Nevertheless, 'ordinary crime discourse' is still informed by it.

Criminology nowadays, as is generally known, has multiple objects and includes very different perspectives. As a branch of the social sciences it lacks coherence and consensus about its object; so much so that one rightly speaks about 'criminologies' (Digneffe 1991) in the plural. And that is not to mention the difficulties some sociologists have to understand criminology as an autonomous scientific discipline (Robert 1999). Although Young's (1986) blanket statement about criminology's continuing theoretical 'standstill' may be too extreme, there seems to be no doubt that the long dispute between on the one hand the positivist-etiological paradigm in criminology, and, on the other, the interpretative-constructivist one, has stifled further theoretical and conceptual development. The result is that rivalling research perspectives now exist side by side without a common conceptual and methodological, let alone theoretical frame of reference.

Consider, for example, David Garland's (2001) critique of present day criminology. Describing several trends of 'new criminologies', Garland essentially focuses on two currents which he identifies as being relatively new. These are the 'criminology of every day life' which includes a large number of different approaches ('rational choice', 'crime as opportunity', 'situational crime prevention', etc.), on the one hand, and what he calls the 'criminology of the other' on the other. According to the former, crime has become a normal aspect of everyday life and people have become accustomed to it. According to the latter, crime is a serious threat, and criminals are dangerous people and somehow different from us, i.e. 'other'. To compare both: 'If the criminology of every day life de-dramatizes crime, treating it as a routine part of the normal scheme of things, this other criminology re-dramatizes it – depicting it in melodramatic terms, viewing it as a catastrophe, framing it in the language of warfare and social defence' (Garland 2001, 184).

Now, let us look at what goes without saying for Garland, that is, let us look at the frame he is using. It is characteristic, I think, that he is concerned with the question of adequate 'dramatisation', that is, with the realistic mode of story-telling about crime. Drama is a form of narrative. It is the specific mode of fiction represented in performance. The word is derived from the Greek word *drama*, meaning 'action'. A drama is performed by actors and takes place on a stage before an audience. It follows plot lines, it develops through 'acts', from the beginning to the end. In fact, as an observer, Garland looks on individuals and society, discerns crimes and normal schemes of things, and watches agents acting and observers observing (and perhaps misrepresenting) facts. Not unlike Sutherland, Garland is interested in the just ordering of 'social order', as evidenced by the title of his book that includes the phrase 'social control' (coined in 1907 by Edward Ross). And he too presumes as axiomatic the Westphalian framing of the political. One could argue that Garland subscribes to the premise of 'ordinary crime discourse'.

Arguments about crime assume a double guise. On the one hand, they concern first-order questions. At this level, the problematic is still that of criminology's 'what'. There are various 'criminologies' that couch their descriptions of different objects in a variety of idioms. Each is focused on devising the criteria for measuring and confronting their particular objects. But above and beyond first-order observations, they also concern second-order observations. At this level, the problematic is about the framing of criminology's object. Here the issue is about thinking through how to 'translate' different descriptions, different frames. Which description –or frame- is true? Is there an objective reality – beyond framing – that can ground our view? Our example has been the political, 'Westphalian' mode of framing: the hegemonic, naturalised, taken-for-granted frame of the modern territorial State as a unit. Theories that are preoccupied largely with first-order issues, have so far failed to develop conceptual resources for (second-order) reflections on frames and framing.

The above refers to paradigm conflicts. It is about interpretations that routinely run up against other interpretations whose underlying ontological assumptions they do not share. For example, positivists looking to identify and incapacitate 'dangerous' people clash not only with those who defend the rehabilitation of offenders, but also with human-rights activists, or with those who are trying to show that 'crime' is a mere label and 'criminal' a mark that only indicates the outcome of successful criminalisation processes. The question here is not simply, 'crime or not-crime?' Nor is it, 'punishment, rehabilitation, or abolition: how much or how little?' What is disputed are not just conflicting interpretations of crime but conflicting views of the 'substance' of crime. The conflict here is between *ontologies*.

This poses a radical challenge to theories of crime and justice. The plurality of observers/narratives – each potentially with their own, differently framed *ontology* of crime – threatens the traditional image of the disinterested, detached observer. There is no point of view that is not someone's point of view. All views are relative to observers. There is no firm 'foundation' for any of them, and none is privileged. But there's more: if conflicting ontologies imply conflicting criteria for observing facts, how can we be sure that interpretations refer to the same objects and to the same reality? Do substantively (i.e. ontologically) heterogeneous descriptions really refer to the same frame of reference, the same world? Given the plurality of conceptions, how should we critically decide what is or what counts as crime? Given the plurality of conventional (political, economic, cultural) framings of crime and justice, how should we critically determine which one is correct?

These questions lead us to another unexamined issue which concerns the question of how to determine ('critically', i.e. in a *discerning* way) the framing of crime. There seems to be a tacit agreement among scholars and researchers that disputes about the relativity of crime can and should be resolved scientifically, by applying a scientific method or procedure. However, given that views of crime and justice are grounded in specific modes of framing, they can only be adequately grasped through a theory that conceptualises forms of communication (Luhmann 1995). From this theory we must expect no definition of crime. Rather than celebrating abnormality or rushing to re-instate a norm, this theory might be expected to consider dichotomies such as crime/not-crime, normal/abnormal, standard/not-standard as coded distinctions deployed, evoked, or used by an *observer*. Thus this theoretical model will observe who (which observer) operates (i.e. observes and describes) with which concepts (coded distinctions). Since no exception can be made for its own mode of observation, it will claim for the knowledge so produced neither critical awareness nor superiority, only difference.

One step back: two models of theory

One could distinguish two forms of modern scientific discourse: fundamentalist, and interpretative (or contextualist) thinking. The fundamentalist model of inquiry seeks to identify, beyond the concrete objects it is concerned with, a logical form, a law or a universal structure in order to explain the particular phenomena it is studying as partial and incomplete manifestations of it. We may call fundamentalist any attempt to ground observation and communication in something more solid and stable than mere belief or practice. The fundamentalist strategy is to, first, identify a ground, and then to order events in such a way that they become anchored to it, and are thereby rendered 'objective' and principled. The ground is a valid ground, if it has certain characteristics. It must be invariant across contexts and cultures; it must stand apart from 'subjective' positions, points of view and interests; and it must provide a reference point against which claims to knowledge (and action) can be measured. In the history of criminology, the status of a 'ground' has been attributed, for example, to God (crime as 'sin'), nature ('criminal energy', or anti-social instincts), society ('disorder', 'maladjustment'), language ('restricted codes'), rationality (crime as 'rational choice'), and the canon of values. The assumption of the existence of one or more grounds determines the direction in which this model elaborates its research programme. If the project is successful, we have a method at hand which, when correctly applied, will produce correct results. Positivist criminologists, for example, believe that crime is ontologically given, that it exists (just like mountains, or pizzas). They will then proceed to consider problems such as 'who or what is criminal', 'why one becomes criminal', 'what are the best means to fight crime and criminality'.

The interpretative model, in contrast, assumes that knowledge is constituted in a circular way. This way of thinking postulates the 'subjective' origins of knowledge and action, and gives up strategies that seek to objectify the world and experience, that is, strategies that rest on the assumption that it is possible to detach the subject from the 'objective' world (and vice versa). Questions of fact, truth, reliability, validity and clarity can neither be posed nor answered in reference to an a-historical, non-situational reality. Foundations are possible, we can give reasons for our acting and thinking, but such grounds do not function as 'a sort of full stop at the end of the line of explanation' (Bateson 1972, 40). Rather, it is contexts, situations, and perspectives that give shape to the contextually and situationally differing meaning of facts and truths. Accordingly, the contextualist strategy does not consist in replacing the fundamentalist model of thought. Instead, it merely denies the elements in the latter's world view the qualities of stability and independence. That does not mean that, since whatever is said will be said from a certain point of view one could never say 'what really happens'. Indeed, *all* descriptions seek to tell 'what really happens'. Therefore, a description is rejected, if it is rejected, not by independent or 'objective' facts, but by a contesting description. The question of 'reality', in the interpretative model, can only arise (hypothetically) when 'what really happens' means 'what really happens after all *descriptions* have been set aside'. But what remains after '*all* descriptions have been set aside' could then not be a description. It is what can not be said (or described), not because it remains hidden as the real truth behind things, but because there is nothing to tell. The thesis of contextualism is not: 'there is no sense', but, rather: 'it makes no sense to ask for a plain sense that would be independent from the observer and his/her context'. Labelling theorists, for example, consider crime not as a natural phenomenon, but as a *construction* produced through social processes of attribution and imputation. They are concerned with problems such as 'what groups are defined as deviant', 'what are the effects of labelling on the individual', 'under what conditions could this or that definition be successful', or 'who has the power to define whom', and so on.

The difference between the two ways of thinking is the difference between a notion of truth as something independent from limited perspectives and a notion of truth as whatever seems to be clear and manifest to observers who are situated in a local, situated, and therefore partial perspective. It is the difference between a truth that measures and evaluates cognitive achievements and a truth that is itself a cognitive achievement. Only the first form of truth guarantees a principled order.

'Being situated' does not mean that we are adrift in a world that we can only make and remake and never finish. It means that all interests and preferences are anchored in a particular situation or context. The situated observer him or herself (or itself) is a function of the possibilities built into this or that context which it operates in. He or she (or it) is tethered by local or community standards that constitute them and enable them to act, e.g. 'rationally'. The one thing the observer could not do is produce his own language his own set of isolated beliefs, or his own 'private' world. In short, he could not create a totally new sense of the world. Whatever the world he is making and remaking is, his will be a position based on a contextual, situated (and hence: particular) presupposition of sense, semantics, discourses. This implies that all principles are preferences since every principle is the extension of a particular and questionable articulation of the world. There is no universal point of view. Preferences are partisan *claims* of principle. In this sense, they are determined by the power, violence, and force of rhetoric rather than by the 'forceless force' of the better argument. It makes no difference whether they openly express the aspect of 'sheer power' and 'mere violence' or, instead, assume the shape of a world view that includes a variety of scopes, norms, reasons and rules (Foucault 1976).

Therefore, the power to enforce a certain view depends not so much on a partisan epistemology, but upon politics and rhetoric. Effects of politics and rhetoric are necessarily objectifying for being influenced by them means being convinced, and being convinced means to start observing the world from a particular point of reference in relation to which other views are then 'obviously' untrue. Our beliefs are all we have: we know something only by being convinced of it. Thus, theory acquires real power when it becomes a community's common sense, when it becomes a *way of seeing and telling* so widespread within a culture that it seems to provide stable (and often quite simple) descriptions of what then seem to be independent, 'objective' realities.

But, one might ask, are there no 'higher' principles which we could orient ourselves towards? This is not the case because there are no limitations, no levels of restriction, no rules which would be 'higher', that is more general, than those already posed by the practices which we are actually engaged in. There are only *different* ones. As Wittgenstein (1953) has shown, it is impossible to think a rule, law, or principle without presupposing a context of life forms that render it intelligible. Whenever one appeals to higher, external, independent rules, one does this on the basis of a *particular* agenda or project that is *already* in operation.

Thus, the idea of the researcher as a detached observer who is observing from a 'neutral' or 'impartial' viewpoint falls apart. Moreover, the definition of what should count and what should not count as an 'impartial' mode of observation is itself an act within the frame of reference of a set of assumptions about what are and are not criteria of judgment and evidence, that is, assumptions that are constitutive of and inseparable from a certain world view. When we act in a 'detached' or 'impartial' way we do so within the frames of our particular angle, with our particular criteria of what 'acting impartially' means 'in our eyes'. We could, of course, reflect 'critically' upon what we do, but that we could only in virtue of, rather than independently from, the accepted norms and standards which are the conditions of the possibility of us seeing what we see.

But is this approach not in contradiction with itself? It isn't. The thesis of contextualism is not that there are no foundations. It merely asserts that whatever the foundation at hand, it will have been established in the course of argument and counter-argument, on the basis of evidence and example which, again, depend on context. As this thesis is self-referential, the contextualist position is not self-contradictory. Self-contradictory would be the (fundamentalist) claim that foundations are impossible.

To sum up: contextualist-interpretative thinking does not sit happily along the fundamentalist faith in scientific method and truth. It claims, first, that facts are filtered and conditioned by the language, the symbolic forms and the discourse formations produced and used to describe and prove them. Hence, it is concerned with the role of difference and opposition within systems of signification. To ascertain, discern, or describe facts would not be possible without the latter. Second, it highlights the operative use of sense (or meaning) as a communicative use. The making of sense occurs as social construction. Hence, sense and meaning can not be perceived or detected as such, they are conceived as outcomes of processes of signification. Signification is the *conditio sine qua non* for there to be any experience of reality at all. All observation and 'telling' is sign and interpretation of signs.

One more step back: a constructivist approach

Ontology and epistemology

Every scientific position entails ontology and epistemology. Ontology is concerned with the question of basic assumptions about the world and the being of the world. Epistemology is concerned with the question of basic assumptions about the preconditions of knowledge about the world. As the previous section already shows, starting positions are fundamentally different. Ontologically over-determined theories take off by asking 'what' questions. Their principal concern is with methodology: which procedures and rules are required in order to obtain true knowledge of the world? Method decides what exists and what reality is. Paradigmatic is the fundamentalist attempt to trace back the great chain of being all the way up to the origins of things. Contextualist-interpretative thinking, in contrast, takes into account the fact that besides the order of things there is also an order of words and signs, and that there is no stable correlation between the two. Accordingly, it distrusts fixed dualistic terms such as 'self and world', 'body and soul', 'subject and object', 'form and content'. It starts, instead, with a reflection on the prerequisites of its project. Being a 'second order' perspective, it seems to be closer to epistemology's aim of questioning not 'what' we know, but 'how' we know what we know.

Of course, one cannot simply escape ontology. Every epistemology entails an ontology. But one can work with a bracketed ontology that suspends judgment about the existence of objects in favour of the observation of operations required to arrive at judgment. In its approach to reality ontology here is restricted to saying (quite tautologically) 'whatever reality is, it is what it is'. This way, epistemology can focus on how 'a world comes into being' (Spencer-Brown 1997, xxxv) as a direct result of the specific operations actualised by individuals, organisations, or systems.

Realism and constructivism

It is true that every epistemology entails ontology. One can pose the question of reality only by actually asking it, i.e. in a reality which is maintained by doing so. But it is also true that not every epistemology entails realism. Realism is an epistemological habit in which it is assumed that 'reality' exists independently from the observer. Reality is given, and is the precondition of cognition. Cognition should mirror reality. Constructivism, on the other hand, relates to a philosophical tradition that is concerned with the internal conditions of thinking. The point is not to delineate the existence of something, but, instead, to ask how objects are distinguished as objects and how they are thereby constituted as this or that 'something'. Reality here appears as the product of cognition, rather than as its criterion.

Constructivism focuses on the observer. From its point of view the perspective constructs both the observer and the observed (Messner 2004b, 67ff). Its specific 'second order' question is the one about how the observer will construct the observations of others to be the object of his own observations in order to describe the space from which he describes.

Suppose the observed here is ontology. Ontology, in this light, means that an observer operates with the distinction 'being/not being'. By means of this distinction the observer indicates what he or she considers as relevant, i.e. as 'being'. The observer disposes of only this logical value (i.e. 'being') in order to indicate existence. The second value (i.e. 'not-being') is used only to verify observations, or to reflect upon them, or to point out mistakes. 'Not-being' has no reality correlate for this observer: not-being is not (and is therefore irrelevant). Conditions here are assumed not to be different for different observers. They can inform each other about mistakes and overcome the operative obstacle of observation, i.e. the fact that the observer, while observing, can not distinguish cognition and error. Observers can learn from one another for they all have the same and only resource for indicating reality and so they must, therefore, arrive at an agreement. Ontology thus limits observations of observers to two functions: learning and critique. But at the end of the day, for these observers there exists only one world - even though they also observe each other in all their difference (dispute then is never-ending).

Now suppose the observed here is contextualist-interpretative thinking. That strand of thinking too seems to be committed to the aforementioned view. The observers taken into consideration here are immediate observers who are embedded -all in the same way- in their own 'real' contexts. Observation, then, still means empirical observation (i.e. the observation of observers doing their situated observing in their context). From this perspective it is possible to describe something as this 'something' only through a communication between a sender and a receiver. Someone indicates something as 'crime', for example, and someone else understands the indicated meaning as a piece of information about the world. A world of mutual understanding (or as the case may be: differing) is made up between sender and receiver. 'Second order' observation here is the same as a change of perspective, and boils down to a move from an internal point of view, where one practises inter-subjectively shared views and standards that almost come naturally, to an external point of view from which one observes the views and standards of a community without sharing them.

Let us now move on to constructivism. The constructivist approach, in comparison, puts forward a radicalised and highly abstract concept of observation. Here it means the actual use of a distinction to indicate one side rather than another. Distinction does not depend upon the difference between 'real' facts, or between contextual perspectives, but is an act that is required each and every time an observation or description –and therefore also: a 'critical' distinction- is to be performed. The actual structure of a distinction is never given beforehand. It emerges anew in every communication.

However, the distinction used in order to indicate and observe something can not itself be distinguished while it is in use. The operatively used but non-observable distinction constitutes the *blind spot* of the observer. Indeed: any observation will rest on its operative distinction, but that distinction produces its corresponding observation (and nothing else), and thus is bound to remain blind to what falls *outside* the scope of its observation. To formulate it in terms of logic: the observer is the *tertium*, the 'excluded middle', of his own observation. According to Michel Serres (1980) he is not the 'subject', he is the 'parasite' of his own observing. The parasite, the disturbance, the malfunction, is to be regarded as part of the observing system.

The issue, in a word, is that of the distinctions used by observers. Hence, we may conclude that those who theorise crime should investigate neither words nor things, but should, rather, observe how observers of crime use their guiding distinction in order to produce further distinctions. This might enable them to see what observers of crime themselves can not see because of their own *blind spot*.

However, it should go without saying that the constructivist programme should now also be turned on itself. All observation depends on distinctions. The blind spot of cognition is constituted precisely by the distinctions used in producing it. If this is true, one has to give up all attempts to persuade the observed observers or to convert them to one's own distinctions and observations. What is needed is a kind of thinking that is able to recognize and accept its own blindness, rather than a theory that will strive to eliminate it (in vain).

Consequences

There is no such thing as plain sense. All that exists, exists because of an observer's selective blindness. We may separate crime from justice, the sane from the insane, the normal from the abnormal, but distinctions made and lines drawn will depend upon our decisions (and choices) rather than on unshakable foundations. At the end of this chapter, I will not attempt to close the discussion. There is no conclusion. Allow me to illustrate some consequences of the above with the assistance of Robert Musil's character Moosbrugger, a maniacal murderer and rapist who is condemned for the murder of a prostitute. Various scenes in the novel throw light on this character and on his trial's proceedings.

Moosbrugger is introduced as a person of public interest. All his terrible excesses had been described in a meticulously exact manner by modern professional observers of incidents and crises, i.e. the media. From the horrors seen, Musil writes, reporters

> could not find their way back to Moosbrugger's good-natured face, although they were themselves good-natured men who had nevertheless described what had happened in a factual, expert manner and, evidently, in breathless excitement. They hardly availed themselves of even the most obvious explanation, that the man before them was insane - for Moosbrugger had already been in various mental hospitals several times for similar crimes - even though a good reporter is very well informed on such questions these days; it looked as though they were still reluctant to give up the idea of the villain, to banish the incident from their own world into the world of the insane. Their attitude was matched by that of the psychiatrists, who had already declared him normal just as often as they had declared him not accountable for his actions (Musil 1953, 67/68).

But perplexity is growing. Whilst there is no doubt about the facts, what is on trial here are precisely those categories of 'good', 'sane', and 'responsible'. It seems to be the mad man Moosbrugger himself who questions them by

> ... demanding to have his murder regarded as a political crime, and he sometimes conveyed the impression that he was righting, not for himself at all, but for this interpretation of the legal situation ... (Musil 1953, 84).

'Political crime' means 'not an ordinary crime'. But Moosbrugger is all but a terrorist. On the other hand, ordinary crime discourse actually is, as we have seen, political crime discourse. Accordingly, the 'normal' case of murder is the political case – which becomes 'abnormal' when it comes in the guise of the 'normal'. Hence, Moosbrugger is not 'righting', i.e. defending a claim within a given legal situation. Musil's original text says indeed that he is 'fighting'. From the judge's point of view all this is a matter of 'litigation' (Lyotard 1983). For Moosbrugger it is a conflict (a matter of 'fighting') that questions the very right of the legal proceedings. He vindicates, as the German text says, his own 'construction of the law'. Moosbrugger's thought, then, is indeed of a different kind, maybe a kind of 'differentthink'. In George Orwell's novel *Nineteen Eighty-Four*, a totalitarian regime aims to make all alternative or dissident thought – 'crimethink' – impossible.

The passage continues:

> The tactics that the judge employed against this were the usual ones of seeing in everything a murderer's clumsily sly efforts to divest himself of his responsibility. (...) This judge rolled everything up into one ...

The judge, of course, does what judges do: he is producing a sentence in the shape of a synthesis. Musil however presents the trial proceedings as a system of communication whereby discourses are partisan moves aimed to construct realities. Hence, the plot also describes the construction of a plot, of narratives. Incidents, actions and discourses, everything implicated is explained by gathering it into 'one': one act, one bundle of papers, one action, one act of a play. The product – a construction of and by the law – is then transmitted to Moosbrugger:

> ... and then presented it to Moosbrugger as his guilt. But for Moosbrugger it all consisted of separate incidents that had nothing to do with each other, each of them with a different cause, which lay outside Moosbrugger and somewhere in the world as a whole. In the judge's eyes his acts were something that issued from him; in his, they had come towards him the way birds come flying along. For the judge Moosbrugger was a special case; for himself he was a world, and it is very difficult to say something convincing about a world (Musil 1953, 84).

The one and the many, the parts and the whole, analytic and synthetic methods ... The 'case' (Messner 2004b) is the interface between the law and the discourses of medicine, literature, history, and psychiatry or psychology. The case has a *genesis*: it has an origin as well as a development, or history. It has one or more protagonists and it leads to a result that is dealt within the designated competent discipline (Foucault 1975). Therefore, every case is an individual case. Linking up power, law and truth in institutionalised practises, the case gains importance for disciplinary discourses. It can be regarded as what Foucault (1977) calls a *dispositif*, that is, an ensemble of discursive practices, e.g. texts or theories, and non-discursive practices such as the know-how and skills.

Moosbrugger looks at himself in a way that is different from the judge's. By using the distinction 'inside/outside' he constitutes himself as an observer who is in the position to observe the social system where he is a participant. Moosbrugger observes Moosbrugger accordingly as 'a world' of consciousness, properly speaking as a psychic system that absolutely 'would think. That was what he called it, because this word had always impressed him' (Musil 1953, 285). When above we elaborated on the difficulties ontology and its contextualist critics had to say something true 'about the world and the being of the world', we noted why it would be hard 'to say something convincing' about it. Convinced we are when the right words or sentences have been spoken. To convince is to 'hit the mark' with words. However, in the present context, Musil seems to go beyond ontology and epistemology. He aims for the heart of our culture, i.e. the mythical faith that words could liberate from what is merely given. In other words: theory's hope that the right description would enable us to control the course of the world, and critical theory's promise that a critical awareness about theory's shortcomings would place us in a better position. Both believe in the force of myths: of stories, of narratives. To be sure, uncertainty, incident, chaos are banned only by the right word, the *orthos logos*. 'To miss the right logos in action as well as in thought is *hamartema*, the Greek word for failing to hit the mark, the word used in the Bible where the English text says *sin*' (Tillich 1989, 239f). Moosbrugger, then, is not merely a 'hard case' for lawyers, he is a monster because his sheer existence confronts us with 'undecidable questions' (von Förster 2002, 152ff.).

Moosbrugger, in a word, is contingency embodied. Moosbrugger has never become what Heinz von Förster (2002, 54ff.) calls a 'trivial machine'. Trivial machines such as cars or vending machines transform some inputs in certain outputs. Operative rules are given, and the same function will always produce out of particular inputs the same result. This type of machine is dependable. Trivial machines are reliable and predictable because they always give the same expected answer. 'Nontrivial machines' (living or social systems such as trees, dogs, or economies) are able to constantly modify their own structure as well as the rules of operation and transformation. As rules of transformation depend on a system's past as well as on its anticipation of the future, outputs will never be predictable. This raises an irresolvable problem: identical inputs may cause different outputs, and different inputs may cause similar or same outputs.

Take children. One asks 'what does two and two make?', and they answer 'birds'. This is known to be an inadmissible answer. Would you leave such an immature child at home alone? Can you hear the sound of broken windows? Where might things end up? Fortunately, 'homologation institutes' (von Förster 2002, 56), officially called 'schools' or 'homes', do exist where children gradually are transformed in trivial machines that always (or mostly at least, hopefully) respond in the desired manner, thus avoiding all kinds of unwelcome surprise.

> And good heavens, how interested the psychiatrists made believe they were when they showed Moosbrugger a painted picture of a squirrel and he told them: 'That'd be a fox, or maybe a hare. Or it might be a cat, or some such'. Every time then they would ask him as fast as anything: 'What does fourteen and fourteen make?' And he would answer slowly and thoughtfully: 'Well, about twenty-eight to forty'. This 'about' caused them difficulties that made Moosbrugger smirk. For it was quite simple: he too knew that one gets to twenty-eight if one goes fourteen further on from fourteen—but who's to say that one has got to stop there? ... And if an oak-pussy is not a cat and not a fox ... one doesn't need to be so particular about the whole thing; somehow or other it's patched together out of all of it and goes scampering over the trees. Moosbrugger's experience and conviction was that one could not pick any one thing out all by itself, because each one hangs together with the next one (Musil 1953, 284f).

The Moosbrugger case is shown to be a block to the routine ways of exact juridical thinking: it causes the juridical system of distinction and judgment to bring about its own uncertainties and paradoxes. Moosbrugger falls under no category, he is not subsumable under a general rule. He is a case that requires the precise observation of what is 'special', about the character. But precise observation brings no solution. It only leads to the dissolution of the object under scrutiny into multitudes of information, motives, reasons, and hints. It dissolves in the inscrutable complexity of the psychic system.

> In this manner an endless system of relationships arose in which there was no longer any such thing as independent meanings, such as in ordinary life, at a crude first approach, are ascribed to actions and qualities. In this system the seemingly solid became a porous pretext for many other meanings; what was happening became the symbol of something that was perhaps not happening but was felt through the medium of the first; and man as the quintessence of human possibilities, potential man, the unwritten poem of his own existence, materialised as a record, a reality, and a character, confronting man in general (Musil 1953, 298).

The pedantic procedure of repeating the singular within the universal is contrasted with a kind of analysis that aims at a 'fantastical kind of precision':

> Precision, as a human attitude, also requires precise action and precise living. It makes maximal demands on action and living. But here a distinction must be made. For in reality, after all, there is not only the fantastical kind of precision (which does not yet exist in reality, of course) but also a pedantical one, and these two are distinct from each other in that the fantastical keeps to facts and the pedantical to the products of fantasy. The precision, for instance, with which the strange mind that was Moosbrugger's was fitted into a system of two-thousand-year-old legal concepts resembled a madman's pedantic efforts to spit a free-flying bird upon a pin; it was not in the least concerned with the facts, but only with the fantastic concept of the whole traditional code of laws' (Musil 1953, 294).

'Fantastical precision', in Musil, on the other hand, replaces the pedantic approach. In order to observe the many branches of a concrete 'something', it passes to an infinitely high resolution adjustment. This way, it penetrates into the 'folds' of facts (Deleuze 2006) and brings about an art of the 'discerning judgment' that is 'critical' only insofar as it causes the 'crisis', that is: the collapse of judgement regimes.

References

Bateson, Gregory. 1972. *Steps to an Ecology of Mind.* New York: Ballantine Books.

Deleuze, Gilles. 2006. *The Fold: Leibniz and the Baroque,* transl. Tom Conley. London New York: Continuum.

Derrida, Jacques. 1990. 'Force de Loi. Le 'Fondement Mystique de l'Autorité''. *The Cardozo Law Review,* 11: 5-6 *(Deconstruction and the Possibility of Justice).*

Digneffe, Françoise. 1991. La criminologie et son histoire. Réflexions à propos de quelques questions d'objet(s) et de méthode(s). *Revue Internationale de Criminologie* 54, 3: 299- 319.

Förster, Heinz von. 2002. *Understanding Systems: Conversations on Epistemology and Ethics,* New York: Kluwer Academic/ Plenum Publishers.

Foucault, Michel. 1976. *Histoire de la Sexualité. La Volonté de Savoir,* Paris: Gallimard.

Foucault, Michel (ed.). 1975. *I, Pierre Rivière, Having Slaughtered my Mother, my Sister, and my Brother ... : A Case of Parricide in the 19th century,* transl. Frank Jellinek. New York: Pantheon Books.

Foucault, Michel. 1977. 'Entretiens avec Michel Foucault' In *Dits et Écrits*, ed. D. Defert/ F. Ewald. Paris: Gallimard, 1994., Nr. 192. Originally published in *Microfisica del potere*, ed. Alessandro Fontana/ Pasquale Pasquino, Torino: Einaudi, pp. 3- 28.

Fraser, Nancy. 2008. *Scales of Justice*, Cambridge: Polity Press.

Garland, David. 2001. *The Culture of Control*. Oxford: Oxford University Press.

Luhmann, Niklas. 1995. *Social Systems*, transl. John Bednarz, Jr./ Dirk Baecker. Stanford, Calif.: Stanford University Press.

Lyotard, Jean-François. 1983. *Le Différend*. Paris: Minuit.

Messner, Claudius. 2004a. 'Observing Victims. Global Insecurities and the Systemic Imagination of Justice in World Society'. In *Imaginary Boundaries of Justice*, ed. Ronnie Lippens, 185- 202, Oxford and Portland: Hart.

Messner, Claudius. 2004b. 'Fall des Ikarus. Vom menschlichen Leiden und seinen Beobachtern' In *Peter Wust - Aspekte seines Denkens*, ed. Ekkehard Blattmann. Münster: LIT, 253- 272.

Messner, Claudius. 2000. Vittimità e prudenzialismo. Nuove forme del controllo sociale tra individualizzazione e globalizzazione. *Sociologia del Diritto* 31, 2: 135-169.

Musil, Robert. 1953. *The Man Without Qualities*, transl. Eithne Wilkins/ Ernst Kaiser. London: Secker & Warburg.

Robert, Philippe. 1999. *Le citoyen, le crime et l'état*, Genève: Droz.

Serres, Michel. 1980. *Le Parasite*, Paris: Grasset.

Spencer-Brown, George. 1997. *Laws of For -/ Gesetze der Form*. Lübeck: Bohmeier.

Sutherland, Edwin H. 1934. *Principles of Criminology*, Chicago Philadelphia: Lippincott.

Tillich, Paul. 1989. 'Anxiety-Reducing Agencies in our Culture' In *Main Works*, vol. II, ed. C. H. Ratschow, Berlin-New York: de Gruyter, pp. 239-248.

Wittgenstein, Ludwig. 1953. *Philosophical Investigations*. Oxford: Blackwell.

Young, Jock. 1986. 'Il fallimento della criminologia: Per un realismo radicale'. *Dei Delitti e Delle Pene* 4: 387- 415.

Notes on Monstrosity. A Constructivist Deconstruction of Criminology

Luciano NUZZO
University of Salento (Italy)

Criminology's Code

Criminology, as the etymology of the word indicates, is the field dedicated to the study of crime. A definition of the concept 'crime', then, must indicate what differentiates criminology as an autonomous body of knowledge. But 'autonomy' is itself a concept that must be clarified. Autonomy cannot be a characteristic of the object of criminology itself, since this object, crime, refers to behaviour or to actions that are in breach of, or offend against legal norms. Crime is itself a relational concept. If one seeks the answer to this problem within the criminological debate, one is bound to end up disappointed (Messner, 2001, 181). Many scholars, in fact, have emphasized that the area of the object of the discipline of criminology is greatly varied. Equally varied are the prospective methodologies with which to observe and describe the phenomenon of crime (Messner 2001; Robert 1996; Digneffe 1991). But what if we consider the object of criminology to be 'deviance', rather than crime. It would seem that 'deviance' solves the problem. The concept of 'deviance', in fact, has a broader heuristic capacity and above all fewer moral connotations than the concepts of 'crime' or 'criminal'. Deviance would cover all those behaviours or actions which, while not punishable by criminal law, nevertheless deviate from social norms, i.e. norms that do not have a specific formal punishment in the justice system, but that, all the same, are widely known to be binding.

Deviance, therefore, indicates deviation from or violation of norms that are perceived, within a given context, as socially legitimate. The distinction between criminal and not criminal therefore is substituted by the distinction between conforming and deviant. But even in this case 'deviance' is a question, indeed a concept of relation. Deviance must be determined *in relation* to the other part of the distinction (e.g. 'conformity', or perhaps 'normal').

What does normal mean? Originally the term deviance was associated, during the 19th century, with measurements of physical and psychological traits of human beings. In the fields of anthropometric, biometric, and psychometric research, for instance, 'differences' that were present within a given population were measured against the establishment of a 'statistical norm'. It was the norm that indicated the distribution of certain traits within a given sample. The statistical norm indicated the regularity of certain behaviours. Social norms, however, do not indicate the frequency of certain behaviours or actions but rather the behavioural *expectations*. The behaviours or actions refer back to expectations that are attributed to the situation. When these expectations are generalized temporally, materially, and socially, they can be considered norms. In this way expectations take on a form that allows for the conformity – deviance distinction (Luhmann, 1993; Luhmann, 1977; De Giorgi, 1998a).

The problem, however, as to how to find a univocal definition of the object, remains. In fact, both in the case in which crime is taken as the object and that in which deviance is taken as the object, criminology seems to continue to ignore the need for a method that makes possible a reflective access to one's own object (Messner, 2001; Kunz, 2004). On the one hand, the workings and functioning of the legal system remain largely out of its scope, while it continues to assume that, in order to determine its object, a mere reference to social order is sufficient. On the other hand, and if the object of criminology is *society*, criminology does not clarify the 'place' in society from which one can describe society. In other words, the central problem for any social theory, i.e. that of being part of the object sought to be described, is not addressed.

But we accept the hypothesis according to which in modern society there are no places from which one could correctly describe the world. Pre-modern societies were used to the possibility of thinking of the unity of the world from a privileged position, 'from the peak of the hierarchy, which was identified with the nobility, and from the center of society, which was identified with the city' (Luhmann & De Giorgi, 1992). In these societies, therefore, order could be thought of as 'natural order', and that which exceeded it as 'disorder'. 'These societies could easily describe law as natural law. Within old mythical traditions the genesis of order was conceived as emanation' (Luhmann, 1988, 156). Modern society, instead, precisely because of the form of the differentiation that characterizes it, defines itself by the autonomy of its own systems of functions. This also means that there are not the necessary conditions for observation from a privileged position. 'There does not exist a unitary form of self-description that can avoid the paradox of identity, the paradox of unity that is multiplicity. Modern society must find a way out without being able to provide a representation of society within society' (Luhmann & De Giorgi, 1992, 362).

From the lack of a solution to this problem derives what has been defined as the crisis of criminological knowledge (Messner 2001; Quensel 1989). In the construction of its object of knowledge, criminology continues to use Enlightenment conceptual schemes, such as the distinction between subject and object (Luhmann 1984; De Giorgi 2006a). This rests on the assumption that there is a transcendental subject of knowledge that, by virtue of its place, that is by virtue of the distance that separates it from the object, is able to know the object. In front of the subject a reality is then assumed to appear; a reality whose contours are independent of the operations of observation and therefore of the observers that observe it. Much in criminology –as is the case with most forms of knowledge about society- is still bound to that scheme. As a result, one could argue that the basic distinction which criminology uses to observe and construct the world it observes 'in front of itself', is that between criminal/not-criminal. The problem of the *distinction of the distinction* remains open. In other words, how it is possible to distinguish between what is criminal and what is not-criminal. It becomes clear then that if one wishes to respond to this problem, it is necessary to say who the observer is and at the same time indicate with what distinction he or she distinguishes. If to the distinction criminal/not-criminal we add and apply the legal code, that is, the coded distinction legal/illegal, a criminal is he who violates the criminal law. If we adopt the moral code, or the coded distinction good/evil, the criminal is he who performs acts that are morally reprehensible. Naturally in modern society there is a variety of different social systems that have the function of resolving specific problems. The social system that has the exclusive task of marking the distinction between legal and illegal, for example, is the legal system (Luhmann 1993). And in particular, within the bounds of the legal system, the penal system has the duty to distinguish between legal act and offense (De Giorgi 2006b). That implies that the definition of criminal is entrusted to the law, and specifically to penal law, and not to political or moral law. Corruption of codes (i.e. coded distinctions) is always a possibility. It is possible, for instance, that the legal code be substituted by the specific code of another social subsystem. Such a hypothesis of superimposition of codes is often found in extreme or exceptional cases. Think for example of the 'ticking bomb scenario' (i.e. what to do with the terrorist who's just been arrested and who's the only one who knows how to switch off a ticking nuclear device that's about to explode; shall we act within the law, or shall we allow ourselves to act without the law?), or emergency anti-terrorism laws. In all these cases the resort to extra-legal violence would be legitimized by the use of another code. The moral code good/evil or the political code, friend/enemy, would then be superimposed on, or in the worst case, substituted for, the legal code (Messner 2010; Nuzzo 2008; Resta 2008).

Circularity of Power/Knowledge

The conclusions reached above allow us now to return to a reflection on the way in which criminology tends to construct its own code of distinction. Let us look at this more analytically. The distinction which criminology uses to observe its object is set up in such a way that the two parts are placed in opposition as if they were two distinct realities. On one hand the legal act, on the other the offence; on one hand conformity, on the other deviance; on one hand normalcy, on the other abnormality. This way the two realities can be observed distinctly. Once the two parts of the distinction are treated as different and opposing realities, observations can oscillate continually between one part and the other of the distinction. The recursive oscillation of such observations produces self-defined values. These self-defined values are then treated as objects that have their own existence (Förster 1981; 2002; De Giorgi 2006a; 2003). 'Deviance' and' crime' are indeed self-defined values produced by observation. Criminology describes these self-defined values as objects. Criminology hereby tends to consider crime and deviance not so much as parts of a single form with two sides of which one is crime and the other legal action, as single, separate realities. In other words, the immanence of the unity of the distinction becomes obscured. As long as criminology believes it is describing a single, separate reality, it remains on a first order level of observation. On this level it cannot observe itself. That is, it does not have the possibility of reflective access to its own object. Only if it is placed on a second order level of observation, that is, if observations of other observers are observed, then it becomes possible to see the distinctions that are used by oneself to construct the world (Luhmann, 1984).

Deviance is deviance in relation to something. If that in relation to which deviance is deviance changes, then 'deviance' is no longer deviance. Between norm and deviance, therefore, exists a circular relationship. As long as linear type conceptual schemes are used according to which the two terms of the relation are opposed, one remains on a first order level of observation: an observer observes the object that is in front of him. It is impossible to observe the unity of the difference between legal act and offence or between normalcy and deviance. In other words, one must presume a given reality. In the case of criminology the reality which one must presume is that of the social order (on the condition of course of not rendering problematic the concept of social order itself, that is, on the condition of not questioning the plausibility of the distinction order/disorder for describing the complexity of modern society or again on the condition of not asking 'how a social order is possible').

Criminology describes itself as the science that has as its own object of knowledge and analysis that very reality. If criminality is a 'reality', it becomes possible to define its nature, dimensions, qualities, and quantities; to individuate and differentiate the different typologies of crimes and to classify them; to inquire into the etiology of crime; to indicate the causes of criminal behaviour; and to describe political, legal, clinical, and social programs for their treatment. Criminology thus often presents itself as a predictive knowledge. Its capacity to prescribe solutions to problems (i.e. of 'crime') is then legitimized on the basis of its supposed ability to objectively know the phenomena it describes. But the problem of the object in this case presents itself as a circle of knowledge/power. In other words, the conditions of its knowledge are not outside the field it intends to describe (i.e. 'crime') but are determined by it (Foucault 1969; Foucault 1976; Foucault 1993). Again, therefore, from the perspective of the knowledge/power relation, the problems set out at the beginning of this chapter re-emerge, i.e. the problem of the truth or the scientific nature of observations and the problem of self-observation. The problem, that is, is about the question whether it's possible to elaborate a theory that includes awareness of the implication of itself in its own production. The problem is not a problem of logic but, rather, a problem that refers to connections of operations. The object, i.e. that which is constructed as the object by the observer, is a connection of operations, for which each operation constructs its own beginning.

To observe deviance means to observe society. A theory of deviance is a form of social communication. The theory, in other words, is a way of producing society. This means that the theory always implies itself as part of the object it describes. To describe means to observe, and every observation is an operation by means of which society is constructed. To construct society means, therefore, that by means of each operation the context of the operations is produced as a result of those very operations. In other words, those operations are made possible by the context of operations and at the same time the context is made possible through the operations. We are like Wittgenstein's flies, trapped in a glass (Wittgenstein, 1999). For Wittgenstein (1961; 2003) there is no possibility of exceeding the limits of language. The only possibility of access to reality, claims Wittgenstein, is through language. But this position, while it represents a break with positivistic paradigms, at the same time does not appear sufficient. The limit would be that of continuing to presume the existence of a reality that is not reducible to a mere linguistic game. To claim, for instance, that crime as object to be 'constituted by the use of particular *language games* without any reference to its materiality', is one thing, but another is to see how the scientific character of knowledge remains based 'on an access to reality which is more than a mere language game' (Carrier, 2008, 171). Using Luhmann's thought and radical constructivism it is possible to go *beyond* Wittgenstein and his followers to say that 'the world as it is and the world as it is observed cannot be distinguished' (Luhmann, 2002, 11). Observation does not represent the world (only) linguistically, but it does construct it in a certain way. What does all this mean in relation to what we have said about criminological knowledge? The object would not be found outside itself, somewhere 'out there' in society, i.e. 'deviance', or 'crime'. Its object, rather, is to be found inside *itself*. In order to trace the circularity of observation and construction *within* the field of criminology, it is, however, necessary to observe criminology from without.

The route I intend to follow below to demonstrate this logic of the circularity that breaks with the linear distinctions of the type subject/object, cause/effect, and beginning/end develops in two further analytical steps. In the first I take the reader into the field of art, in particular to a very famous movie by Fritz Lang, *'M' the Monster of Düsseldorf* (1931). In the second I draw attention to the reflections of M. Foucault. Even though, or perhaps because of the fact that Foucault was not a criminologist, he has been able to deconstruct the schemata used by criminologists to justify their own object. At the same time his analyses make possible descriptions that are adequate to the levels of complexity that characterize modern society. In particular I will refer to the *Lectures on Abnormals* held at the Collège de France in 1974-1975, and specifically on those lectures in which, by means of the genealogy of the figure of the monster, Foucault shows the circularity of the knowledge/power relation in the construction of 'crime' and 'deviance'.

Fritz Lang's 'M'

On the 11th of May 1931 Fritz Lang's film *'M' the Monster of Düsseldorf* came to movie theatres. The title of the film was to have been *'ein Mörder unter Uns' (A Murderer among Us)*. This title, which appeared in newspapers before the start of production, had stirred the National Socialist Party who feared that the film's subject was political and that it alluded to violence, organized by the National Socialist Party in German cities, against their opponents. The director of Zeppelin production studios not only denied Lang the use of the Zeppelin studios but also advised against releasing the film because it would hurt 'the feelings of many people who are going to become very important' (Kracauer, 1977; Eisner, 1978). Lang said that he understood who the Zeppelin director referred to when during the dispute that followed the discussion he noticed on the lapel of the Zeppelin director's jacket the symbol of the National Socialist Party. The title had misled the Zeppelin director into suspecting that the film was against Hitler and his followers in those years in Germany when they were beginning to come to power. Only after he had explained that the film told a news story that had earlier shaken German public opinion did the director Lang, succeed in obtaining permission to use the Zeppelin studios.

The film opens with the story of Elsie. The last child victim of the monster is awaited in vain by her mother at home. She has been killed in the woods. Elsie's killing is one in a series of murders. Panic spreads through the city. The police, goaded by a hysterical minister who fears public opinion, multiply their efforts. The murderer meanwhile seems to have been recognized almost everywhere. Everyone suspects everyone else. The city is besieged, every quarter combed, every house searched. But despite the exceptional measures adopted, the police do not know which lead or track to follow. The only result that the new security measures succeed in producing is to obstruct the normal activities of the criminal gangs of the city. These, in a separate meeting contemporaneous with that of the police, decide, led by their leader Schränker, to eliminate the monster. The pressures of the police on the criminal quarter have reached the point of impeding the 'normal' flow of 'business'. Thus, while the police put their trust in clinical and criminological know-how and by means of graphological analysis conduct what today we would call profiling of the murderer, the criminals themselves mobilize beggars in order to catch the murderer.

The criminal profiles lead the police to concentrate their investigations on persons who are confined in asylums, or who had psychiatric problems and have been released. The criminals instead, using the network of beggars, go through the entire city with a fine-toothed comb. Through a system of signals they warn of the presence of every potential suspect. The police succeed in discovering the identity of the murderer, but they fail to apprehend him. A blind beggar however recognizes an aria by Grieg that he had heard whistled when he had sold a balloon to an unknown person who accompanied a little girl. A particular sign, the whistle of the murderer, is revealed to be of fundamental importance. The blind man gives the alarm. The signs are repeated. To make the murderer recognizable, he who shadows him marks him with an M on the right shoulder of his coat. From this moment on the monster has a face. It is the frightened face of Mr. Becker (played by Peter Lorre) who flees in the vain hope of saving himself. But he has no way out. He hides in a large building which houses the Savings Bank. The teams of criminals surround the building. As soon as the employees exit, the criminals enter the bank lea by their leader who is dressed as a police officer. The gangsters search for the Monster room by room. Another sign, that of a knife tapping insistently on the pavement, betrays M's presence in the building. Shortly before the police, alerted by a guard, burst in, the criminals manage to flush out the monster and take him to an abandoned distillery. Here, before a jury of 'infamous men' with grim and vindictive faces, Schränker, the leader of the city's criminals, begins the trial in the role of an impeccable tribunal president. The trial is grotesque. It reproduces the ritual but it is devoid of all meaning. The verdict is rendered. The murderer has confessed his horrible crimes, the attorney has uselessly argued that his client lacked mental capacity, the jury, incited by the presiding criminal, pronounces the death penalty. As the crowd throws itself upon the monster to kill him, the police burst into the room. The next scene shows the bar of a tribunal and then the judges that file in to pronounce the sentence. We do not know if Mr. Becker, the monster of Düsseldorf, will be condemned as the criminal Schränker, sustaining the reasons of collective security against those of responsibility and mental capacity, decreed, or whether he will be judged mentally ill and entrusted to the knowledge and care of doctors, as requested by the attorney in the farcical trial. The final scene shows three mothers who warn the spectator of the need to be vigilant so that crimes like these do not happen again.

The first question to ask is this: what does art add to the discourse on crime and deviance, in particular a film that speaks of what we can define as a serial killer *ante litteram? 'M' the Monster of Düsseldorf*, in the language of art, speaks to us of crime, of circularity, of the contingency of distinctions such as normal and abnormal, criminal and not criminal, legal right and crime. Through art it is possible to see that which we cannot see from other perspectives of observation, i.e. the plurality and contingency of possible constructions. Through art the observer can see the blind spots of his own observations. He can use, at the same time, both sides of coded distinctions. He can observe their unity. He notices, in art, the contingency of the distinction which he uses in the very moment of observation. Art allows the observer to see that which he treats as separate objects, in our case 'crime' and 'criminality', are constructions contingent upon the observer's perspective. This contingency appears in its typically artistic dimension, i.e. pretend reality and real pretense (Luhmann, 1997).

Lang's film is constructed as a documentary, as if he were covering a news story, something of which we already know the ending. But the film deconstructs the facts that we think we know. It decomposes the linear sequence and shows them to us from a variety of different points of observation, to then recompose them into a new sequence. This way it becomes clear that there does not exist one reality but rather as many as there are observers who construct it with, or in their operations. Through film editing techniques the director makes us see that which a single observer cannot see, i.e. the events in the simultaneity of their occurring (Kracauer, 1995).

Again, the artistic construction of a theme or a problem allows for a more reflective attitude. It permits the description of 'the paradoxes that the structure of society hides from itself to make possible its operations' (De Giorgi, 1998b, 22). The themes of crime, of its causes, of the social reaction they produce and the processes of labeling they generate appear in their artificial dimension of construction by an observer. The way in which Lang's films addresses the themes of crime, pathology, and the fear that it generates, may lead one to understand how every description, whether artistic, sociological, or juridical, offers only *a* construction of the real among many other possible constructions. The privilege of art is that of showing the plurality and the contingency of possible constructions, and therefore to render visible even that which Walter Benjamin defined as the possibility of the impossible (Adorno, 1977; Derrida, 2003). Art not only interrupts the distance between the spectator and that which he sees, thus involving the observer with the object itself. It also imposes a reflective movement through which the observer becomes an object of his own observation.

Fritz Lang, as has been noted, was inspired by a news story, i.e. that of Peter Kürten who had assaulted and killed several girls in Düsseldorf. The police had had many difficulties in arresting the murderer. Kürten in fact was a lower middle-class person above suspicion. He had an absolutely 'normal' life style which was difficult to fit into a criminal typology. This 'normality' of the murderer on the one hand and the brutality of his crimes on the other hand had contributed to widespread feelings of powerlessness and fear. In Lang's film this story becomes the pretext for a grandiose construction of reality. This is a reality in which murderers and children, police and criminals, are on the move. All of them construct the other and are in turn the result of their reciprocal constructions. At the same time they construct the context in which they move, the context in which the story takes place (i.e. the city) not as an amorphous space, but as a space of tension, of relations, of communications. The story could not have taken place in any other setting but within a large metropolis.

'The murderer is one of us' is the message that the film seems to communicate to us. Fear is fed by the fact that he is not something external that comes from the outside, something alien against which we could, if necessary, defend ourselves. The monster is ordinary and exotic at the same time, familiar *and* strange. In children he evokes the ogre, the bogeyman, or a deep fear as it announces itself in the first scene of the film, when the children sing a nursery rhyme which threatens the arrival of the bogeyman. The adults do not have at their disposal a language to neutralize this fear. They need to give it (or him) a face, and box him in a taxonomy.

'Who is the murderer?', it says on the poster affixed to the walls in the city. The entire first part of the film seeks to give an answer to this question. The murderer is not a foreigner, not someone who comes from outside and who places in doubt the order on which the political community is based. The murderer can commit his crimes precisely because he is not identifiable as a criminal. This allows him to escape the network of control of the police and of the criminals themselves. The film therefore describes for us the *normalcy* of the monster. The monster of the film represents the *unity of the distinction* normal/pathological. It is the 'normal' Mr. Becker who the landlady –interrogated by the inspector- describes as a well-mannered person. The face of the actor, Peter Lorre, follows these oscillations from normal to pathological and vice versa. At one time his is the relaxed face of the man who buys candies for a little girl and at another time it's the wide eyed face given over to uncontrollable desire when he sees a potential victim. This of course relates to the theme of man's Janus-faced double nature, a theme which literature and then film had already plumbed. Think of figures such as Frankenstein, Doctor Jekyll and Mr. Hyde, but also of all those figures that people the detective fiction of the 19th and 20th centuries (Kracauer 1974). Psychiatry and criminology had already begun to inquire into the *nature* of 'crime'. We think of the publication in the second half of the 19th century of the analyses of criminal anthropology of Cesare Lombroso (1897) who reduced crime to the pathological nature of the criminal. As M. Foucault explains, during those years we see the shift from crime to 'the criminal inasmuch as the criminal could effectively be a sick person' (Foucault, 2004, p. 88).

The problem that the monster poses is given by the fact that his behaviour cannot be rationally understood, but this also means a resistance to being boxed within a particular discourse. And even when disciplinary knowledge and control practices do box him in, the problem posed by the monster continues to exceed those disciplines and practices. The monster's is a subversive potential that places in discussion the discursive categories with which it is described, starting with that of rational/irrational.

The actions of the monster, dictated as they seem to be by an irrepressible impulse for the satisfaction of personal desire and self-interest, deny the process of civilization as intended (from Hobbes on) as a process of subjugation and rationalization of the instinct. The unconstrained satisfaction of one's own pleasure is nothing to do with the rational since it goes against the exigencies of economic calculation (which middle class respectable citizens such as M's persona ought to respect). Organized criminality itself in fact does not perceive

M, the murderer of little girls, as a criminal, not for reasons of moral character (or lack of it) but rather because his actions do not pursue any profit; they are not understandable through instrumental reason, a principle which organizations, be they state or criminal, must necessarily share to be able to continue to exist.

The monster also unhinges the distinction internal/external. The monster is at one and the same time 'internal', i.e. a respectable citizen, member of the lower middle class that shares a series of institutionalized social values, and 'external' in an absolute sense, because his actions cannot be understood and therefore they are placed beyond the threshold of the human. The other distinctions that follow from the above are lessened, confounded, and undermined. The monster as monster is neither enemy nor criminal, or better, he is both. The reaction against his crimes can only be exceptional. It requires a total mobilization like that which had involved the European population during the First World War and which Ernst Jünger had described in an essay in 1930 (Jünger, 1997). The question that guides the observation of the spectator and that of the parties of the drama, namely, the police, the frightened populace, the criminals, and the murderer himself, I have already said, is 'Who is the murderer?' Medical and legal know-how and formal and informal control practices seek the signs that allow one to give a face to the crime. But what happens when the 'mark' is placed and it permits the recognition of Mr. Becker as the murderer? From that moment on, I think, the spectator begins to change perspective. In the dramatic scene of the trial before the jury of criminals we hear, for the first time, the monster speak. 'Who are you to judge me?' is the question he levels at the criminals. The echo of this question however exits from the rooms of the old, abandoned distillery to reach the spectator himself, to interrogate him on the construction of his own observation.

Foucault's Observations

In his Course at the Collège de France in 1974-1975, dedicated to the *Abnormals*, Foucault describes the genealogy of the monster. The monster is a legal notion that is distinguished from defectiveness or infirmity. The latter indicate violations of nature which however find a place in and are anticipated and disciplined by civil and canon law. The monster, on the other hand, not only violates the law of nature, but that violation of nature constitutes an infraction of these same civil and religious laws. In order to be monstrous, therefore, it is not enough to be simply infirm or defective. It is necessary instead that the transgression of nature be such as to refer to the transgression of an interdiction posted in the law. The monster, therefore, is the *against-nature* which puts into discussion law, which paralyzes its functioning. In the face of monstrosity, legal discourse is impotent, and, as in a mirror, Foucault tells us, the law is constrained to render accounts using its own fundamental logic. In other words, the monster is a disorder which exceeds the order of legal discourse. It does not let itself be boxed into the categories and distinctions that the law uses, and, for that reason, it brings about a paralysis of the law.

The figure of the monster from medieval times up through the 18th century was characterized by 'double nature'. It was the double nature of 'monsters' that typified the latter. The monster is a mixture, of two kingdoms, man and animal, of two species, or of two sexes, man and woman together. Classical examples are the centaur, the Minotaur, the Cyclops. But every age, Foucault argues, appeals to a certain figure of monster. During medieval times the monster is mainly the union of two kingdoms, man and beast. During the Renaissance, the prevalent figure of the monster is that of Siamese twins. In the 1600s the monster is usually the hermaphrodite, man and woman at the same time. Every age, in other words, reflects in the figure of the monster a series of theological, political, and legal issues. For example, the monstrosity of the Siamese twins is the image of the kingdom, but also Christianity, divided. But with the figure of the hermaphrodite begins a change in the perception of the monster and a shift from the legal-*natural* conception of monstrosity to a legal-*moral* type of conception instead. Examining certain cases, Foucault shows us how this change came about. If until the 1600s the double nature of the hermaphrodite, the being man and woman at the same time, is automatically the indication of legal monstrosity, from the 1600s onwards natural monstrosity does not imply directly legal or *moral* monstrosity. Monstrosity is no longer understood as a mixture of opposites, of that which nature has prescribed be kept distinct. Monstrosity is an irregularity, a deviation that constitutes behaviours that are monstrous because they do not conform to legal or religious prescriptions. That which crystallizes in a clear way at the end of the 18th century, but which had already emerged during the 17th, is moral monstrosity (which is autonomous and different from natural monstrosity): 'With the idea of a monstrosity of behaviour, the old category of the monster has been transposed from the realm of somatic and natural disorder to criminality pure and simple' (Foucault, 2004, 73). With the movement from the figure of the natural monster to the moral monster, from monstrous nature to monstrous behaviour, the concept of criminality associated with the two figures changes. Criminality during the 17th century was associated with the *against-nature* of the monster. The monster was ontologically criminal. Beginning during the second half of the 18th century, however, criminality is no longer determined by nature but by behaviour. The discourse that will continue to be increasingly affirmed will be that at the base of criminal behaviour is a monstrosity. The task of medical knowledge is to individuate the monstrous *character* that lurks at the base of criminal behaviour. According to the criterion of legal-natural monstrosity the monstrous individual was always associated with criminality. According to the criterion of moral monstrosity, 'the relation is inverted and one will have that which we could define the systematic suspicion of monstrosity beneath every criminality' (Foucault, 2004, p. 79).

The question that Foucault poses is how it is that, from a certain point in time onwards, the power to punish has had to refer to the nature of the crime. In other words, in what way and why the distinction between 'legal' and 'illegal' became specified as that between 'normal' and 'abnormal.' The genealogy of the monster, the passage from the *natural* monster to the *moral* monster therefore occupies the centre of a complex transformation of the technologies of power. The 18th and 19th centuries witnessed the affirmation of a new form of power of which the disciplines constitute the essential walls. This transformation includes, beginning in the 18th century, the progressive passage from the sovereign and territorial power of the *Ancien Régime* to modern biopower, i.e. a power that assumes the form of a government of men and of things, of an 'economy' (Foucault, 1976). To summarize in a few words these two models of power I will refer to two paradigmatic events, i.e. leprosy and the plague that M. Foucault analyzes in his lectures on abnormality (Foucault 2004) and then in *Discipline and Punish* (Foucault, 1993).

The paradigm of leprosy is that of exclusion. Lepers are expelled from the city into strictly separate areas. Through isolation of the lepers the objective is to purify the community. The ideal is that of a pure community. The plague, on the other hand, implies a completely different paradigm. With the explosion of the epidemic it is no longer possible to expel the plague-ridden from the city. The city itself is divided into zones. Each zone is distinct by virtue of the intensity of the epidemic, of the disinfections, and of the quarantines. Here it is necessary to implement thorough and generalized systems of control. The population is registered. Every quarter is placed under the watch and guard of an overseer. Soldiers, doctors, and grave-diggers, the only ones who can circulate freely throughout the city, must exercise control over the population, ascertaining the conditions of health of each family, and distributing medicines and victuals (Foucault, 2004; 1993).

Leprosy therefore harks to the model of 'sovereign' power that is articulated around the principle of self-preservation of the sovereign. This is a power centered on the interdictory character of the law. It manifests itself as exclusion, banishment, marginalization, and repression. The plague, on the other hand, refers to a model of power that Foucault defines as *biopower*. Biopower is exercised through two different technologies that however find their unity in reference to life. On one hand through a conjunction of knowledge and techniques that are concerned with the body-organism of the individual person and that are defined within a specific disciplinary apparatus. On the other hand through a series of disciplines that are concerned with the body-species of the population (Foucault, 1976).

The transition from sovereign power – the *power to make die or let live* – to biopower – the *power to make live and to push out into death* – also brings a new *economy* of penalties and therefore a new conception of crime. Crime is no longer considered simply an attempt on the person of the sovereign, which therefore legitimated vengeance exercised through the spectacle of physical and capital punishment, or through the exclusion from the community of he who is *banished* (Agamben, 1995; Foucault, 1993). The crime in the new economy of power is a behaviour that violates the social covenant (or contract). Crime is animated by a specific interest, i.e. an irrational interest that contradicts itself in the moment it is satisfied because it engenders (a) punishment (Foucault, 2004). It is necessary, however, in order to be able to apply punishment and in order to avoid repetition of the crime, to inquire into the nature of the crime, that is, to try and understand the interest that caused the criminal to commit the offence. But if it is true that the interest at the base of crime constitutes the principle of its intelligibility at the same time, it is an interest that has to be irrational, because in denying the interest of one's fellows and following one's own personal egoisms, the criminal must indeed be 'irrational'. In the 'irrational' criminal the wild and natural instinct prevails over civility and order. In the form of the criminal we see the 'nature against nature' that characterized the monster reappear again.

The criminal is characterized at the level of his own nature by his 'criminality'. The knowledge of crime and of the criminal in this new setting must be a *naturalist knowledge of criminality* (Foucault, 2004, 87). The criminal as criminal is brought again into the realm of the pathological. The issues of the illegal and of the pathological are here inextricably woven together. At the core of every criminal lurks a monster, where the monstrosity is given by the pathological character of the criminal. The figure of the monster, precisely by its exceptional character, provides a principle of intelligibility for understanding deviance. But it tells us also something more about the mode of construction of the object on the part of medical, legal, and social knowledge of criminality. In fact, the knowledge of pathological and monstrous anomaly is in some way tautological in that it finds in itself the principle of explanation of that which itself describes scientifically and objectively.

Through the definitions, classifications, and distinctions, the discourse on criminality and on deviance contributes to create the object behaviour as a social problem, reproducing, at the discursive level, those same mechanisms that the practices of power render concretely visible. As Dreyfus and Rabinow (1989) have observed, specialist knowledge 'objectified man, contributing to producing the nosological categories that the disciplinary technologies were made to manage [...]. The criminal became an almost natural species, that could be identified, isolated, and studied by the new emerging human sciences such as psychiatry and criminology' (Dreyfus & Rabinow, 1989, 221). Foucault shows us how criminological knowledge operates within certain institutions and how it constructs its reality. His research reveals the discursive mechanisms and the practices of power through which this reality is produced.

Conclusion

From the time when criminological reflection claimed for itself the status of autonomous science of crime or of deviant behaviour, numerous criminologies have emerged. Each claimed to demonstrate that which the others could not. Each began with the criticism of the others. Each emerges between, on the one hand, the past, i.e. the wreckage of other theories, and, on the other, a future of new theories with, again, cognitive promises and theoretical expectations.

In reality the structure of criminological constructions was always the same. The only exception in this rather desolate panorama seems to us to be constituted by the labeling approach. Still, this latter model's claim to have used a different perspective notwithstanding, it too lacks that which lacks in all the others, i.e. a theory of society that allows for the observation of how the circularity of the constructions of self-defined values produce 'objects' that are (supposedly) separate from the observer and that are opposed to it. In other words, what is missing in all theories is the theoretical possibility of representing the processes through which from the circularity of the paradox one arrives at the representation of the contradictions that are materialized in the distinctions that are used by the theories. More than any other theoretical analysis and critique, we hold that the visual images of a work of art like Fritz Lang's 'M', or the marvelous pages in which Foucault describes the monster, and condenses the archeology of the circularity of knowledge and power, intimate the discourse on theory that we have rendered above.

The great German penologist of the last century, Gustav Radbruch (1992), affirmed that what was needed was not a better criminal law but something better than the criminal law. In the same way we state that as long as criminology will continues to construct its object opposing itself to it as to an external reality, it will not be able to furnish any knowledge of the (supposedly separate) object. Only when criminology represents itself as part of its object, will it furnish useful knowledge. Let us be clear: this knowledge will permit us to see how (criminal) law constructs that which it then uses as reality and how the criminological observer hides this process. However, when society has elaborated within itself a variety of techniques of construction of reality that are different from those used by the criminal law, there will probably no longer be any need for criminological knowledge proper. We should then be able to produce a much vaster knowledge that describes how society has hitherto been producing the 'other', or 'difference', continually, with less than desirable consequences.

References

Agamben, G. 1995. *Homo Sacer*. Torino: Einaudi.

De Giorgi, R. 1998a. *Scienza del Diritto e Legittimazione*. Lecce: Pensa.

De Giorgi, R. 1998b. 'Redes de la Inclusión'. In Castañeda Sabido, F. & Cuéllar Vazquez, A (Eds), *Redes de Inclusión,* 17-28. México: Facultad de Ciencias Políticas y Sociales UNAM.

De Giorgi, R. & Luhmann, N. 1992. *Teoria della Società.* Milano: Franco Angeli.

De Giorgi, R. 2006a. 'Il Diritto nella Società del Rischio'. In De Giorgi, R., *Temi di Filosofia del Diritto.* Lecce: Pensa.

De Giorgi, R. 2006b. 'Diritto e Reato nel Secolo XXI'. In De Giorgi, R., *Temi di Filosofia del Diritto.* Lecce: Pensa.

De Giorgi, R. 2003. Heinz von Foerster (1911-2002). Eine Beobachtung'. *Recthsgeschichte. Zeitschrift des Max-Planck-Instituts für europäische Rechtsgeschichte,* 2, 161-167.

Derrida, J. 2003. *Il Sogno di Benjamin.* Milano: Bompiani.

Digneffe, F. 1991. 'La Criminologie et son Histoire. Reflexions a Propos de Quelques Questions d'Objet(s) et de Méthode(s)'. *Revue Internationale de Criminologie,* XLIV, H. 3, 299-319.

Dreyfus, H. & Rabinow, P. 1989. *La Ricerca di M. Foucault. Analitica della Verità e Storia del Presente.* Firenze: Ponte delle Grazie.

Eisner, L. H. 1978. *Fritz Lang.* Milano: Gabriele Mazzotta Editore.

Förster, H. von. 1981. *Observing Systems: Selected Papers of Heinz von Förster. Seaside,* CA: Intersystems Publications.

Förster, H. von. 2002. *Understanding Systems: Convesations on Epistemology and Ethics,* New York: Kluwer Academic/Plenum Publishers.

Foucault, M.. 2004. *Gli Anormali. Corso al Collège de France (1974-1975).* Milano: Feltrinelli.

Foucault, M. 1993. *Surveiller et Punir.* Paris: Gallimard.

Foucault, M.. 1976. *La Volonté de Savoir.* Paris: Gallimard.

Foucault, M.. 1969. *L'Archéologie du Savoir.* Paris: Gallimard.

Junger, E. 1930. 'La Mobilitazione Totale'. In: *Foglie e Pietre* (1997). Milano: Adelphi.

Kracauer, S.. 1977. *Cinema Tedesco. Dal Gabinetto del Dottor Caligaris a Hitler.* Milano: Mondadori.

Kracauer, S. 1974. 'Sociologia del Romanzo Polizesco' In: *Saggi di Sociologia Critica,* Bari: De Donato. 101-207

Kracauer, S. 1995. *Teoria del Film.* Milano: il Saggiatore.

Kunz, K. L. 2004. *Kriminologie. Eine Grundlegung.* Bern: Haupt.

Lombroso, C. 1897. *L'Uomo Delinquente.* Milano: Hoepli.

Luhmann, N. 1977. *Sociologia del Diritto.* Bari: Laterza.

Luhmann, N.. 1984. *Soziale System. Grundriss einen allgemeinen Theorie.* Frankfurt a. M.: Suhrkamp.

Luhmann, N.. 1988. 'The Third Question: The Creative Use of Paradoxes in Law and in Legal History' *Journal of Law and Society,* 15, 153-165.

Luhmann, N.. 1993. *Das Recht der Gesellschaft.* Frankfurt a.M.: Suhrkamp.

Luhmann, N.. 1997. *Die Kunst der Gesellschaft.* Frankfurt a. M.: Suhrkamp.

Luhmann, N.. 2002. *Theories of Distinctions. Redescribing the Description of Modernity*. Stanford:Stanford University Press.

Messner, C. 2001, *Osservando il Soggetto*, Lecce: Pensa.

Messner, C. 2010. 'Diritto, Politica, Tortura e altri 'States of Concernes'. *Materiali per una storia della cultura giuridica, 1*, (forthcoming).

Nuzzo, L. 2008. *Le Anticamere del Diritto*. Lecce: Pensa.

Quensel, S. 1989, ‚Krise der Kriminologie: Chancen für eine interdisziplinäre Renaissance?'. *Monatsschrift für Kriminologie und Strafrechtsreform*, 74, H. 2, 65-79.

Radbruch, G. 1992. *Gesamtausgabe. Band 9: Straftsrechtreform*. C.F. Muller Verlag.

Resta, E. 2008. *Il Diritto Vivente*. Bari: Laterza

Robert, Ph. 1996. ‚Verbrechen, Recht und Staat.' In Trotha (Ed.) *Politisher Wandel, Gesellschaft und Kriminalitätsdiskurse. Beiträge zur interdisziplinären wissenschaftlichen Kriminologie*. Baden Baden: Nomos, 51-76.

Wittgenstein, L. 1961. *Tractatus Logico-Philosophicus*. London: Routledge & Kegan Paul Ltd.

Wittgenstein, L. 1999. *Ricerche Filosofiche*, Torino: Einaudi

Wittgenstein, L. 2003. *On Certainty*. Oxford: Blackwell Publishing Ltd.

On Gabriel Tarde, Complexity Theory and Complex Interactions

Patrick VAN CALSTER and Marc SCHUILENBURG
University of Leyden and University of Amsterdam
(The Netherlands)

'Do I really look like a guy with a plan? You know what I am? I am a dog chasing cars. I wouldn't know what to do with one if I caught it. You know, I just ... do things. The mob has plans, the cops have plans, Gordon's got plans. You know, they're schemers. Schemers trying to control their little worlds. I'm not a schemer. I try to show the schemers how pathetic their attempts to control things really are.'
The Joker (*The Dark Knight*, 2008)

Introduction

In *The Dark Knight* (2008), the only Batman film without the word 'Batman' in the title, the Joker – brilliantly played by Heath Ledger – likes to emphasize the need to create a little chaos in Gotham City's civil life. Since it is in moments of chaos that everyone becomes more aware of what is really at stake, it is important to disturb and break the order every now and then, the Joker explains, sitting by the sickbed of Harvey Dent, the district attorney charged with responsibility for investigating and prosecuting organized crime in Gotham City. 'Introduce a little anarchy. Upset the established order, and everything becomes chaos. I am an agent of chaos. Oh, and you know the thing about chaos? It's fair!' For those acquainted with reflections upon the relationship between chaos and order, the Joker's attempts to derange the order in Gotham City are akin to the occurrence of a forceful event that manages to upset established forms of knowing (Badiou, 2005). In such an approach, popular opinion is challenged so fundamentally that everyone is forced to reassess their position in the light of the event. In philosophical terms this means opening up new space in which what Badiou (2002: 42) calls a 'truth-process' begins. By consistently studying each specific situation in relation to that event, the life of Gotham City's citizens will again be given unity and direction. The individual - the subject of loyalty - thus never precedes the event. Here, truth and subject are post-evental.

Alain Badiou (2002; 2005) and Slavoj Žižek (2002) argue that such events usually manifest themselves through revolutionary turns. These turns 'punch a "hole" in the knowledges' (Badiou, 2002: 43), implying a distinction between 'knowledge' and 'truth' and that truth is not part of 'knowledge'. For Badiou, the introduction of different party politics or a different state apparatus are not the objective of such a revolutionary turn. Revolution constitutes a clean break with the past. By this, Badiou undeniably upholds the modern view that, in politics, the new can only emerge from revolutionary thinking (Schuilenburg, 2006). A more modest perspective could be opted for by studying the impact of events on everyday life and social change. Without introducing the political event of a revolution that is beyond any form of representation, one could attempt to show how, at the most basic level of social existence, interpersonal interactions cause the disruption of an existing socio-cultural field, which subsequently develops in unexpected ways. This approach is best expressed in the work of the French sociologist Gabriel Tarde (1843-1904).

Tarde was a contemporary of Emile Durkheim (1858-1917) and one of the founders of French sociology. While Durkheim, and later the majority of social scientists, criminologists included, focused on large collective structures ('culture', 'the organization' and 'society'), Tarde emphasized the small changes and details in social life. He depicted these changes in *Les lois de l'imitation* (1890), *La philosophie pénale* (1890) and *Les lois sociales* (1898), using interactions he described in terms of 'imitation' and 'invention'. In this chapter we consider the importance of Tarde's work for criminal policy and criminal justice. We do this by situating his work in the history of social science and, more specifically, by showing how Tarde's way of thinking relates to Durkheim's definition of a social fact. Subsequently, we discuss his concepts of 'imitation' and 'invention', and explain how these can be understood as series of interactions ('process thinking') that continually ramify and multiply. These 19th-century concepts have recently been given a scientific foundation by and in complexity research. We conclude this chapter by providing concrete suggestions as to how this process thinking can be deployed to resolve criminological issues, to which end we make reference to developments in complexity sciences.

Durkheim: social fact

Although Gilles Deleuze writes in praising terms about Tarde's insights in *Difference and Repetition* (1968) and, together with Félix Guattari, pays homage (1987: 218) to his work in *A Thousand Plateaus*, Tarde has for a relatively long time received only marginal attention. This has gradually changed over the past few years, mainly owing to Eric Alliez's efforts to have Tarde's entire oeuvre republished and to Bruno Latour's admission that it was Tarde who provided the basis for his *Actor Network Theory* (2002; 2007). Apart from the importance of Tarde's insights for Deleuze's differential philosophy and Latour's theoretical sociology, Tarde himself was active in many areas. In addition to being a lawyer and criminologist, he was intensively involved in statistics and social psychology. He was a magistrate in his home town of Sarlat, a director of the Ministry of Justice's Bureau of Statistics in Paris and a professor of modern philosophy at the *Collège* de France. He also found time to write essays and a science-fiction novel entitled *Underground Man* (1905), a novel about an ice-covered world where people live underground and art and music are the most important aspects of life.

So why then has Tarde's work received so little attention over the years? This is largely due to his debate with Emile Durkheim, who was appointed to a Professorship at the Sorbonne in 1902, two years after Tarde. Durkheim went on to become Professor of Pedagogy in 1906 and, in 1913, the first person to hold the *Chair de Sociologie de la Sorbonne*. Tarde's debate with Durkheim revolved around the issue of continuity and change, and the relationship between the whole and its parts in social reality (Van Ginneken, 1992: 203). According to Durkheim, a social fact – in other words, the description of what the social precisely entails or defines – is characterized by the power of external coercion it exerts upon individual behaviour and the influence it has on personal attitudes or needs. An example of such a social fact is the language in which we communicate. The language we learn to speak from birth is inescapably imposed upon us and has a compelling and invisible force that no-one can escape.

According to Durkheim, a social fact is identifiable not only through its external influence on what individuals do and say, but also because it has a reality of its own that cannot be reduced to the qualities of separate individuals. In other words, it is an independent entity that imposes certain views and behaviour on an individual that that individual would not have displayed spontaneously. With his sign theory, for instance, Ferdinand de Saussure showed that an extensive system of rules (*langue*) functioning independently of any single individual's use underpins the individual use of language, i.e. the spoken dimension (*parole*) Although no-one is obliged to accept or follow the rules of language, failure to apply such rules makes natural and normal interpersonal interactions virtually impossible. From that perspective, a social fact is not only coercive and supra-individual, it can also be understood as objective (in the meaning of 'thing'), as Laermans (1995) summarizes Durkheim's views. The characteristics of a social fact feature most clearly in Durkheim's thesis of a *conscience collective*, the largest common denominator of the content of the consciousness of individuals in a society. This collective consciousness manifests itself as a separate variable and forms the foundation for cohesion in a community. Not only does it generate emotions that are qualitatively different from individual perceptions, but it also has specific characteristics (Durkheim, 1977: 12). If we apply those characteristics to society itself, society will have a reality of its own, a philosophical point of departure called 'realism' (Durkheim, 1977: 8-9). In 'realism' society has its own nature. The independence of society as a whole gives rise to convictions, norms, ideas and perceptions that are shared by the members of that society. We should not infer from this, however, that a society exists eternally and completely on its own, as if functioning totally separately from the individuals who compose it. Durkheim opposes a transcendental view of society as an entity operating independently of its constituent individuals. To Durkheim, society, through the associations of individuals, gives rise to specific behaviours that together form a collective unity. In *De la division du travail social* (1893), for example, he analyzed the development of a moral solidarity in different types of society. While the earlier, more primitive society enjoyed a mechanical solidarity based on equality, the modern, industrialized society is characterized by an organic solidarity based on differences and inequality and caused by factors such as the new division of labour and the sharp rise in population that have further increased the number of mutual interactions.

To properly understand the debate between Durkheim and Tarde, it is important to appreciate that both of them considered interpersonal interactions in a society to be social. All things considered, Durkheim would say, these, together with other factors, underlie the changes occurring at the level of moral solidarity in a particular type of society. But, Durkheim emphasizes, they depend primarily on an individual's psychological characteristics and the specific circumstances in which they occur. In that respect, interpersonal interactions are not phenomena that Durkheim considers typical of the science of sociology. He uses the term 'socio-psychological phenomena'; they are of interest to sociologists without being an immediate subject for sociological study. Although psychological insights about associations of individuals can help understand changes in solidarity in a society, it is up to the science of sociology to study that solidarity as an independent social fact. This can be accomplished by using scientific methods and models which, as Durkheim demonstrates, can be applied to objectify and verify statistics about birth, marriage, suicide and crime rates. It is possible to analyze the average numbers of births, marriages and voluntary deaths, and also the degree of criminality that expresses the collective consciousness or morality of a society, without discussing the related individual circumstances (Boutellier, 1993: 17-23).

Tarde: interactions

Whereas Durkheim, simply put, maintained that social facts should be analyzed as separate entities ('as something unique'), Tarde argued that sociology should focus precisely on the interpersonal interactions that provide society with some degree of social structure. Although the two positions are not necessarily diametrically opposed, they do focus on different fields of research. Contrary to Durkheim's structuralist view, which concentrates on studying the shared convictions of a group or a collective as a whole, Tarde considers the interpersonal interactions themselves as a social fact worthy of scientific research. We should take this to mean that the 'metaphysical meaning' that Durkheim attaches to a social fact has no absolute validity or value to Tarde. Tarde's interests could be said to lie in the dynamics of social life. He thus draws our attention to an essential aspect that remains unanswered in Durkheim's thinking. In other words, 'How can so many different individuals together form one whole?' Or, to put it differently, 'How can the resemblance between thousands of different individuals be explained?' (Deleuze, 1994: 314 n.3, Deleuze & Guattari, 1987: 218).

Instead of disputing Durkheim's concept of social facts or questioning his scientific analysis of suicide, criminality and so on, Tarde uses a different approach. On the one hand he questions the rigidity of Durkheim's assumption of a collective whole underlying a society's shared solidarity, morality and culture, while on the other he asks how a social fact can exist outside the individuals themselves (Rhoads, 1991: 119). After all, Durkheim's assumption of a social fact is based on the never-tested assumption that such a 'shared conviction' exists. Tarde does not deny the possibility of solidarity and morality between individuals, but focuses the attention on how resemblances between individuals (that entail a degree of solidarity or morality) arise. Durkheim simply assumed that resemblances multiplied, and that these resemblances formed a reality of their own that more or less transcended the individual level. Acting morally then simply means that someone subjects to the force of a collective externally imposing rules, norms and codes on individuals. But that assumption, Tarde argues, is merely an 'ontological illusion' (1969: 115) and basically implies a revival of Plato's doctrine of Ideas (1969: 117). In a way similar to Durkheim's social facts, Plato sees Ideas as representing eternal, stable and archetypical things that can be known only through spiritual experience. The Ideas themselves are not confined to matter, time and place, but lie in a higher world that, according to Plato, is fixed forever and leads an autonomous existence independent of thought.

Tarde, however, prefers, as he puts it, a 'pure sociology' or a 'general sociology' (1962: ix-x) that interprets the general character of social interactions and can be applied to every social fact. He uses the term 'general laws' (1912: 326) in that respect when discussing series of interpersonal interactions that are perpetual rather than temporary. Although the terms 'general laws' and 'general sociology' seem to suggest otherwise, Tarde's method should not be defined as structuralistic (Barry & Thrift, 2007). While Durkheim places the emphasis of social sciences on structures underlying social relations (i.e. structures that are not directly visible), Tarde focuses attention on concrete relations between people. So before we can deal with the question of whether an underlying structure exists and, if so, how it affects daily life, we should – according to Tarde – explore how resemblances develop in the behaviour of all these different individuals who constitute social life. According to Tarde, such resemblances arise through repetition. 'All resemblance is due to repetition,' he writes in *The Laws of Imitation* (1962: 14). This does not mean, however, that a linear process unfolds in which people continuously repeat each other's behaviour, or in the style of a monomaniac. In *The Laws of Imitation* (1962: 7) Tarde also writes that 'repetition exists for the sake of variation.' And just before the previous excerpt he hypothesizes that 'resemblances and repetitions (...) are the necessary themes of the differences and variations which exist in all phenomena' (1962: 6).

In his 'general sociology' Tarde essentially attempts to find a mean between Scylla's absolute relativism and Charybdis' absolute absolutism. In this approach, a society corresponds with a 'group of beings who are apt to possession of common traits which are ancient copies of the same model' (Tarde, 1962: 68). In *The Laws of Imitation* he analyzes such resemblances as series of imitations that he links with notions such as somnambulism and hypnosis – frequently debated notions in the late 19th century. Entirely in line with his thinking, society then is 'imitation and imitation is a kind of somnambulism' (1962: 87). The emphasis on somnambulism and hypnoses reappears in *Penal Philosophy* (1912: 192-201), where Tarde discusses in detail the idea of hypnosis as 'the experimental junction point of psychology and sociology: it shows us the most simplified sort of psychic life which can be conceived of under the form of the most elementary social relation' (1912: 193). In his later work, somnambulism and hypnosis are relegated to the background, yielding to a more abstract and horizontal approach to interpersonal interactions that he terms 'repetition, opposition, and adaption' (2000: 8). Proceeding from this conditional formulation of action, Tarde further stretches the notion of society. In *Monadologie et sociologie* he writes (1999: 58) that 'all things are society and any phenomenon is a social fact,' a view that Latour (2002) describes as 'a flat society argument.' In the framework of this chapter, however, it is important that, from Tarde's perspective of interactions, the Durkheimian issue of structure and order is a *secondary* issue. Initially there is change, movement, and difference (Tarde, 1962: 71; Latour, 2007: 13-16; Deleuze & Guattari, 1987: 218-219), while order and stability always follow later. They *emerge* from the dynamics of social life, as temporary congealing points of continually branching series of interactions that are not so much 'things' as events that never obtain their final meaning.

Imitation

To answer the question of how interpersonal interactions take place in general and, more specifically, with what variation, Tarde makes a systematic distinction between processes of 'imitation' and 'invention'; two series of interactions, each of which forms a reality in itself, but also influences the other. Tarde (1862: 17) defines imitation as the movement by which something is repeated and diffused. In the preface to the second edition of *The Laws of Imitation,* he speaks of 'the action at a distance of one mind upon another' (1962: xiv) and of 'every inter-psychical photography, so to speak, willed or not willed, passive or active' (1962: xiv). In specific terms, this means that people consciously or unconsciously imitate each other's behaviour. They copy certain methods or preferences, such as the way they work (process or technique), the way they dress (fashion) or the music they prefer. But imitation is found in smaller things as well, such as in the minute adjustments in behaviour seen when youngsters copy each other's body movements or adopt certain expressions. In his book *Kapot moeilijk* De Jong (2007) shows how the behaviour of Moroccan youths reflects shared street values (such as loyalty, courage and success) and related norms about what behaviour is deemed good or bad in specific circumstances. De Jong explains why phrases like 'typically Moroccan' do not adequately explain or capture delinquent group behaviour among Moroccan youths. Explanations that assume a 'cultural' base (such as a 'warrior culture', with typically male virtues such as courage, honour and respect) do not adequately explain why Moroccan youths form groups that the public perceives to be threatening. A better explanation, De Jong writes (2007: 211), can be achieved by considering the dynamics of group processes and the specific circumstances in which youngsters grow up in certain neighbourhoods. It then becomes clear that striking resemblances arise through individuals copying each other's behaviour and attaching a shared meaning to certain actions.

In this respect it is important to point out the branching character of series of imitations. This means that, in the dissemination of behaviour, all kinds of new series will form and may produce new relationships. These in turn may generate other series of imitations. Adding new series to existing ones leaves open the possibility of creation, and keeps the socio-cultural field in motion and thus alive. This is how criminality should also be approached, Tarde writes in *Penal Philosophy* (1912: 362). In other words, as 'a phenomenon of imitative propagation.' Forms of criminality spread 'like every industrial product, like every good or bad idea' (1912: 338). Tarde does not claim here that criminality can be studied as a separate entity, independent of other developments in society. The question, he states (1912: 362), is 'whether the many other phenomena of imitative propagation, which taken all together are called civilization (...), foster or impede the progress of the propagation of crime. Or rather, the aim is to discover, if that were possible, which among these various spreadings of example which are called instruction, religion, politics, commerce, industry, are the ones that foster, and which ones that impede, the expansion of crime.'

Tarde (1962: 140 ff) distinguishes two laws to elucidate the process of imitation. He speaks of a 'logical law', where imitation starts from the idea that it will contribute to a higher objective or is expected to solve a problem better than other inventions. More often, however, than arising from rational or well-thought-out considerations, imitation occurs in response to 'extra-logical laws'. The emphasis in these laws is on cultural elements, but psychological and sociological influences also play a role. Tarde shows that certain forms of crime occur increasingly frequently as the number of interactions between different people increases (through processes of urbanization, for example, or following the move from the aristocracy to the bourgeoisie). He illustrates this with the notorious case of the nursemaid Henriette Cornier, who in 1825 decapitated a 19-month old child and subsequently threw the head out of a window. Not long after, other nursemaids also yielded to an 'irresistible impulse to cut the throats of their employers' children' (Tarde, 1912: 340).[1]

Invention

Tarde uses the term 'general laws' to indicate that the process of imitation not only plays a role in social life, but also in other areas such as geology, astronomy and chemistry. But even though he refers to these laws as 'general', their effect is different in each area. The process of 'invention' is distinctive in this respect. An invention is not social until it is imitated in social life, Tarde writes in *Social Laws* (2000: 23, 78). From a societal point of view, inventions that are not imitated are not relevant (Tarde, 1912: 396 n.1). This means that an invention does not produce effects until it is included in series of imitations 'which have fallen one after another into the domain of the commonplace, the traditional, and the customary' (Tarde, 1912: 118). This includes both small and large imitations; imitations occurring within a short space of time or over a longer period.

Tarde (1969: 153) defines an invention as the combination of dissimilar imitations as, he believes, inventions, too, branch into series, like links in a chain with 'highly variable intervals, sometimes of a few days or months, sometimes of several centuries' (1969: 160). They merge into series of imitations, spreading in turn like an oil stain and leading a socio-cultural field increasingly to achieve sameness. How should we interpret this? Inventions spread, to use one of Tarde's favourite analogies, like ripples in water moving steadily towards the shore until they hit an obstacle. According to Tarde, that obstacle will often be the imitation of a previous invention, and their collision (in dialectic terms 'opposition') will generate a new product: a new invention that may in turn be imitated until it, too, hits new obstacles (Tarde, 1969: 21). Following on from this analogy, society can be seen as one large irrigation system. In other words, a system with constantly moving currents, undercurrents, and countercurrents (Van Ginneken, 1992: 200).

Although invention and imitation should not be considered hierarchical opposites (as they are mutually influencing forces), Tarde seems, in his approach to inventions, to adhere to the classical notion of 'genius' as found *inter alia* in the final of Kant's three *Kritiken*, being *Kritik der Urteilskraft* (1790). According to Kant, a genius is characterized by an autonomous creativity (autonomy literally means 'self-legislating'). He appreciates positively what others

1 Even today, certain incidents, such as stones thrown onto cars from viaducts, or suicides from certain buildings, are kept out of the news for fear of imitation.

consider to be merely coincidental or trivial. In a similar fashion, Tarde attributes inventions to the ability of a 'truly great man'. In *Penal Philosophy* (1912: 164-165), for example, he asserts that such people can reform the crowd and gradually make it conform to themselves. At the same time, Tarde believes that this rationalist view only partly explains why we are 'more imitative than innovative' (1962: 98). Contrary to the more rational approaches of Durkheim and Weber and following Théodule Ribots' *Essai sur l'imagination créatice* (1900), Tarde (1969: 150) also points to other factors that influence the generation of new inventions, such as emotion or desire ('fear or anger, sadness or joy, hate or love'). In *The Laws of Imitation* (1962: xiv), therefore, he refuses to distinguish between conscious and unconscious inventions: 'I have certainly applied this name [invention, PVC & MS] to all individual initiatives, not only without considering the extent to which they are self-conscious – for the individual often innovates unconsciously, and, as a matter of fact, the most imitative man is an innovator on some side or another – but without paying the slightest attention in the world to the degree of difficulty or merit of the innovation in question.'

Tarde seems to imply that an invention is a strictly individual matter, while imitation requires two separate individuals. In other words, to what extent is Tarde's approach simply a plea for practising 'psychologism' or 'spiritualism'? In *Difference and Repetition*, Deleuze refutes the criticism that a psychology lies hidden behind Tarde's '*general sociology*'. According to Deleuze (1994: 313-314 n.3), Tarde realizes a 'microsociology, which is not necessarily concerned with what happens between individuals but with what happens within a single individual: for example, hesitation understood as "infinitesimal social opposition", or invention as "infinitesimal social adaptation".' By this, according to Deleuze, Tarde demonstrates that there is always a second issue besides the issue of structure. More than on the structural level of order and stability, which Deleuze terms 'molar' (1987: 213 ff.), this involves a 'molecular' level (1987: 213 ff.) with a very different rhythm and speed. This level is not necessarily manifest or noticeable, but does have the potential to break open and transform a social-cultural field. Or, as Deleuze and Guattari state in *A Thousand Plateaus* (1987: 215), 'Although it is true that the molecular works in detail and operates in small groups, this does not mean that it is any less coextensive with the entire social field than molar organization.'

Variation and movement

At the risk of simplification, it could be argued that the question of variation and movement is key to Tarde's approach (Alliez, 2001). More specifically, Tarde claims that it is not productive to reason from the mere assumption of a fixed order or structure. In Tarde's words (2000: 93), 'To understand social conditions, we must seize social changes in detail as they pass.' After all, the smallest body movement, such as the knowing wink between board members of a multinational during a meeting, can initiate quite significant change in a socio-cultural field. In this light, the elementary social fact is not the individual or the whole, but a series of interactions that produce a difference, i.e. movements that differentiate something qualitatively and quantitatively (Barry & Thrift, 2007).

It will be obvious by now that we are far removed from the classical way of looking at meaning or purpose in which the human subject is at the centre of attributing meaning and purpose. That classical view is largely inspired by Descartes' magical maxim 'I think, therefore I am.' In this view, a person's actions are the product of a free, autonomous and immutable actor. This individual is in opposition to his immediate environment, without forming part of it. From an external position he is able to comprehend and grasp social reality in its entirety. However, like Tarde, we may wish to assume that interaction cannot be reduced to the action of the individual or the substance or subject it refers or is ascribed to. Interaction is an autonomous process. It expresses a 'becoming', as Deleuze puts it.

The above observations raise questions as to how existing practices and institutions can be transformed, and what attitude should be accepted as regards policy and practice. In other words, how can we demonstrate that 'molar' organizations (Deleuze) are dismantled as a result of the introduction of new openings on a 'molecular' level and the creation of other connections? Can Tarde's body of thought be applied to develop a different approach to criminality and conflict control? And, if so, how?

Reification

Tarde's basic assumption of a molecular 'sublevel' of series of interactions underlying the molar level is not as self-evident as it might seem at first sight. It is, in any event, at odds with the perspectives in which the potential and effect of policy initiatives, or the freedom of choice of governmental and non-governmental actors, are assumed without question. Distinct from the idea that changes can be brought about effectively in society, the idea that 'social change can be effected by government policies' – in other words, deliberately and strategically – might be problematic (Schuilenburg, 2008; Van Calster & Verfaillie, 2007). In this respect, Tarde highlights the dangers of 'reification', an approach to reality in which social phenomena are separated from concrete human action. According to Berger and Luckman (1967: 105-109), reification is the result of an over-applied process of objectification. When, for example, people have applied a process of 'reification', they no longer experience social reality as a product of human interactions. Reality is then given an ontological basis that is detached from all concrete human interaction, and institutions are regarded as independent, as 'natural' and essential. Roles and identities, too, can be the object of reification. In the former – the roles – individuals are no longer able to distinguish between the roles they play and their true self. They limit their own freedom of choice because they feel they have to act in accordance with the position they hold. In the latter – the identity – the individual completely identifies with specific socially attributed characteristics.

According to the Dutch criminologist Bianchi (1980: 384), criminal law and the criminal justice system are such 'false gods'. They are credited with having an immutable life of their own and are subsequently worshipped as something inevitable and necessary. However, when institutions such as the police or the judiciary are reified, they are imagined as a 'thing' and thus as a whole, acting according to their own order (Van Calster, 2005). In other words, we ascribe a purpose to reification and the parts are studied to the extent that they help accomplish that purpose. As a result, the whole is imagined as a determining force, which has to be obeyed by its parts. Consequently, people no longer believe they can exert an influence on or transform their institutions, or rather they assume that the dynamics of those institutions are subjected to forces that are beyond their control.

The only way this framework allows for any real change is by emphasizing the remarkable qualities or views of individual reformers such as scientists, legislators, practitioners, politicians and policymakers. They then are expected not to be subject to the determining forces of the whole. This approach implies that these individuals are somehow *outside* the dynamics of the whole. They evaluate these dynamics as 'outsiders', devise plans and prescribe the correct remedies, which may then subsequently be deployed. This is a very mechanical way of looking at social reality, and ignores the many series of interactions that continuously take place and exert an influence on what occurs at a molar level (Van Calster, 2006).

Processes of interaction

Tarde states that all knowledge (including criminological knowledge) is a social activity that can evoke varied reactions from and within the professional field. Criminologists and policymakers should not, therefore, be placed outside the reality and social dynamics. When, for example, they devise new methods of conflict settlement to be imposed on that reality, they do not do this from 'outside' the system. Researchers unavoidably participate in what they research, while policymakers participate in the policies they design. Hence, they contribute considerably to what they attempt to research or reform (Heisenberg, 1962: 19). It is more plausible, therefore, to define the criminal justice system as a complex social process of interactions (which includes both linguistic and non-linguistic dimensions), not only between people, but also between objects – including abstract items such as rules, regulations and territories (the court, a police station and so on) (Van Calster, 2005). This is because, as Tarde argues, people constantly interact, and it is precisely in and through those series of interactions that all kinds of actions, such as cooperation and conflict, emerge. Those interactions can take many different forms and may include innocent, conformist and deliberate, but also confrontational or unintentional interaction.

A focus on these series of interactions raises the question of *how* reforms actually occur, and what the impact is of the actions of people commonly considered the source of those reforms (legislators, politicians, practitioners in management positions, policymakers or scientists). These reformers, after all, design the desired changes. They devise models and plans and draft legislative texts or policy documents. This process takes form through and in the very interactions these actors have with others – actors with different interests, or conflicts; actors that harbour particular rational and emotional considerations. Hence, at the time when these models, action plans or legislative texts are actually being introduced or implemented, reformers have no certainty about their impact.

In criminal justice, for example, the impact of interactions that the many managers have *with* the lower echelons will undoubtedly be far greater than the impact of interactions *within* and *from* the lower echelons since actors in management positions tend to reach a far greater audience and, in addition, may be able to enforce their decisions and measures. But practitioners in management positions, politicians, policymakers, legislators and criminologists cannot *de facto* determine what the reactions from the professional field to their plans and intentions will be. The value and importance of the measures they take depend, therefore, on how others respond to them. Thus it is in and through series of interactions that the dynamics and developments of the process of criminal justice and its many institutions emerge. No one person will ever be able to determine the dynamics of interactions within an institution or during a collaborative undertaking because those dynamics depend on what others will do. Moreover, the manner in which *external* organizations and actors respond co-determines these dynamics of transformation. In short, the whole process can better be described as – to borrow a notion from complexity sciences – *emergent* as it will never be the exact realization of a preceding design.

Emergence

The question that immediately arises is how can it be that interactions of thousands of people are able to produce, for example, a particular police or penal 'culture'? The answer to this question relates to the intrinsic self-organizing, *emergent* properties of interaction itself (Mainzer, 1997; Taylor, 2001; Kauffman, 1993; 1995). Recent scientific complexity research has shown that, under certain conditions (such as diversity), interactions between large numbers of entities who react to one another's locally-oriented behaviours, customs and principles generate coherent and potentially *renewed* behavioural patterns. To put it differently: interactions possess the inherent capacity to spontaneously form a coherent pattern *in itself*.[2] Abstract systems thus have the ability to self-organize and hence produce patterns and behavioural patterns without these having been imposed. This process of interaction between people who are sufficiently different from each other can thus be described as a self-organizing process with an intrinsic capacity to form behavioural patterns. We define this as a complex process of interaction. We should add, however, that not only does the pattern of interaction organize itself on a molar level, but also on a molecular level. Since these two levels appear together and concurrently, separating them will be problematic. As the scientists Kauffman and Ray have shown, the molecular level forms the molar level, while at the same time it itself is formed by that molar level. Let us examine these complexity sciences in more depth.

In the computer simulations performed by Stuart Kauffman (1993; 1995) and Tom Ray (1992), every agent is represented as a computer program. Each computer program contains a set of rules and instructions determining its interaction with other computer programs. As the emphasis is on an agent-based approach, the research object is represented as a population of agents that interact according to their own local 'if-then' rules (Mainzer, 1997; Lewin, 1993). So, rules or patterns should not be formulated that apply to entire populations, but rather interaction rules for the individual entities that together make up a population or system. A complex adaptive system consequently comprises a large number of agents, with each agent behaving in accordance with its own local interaction rules. No individual agent, or group of agents, determines the behavioural pattern displayed by the system as a whole, or the manner in which this pattern evolves. This approach does not include anything imposing its will from outside the system. There is no blueprint for the organization of the entire system.

Kauffman (1995: 63-64; Mainzer, 1997: 97) used computer simulations to demonstrate that a network consisting of a large number of entities (agents) interacting randomly evolves in a relatively short time into a connected, autocatalytic network. In other words, when entities interact randomly, some of them begin to play a role in the construction of others. This is called the process of catalysis. As time progresses, the behavioural patterns emerging from this catalytic interaction isolate themselves and form autocatalytic networks. In specific terms, this means that entity A plays a role in the construction of B, which plays a role in the construction of C, which in turn plays a role in the construction of A. There is no design or blueprint for this network. It emerges and sustains itself in a self-referential manner. The emerging pattern is self-

2 Relatively accessible studies about this process of self-organization include Nicolis & Prigogine (1989), Prigogine & Stengers (1984), Gell-Mann (1994) Mainzer (1996) and Taylor (2001).

organizing. Here, self-organization is an intrinsic property of interaction, which causes the emergence of patterns (Mertens, 2000).

Note how different this line of thought is from thinking in terms of reification. Reification implies giving a certain content to various concepts, which is then used as a reference to give meaning to social reality. This causes them to become systemic or molar frameworks (feedback mechanisms), where the rules of conduct are seen as being outside the system, and which are referred to in order to correct or streamline behaviour. One consequence of this can be that 'culture' is individualized as a collective to which we can then ascribe values and motives. This way of thinking depicts the collective as an acting individual. The behaviour of members of an organization, a society or, for example, the criminal justice system is then driven by the values of that 'whole'. Hence, norms and values become abstracted from daily life. In short, reification idealizes the collective, which is represented as a personality that can justify the actions of the members. This idealization, however, diverts attention from interactions in everyday life and interactions in the *here-and-now*. And it is precisely this everyday-life dimension which, according to Gabriel Tarde, continuously affects the formation of stabilities and which he believes deserves research attention.

The control of criminality as a process

By taking series of interactions as his point of departure for analyzing life in society, Tarde laid the foundation for what we call 'process thinking'. Process thinking assumes a long concatenation of forms of interaction that have often completely lost their original meaning. The relationship between cause and effect in those concatenations is highly ambiguous and difficult to determine, and it is very difficult to even discern cause and consequence. Take Kauffman´s autocatalytic networks, for example. The problem is aggravated by the many coincidences that look like causes, but are actually relational in nature (Cilliers, 1998). This makes it difficult to accurately predict what will happen in a specific place over a specific period of time. To summarize, if we were to research the operation of the penal system (often labelled as a persistent penal culture or obstinate practice),[3] as a pattern of interaction that is not so much

3 This, of course, does not alter the fact that there are frequently elements of rational planning and determination through and in the many processes of research and policy. Just as it does not alter the fact that intense negotiations (and thus social networks) will be entered into and result in various agreements that may or may not be observed. In other words, from the perspective of process thinking, the issue of control and the extent to which social change can be brought about by government intervention or policy seem only relative. Attempts to achieve them may produce unintended outcomes over which one has little control. For that reason, objectives, models and good intentions often 'lose their innocence' after a 'confrontation' with social reality itself.

the implementation of a preceding design, but rather the result of an ever-emergent process of interactions, the focus of research would be on interaction *themes* that organize experiences, such as themes that are considered unpleasant and are usually avoided (Van Calster, 2005).

It then becomes evident that the criminal justice system is simply a series of temporary 'successful' patterns and themes of interaction, accepted by the participants as 'good enough' to be repeated, and thus becoming organizational customs. The repetition of these patterns and themes creates stability in the collective identity (or organizational culture) and organizes cooperation. These patterns and themes are expressed through a certain organizational language; in other words, in certain ways of doing and saying things. These ways create the collective identity (the criminal justice system, for example), as well as various aspects of their individual identities. The repetition of organizational customs (culture or language) that are 'good enough' will increase efficiency as the constant repetition of these customs in a similar way will improve people's performance. These customs (a certain way of speaking, for instance) are safe themes that organize cooperation. They reflect what has emerged as a standard of conduct, and make prevailing power relations seem natural. Newcomers to 'the criminal justice system' then believe that they have to use this particular way of speaking to express involvement in or commitment to the organization. We hasten to add, however, that these patterns are not recorded anywhere and are not fixed. Precisely because they are repeated constantly – imitated, as Tarde calls it – they always have the potential for transformation and thus for change.

But if the dynamics of the police and the judicial system are emergent and do not necessarily, therefore, correspond with the predetermined designs and intentions, how do these institutions change? As the research by Kauffman (1993: 1995) shows, new patterns, and thus new meanings, arise primarily in interactions that are characterized by diversity. When there is little diversity between people and they have developed solid (and often rigid) conceptions and ways of interacting with each other, their interactions are unlikely to generate anything new. Their patterns of interaction are more likely to be repetitive. Conversely, groups with a full range of diversity will have to contend, incessantly, with dissonance and forms of 'disobedience'. Successful transformation, therefore, falls somewhere in between these two extremes, in a zone Kaufman (1993) calls 'the edge of chaos.'

As we noted earlier, there is a strong probability that behaviours arising from these complex processes of interaction become routines and customs, stabilizing themselves on a molar level. Routines and customs are identifiable by their clear and delineated meaning. That is what determines the reliability and robustness of these routines. If such routines are deemed successful, that success will strengthen them, and this may make them seem rigid to reformers. Routines are often accompanied by a certain formal use of language (usually excluding other forms of interaction), within which tasks and roles are clearly defined. As a result, they exert considerable influence on cooperation. This way, the constant repetition of customs generates stability of the collective and, for example, a penal culture. Criminal law and criminal justice, then, should be considered as stable series of interactions, rather than determining forces. These customs embody the official standards of conduct and generally make the power relationships formed in this process seem natural. Over time, actors tend to abstract, objectify or reify this repetitive behaviour, and consider it to be something that has always existed and as self-evident. In other words, they 'forget' that it has been generated in and through human interactions. People in organizations become habituated to this stability and feel threatened, or may even become aggressive, if new ways of interaction are introduced.

We believe that those applying themselves to studying the criminal justice system must also focus on the smallest deviations or slightest changes in series of interactions. Research by Elias and Scotson (1994) may provide an interesting source of inspiration in this respect. Elias and Scotson examined what happened when a group of workers moved into a new apartment block adjacent to an older one inhabited by other workers. Even though there were no substantial differences between the two groups, hostility soon developed. The older residents started to denigrate the newcomers. Elias and Scotson explained this in terms of cohesion among the older group of workers. The older residents had come to think of themselves as 'we', a group with common attachments, likes and dislikes, and interests that had emerged because of their cooperation. They had developed a sense of identity. The newcomers lacked this cohesive identity because they had no history of working together and that, according to Elias and Scotson, made them vulnerable. The more cohesive group, therefore, was quick to label the newcomers and to attribute to them hateful qualities such as 'dirtiness', 'unreliability' and 'criminal', even though there were no obvious differences between the two groups. One group used the fact that the others were newcomers to generate hatred and thus maintain a power difference.

Conclusion

The Durkheimian strand of thought identifies 'the criminal justice system' with repetitive patterns of language and power, but ignores the complex processes of interaction *from* which this 'order' has emerged. It abstracts and names these repetitive patterns, using the organization's legitimate language as if it were a system that already existed *outside* processes of interaction. This thinking consequently ignores the ever-present potential for transformation. From that perspective, transformation can only be explained as having been imposed by an extra-ordinary individual.

On the other hand, 'process thinking', which is based on Tarde's thought and further developed in complexity sciences, suggests a need to analyse actions within social processes, whereby emphasis is placed on perceptions, world views and interaction styles of all those participating *in* (and not *with*) those processes. This in turn suggests that criminal activity, for example, or attempts to control it are not just a matter of rationality or functionality, and thus of wilful change and control, but rather the effects of various complex processes operating on a molecular level and over which one has little or no control. Far more than focusing on the molar level in isolation, we must also, therefore, look at the molecular level and its ever-emerging effects. For even when everything appears to function well, the smallest of actions and passions – on the molecular level – may have unexpected consequences on the molar level.

Literature

Alliez, E. (2001), 'Différence et répétition de Gabriel Tarde', in: *Multitude Web*, (7): p. 171-176.

Badiou, A. (2002), *Ethics. An Essay on the Understanding of Evil*, Verso: London/New York.

Badiou, A. (2005), *Being and Event*, New York: Continuum.

Barry, A. & Thrift N., (2007), Gabriel Tarde: imitation, invention and economy, in: *Economy and Society*, 36, 4, p. 509-525.

Berger, P.L. & Luckman, T. (1966), *The Social Construction of Reality: A Treatise in the Sociology of Knowledge*, New York: Doubleday.

Bianchi, H. (1980), *Basismodellen in de criminologie*, Deventer: Van Loghum Slaterus.

Boutellier, H. (1993), *Solidariteit en slachtofferschap. De morele betekenis van criminaliteit in een postmoderne cultuur*, Nijmegen: SUN.

Cilliers, P. (1998) *Complexity and Postmodernism. Understanding Complex Systems*, London/New York: Routledge.

Deleuze, G. & Guattari F. (1987), *A Thousand Plateaus. Capitalism and Schizophrenia* (orig. 1980), Minneapolis: University of Minnesota Press.

Deleuze, G. (1994), *Difference and Repetition* (orig. 1968), New York: Columbia University Press.

Durkheim, E. (1977), *Over moraliteit*, Meppel: Boom.

Elias, N. & Scotson, J. (1994), *The Established and the Outsiders*, London: Sage.

Gell-Mann, M. (1994), *The Quark and the Jaguar: Adventures in the Simple and the Complex*, London: Abacus.

Ginneken, J. Van (1992), *Crowds, Psychology, and Politics, 1871-1899*, Cambridge: Cambridge University Press.

Heisenberg, W. (1962), *La Nature Dans la Physique Contemporaine*, Paris : Gallimard.

Jong, J. De (2007) *Kapot Moeilijk*. Amsterdam: Aksant.

Kauffman, S.A. (1993), *Origins of Order. Self-organization and Selection in Evolution,* Oxford: Oxford University Press.

Kauffman, S.A. (1995), *At Home in the Universe,* New York: Oxford University Press.

Laermans, R. (1995), Sociologie vandaag: enkele stellingen en notities, in: *Tijdschrift voor Sociologie,* vol. 16, nr. 2. p. 133-141.

Latour, B. (2002), Gabriel Tarde and the End of the Social, in: *The Social in Question. New Bearings in History and the Social Sciences* (P. Joyce, ed.), London: Routledge, p. 117-132.

Latour, B. (2007), *Reassembling the Social. An Introduction to Actor-Network-Theory,* New York: Oxford University Press.

Mainzer, K. (1996), *Thinking in Complexity. The Complex Dynamics of Matter, Mind, and Mankind,* Heidelberg, New York: Springer-Verlag Berlin.

Nicolis, G. & Prigogine, I. (1989), *Exploring Complexity. An Introduction,* New York: W.H. Freeman & Company.

Prigogine, I. & Stengers, I. (1984), *Order Out of Chaos. Man's New Dialogue with Nature,* New York: Bantam Books.

Rhoads, J.K. (1991), *Critical Issues in Social Theory,* Pennsylvania: The Pennsylvania State University Press.

Schuilenburg, M. (2006), De kracht van een revolutie. Mensenrechten en de democratie, in: *Het Uur van de Waarheid. Alain Badiou – revolutionair denker* (R. de Brabander, ed.), Kampen: Ten Have, p. 101-119.

Schuilenburg, M. (2008), The Dislocating Perspective of Assemblages. Another Look at the Issue of Security, in: *Open. Cahier on art and the public domain,* no. 15 (Rotterdam: NAi Uitgevers), p. 18-35.

Tarde, G. (1999), *Monadologie et sociologie* (orig. 1893), Paris: Les empêcheurs de penser en rond.

Tarde, G. (1912), *Penal Philosophy* (orig. 1890) Boston: Little, Brown, and Company.

Tarde, G. (1962), *The Laws of Imitation* (orig. 1890), Massachusetts: Gloucester.

Tarde, G. (1969), *On communication and social influence* (selected papers. Edited and with an introduction by Terry N. Clark), Chicago: University of Chicago Press.

Tarde, G. (2000), *Social Laws. An outline of sociology* (orig. 1898), Kitchener, Ontario: Batoche Books.

Taylor, M.C. (2001), *The Moment of Complexity. Emerging Network Culture,* Chicago: University of Chicago Press.

Van Calster, P. & Verfaillie, K. (2007) Het strafrechtsysteem als narratief proces. Over de illusie van maakbaarheid en controle, in *Liber Amicorum Christiaen* Eliaerts, (Van Calster, P., J. Christiaens, E. Enhus, A. Nuytiens & S. Snacken, eds.): University Press Brussels, p. 319-332.

Van Calster, P. (2006), Re-visiting Mr. Nice. On Organized Crime as Conversational Interaction, *Crime, Law and Social Change,* 45, 4/5, p. 337-359.

Van Calster, P. (2005), *Georganiseerde Criminaliteit als Emergent Fenomeen van Complexe Wisselwerkingsprocessen*, PhD thesis: Brussels University Press.
Žižek, S. (2002), *Welcome to the Desert of the Real! Five Essays on September 11 and Related Dates,* London/New York: Verso.

Criminological Change: Tribe, Fashion, Image

Ronnie LIPPENS
Keele University (UK)

Introduction

Let us remind ourselves of the three basic questions of criminology. Stanley Cohen is among those who managed to summarize them most succinctly: 'Why are laws made? Why are they broken? What do we do or what should we do about this?' (1988, p. 9). Or, put slightly differently, 'why do definitions of crime change and vary across time and space, and how does that happen?', or 'why and how do particular behaviours and even whole groups or populations get to be criminalized in the first place?'; 'why and how do people offend against norms, including legal norms such as the Criminal Law?'; and 'what should we do with offenders or, more broadly, what should be done about crime, and how?'. A closer look at these questions might perhaps reveal how, at the very heart of each, a more basic one dwells, i.e. 'who, or what, counts as 'in', and who, or what, counts as 'out', and how do such *accounts* come about, emerge, and indeed change, across time and space?'. That is the question we would like to reflect upon in the contribution at hand. At heart this is a question of (and for) anthropology, In what follows we will make an attempt to answer the aforementioned question drawing inspiration mostly from what is commonly known as *actor-network theory* (or ANT). ANT emerged from anthropology (no surprise there either!).

Our focus will be on the emergence, and hence: change, of *accounts* of how behaviours or groups come to be defined 'in', or, as the case may be, 'out'. Such accounts are what we call – or might call – *criminologies*. Our intention, then, is to provide an answer to the question 'Where does newness, or change, in criminological accounts come from?'. The paper originates in a fairly basic desire of its author to provide students with a fairly basic insight into the matter at hand, i.e. the emergence and development of scientific 'newness'. Although the reader will find here references to some of the well-known literatures that may shed a light on the *what* of scientific, or theoretical newness, the contribution at hand shall approach the problem from a slightly different angle. Here we are not so much interested in the *what* of scientific or theoretical newness as in the *how* and *why*. That scientific or theoretical newness is a matter of structured *paradigmatic* struggles in *scientific communities* (Kuhn, 1970), or, in more subtle versions, of 'naturally', more fluidly changing interpretations in *interpretive communities* (Fish, 1989), is something we won't spend any energy refuting here. There is no reason to. We will, on the contrary, focus on how exactly scientific or theoretical newness ('change') emerges, and how it develops. We will also delve a little deeper into the *why* question. Let us briefly state the gist of our argument here. We will argue that scientific or theoretical newness, or change -and we'll focus particularly on criminological newness or change- is, first and foremost, all about image. *Drawing things together* (please keep this phrase in mind) from anthropology (ANT in particular) and from art history and art criticism, we will argue, in what follows, that scientific or theoretical newness can be considered as the result of a tribal process of assemblage and fashionable circulation of images, indeed: of *image*. This process of assemblage and circulation, we will argue, is at the very same time also a process of formation of self and community. The formation of self and of community takes place in and through this very assemblage and circulation of image(s). The boundary between self and community, then, we hope to be able to demonstrate, *is* this process of assemblage and circulation, and, as such, that is, because it *is* a process of assemblage and circulation, this boundary is shot through with the potential for 'change' and 'newness'. In other words, change and newness in science or theory originate in the process in and through which the scientific or theoretical 'self' and the scientific or theoretical 'community' -any particular 'self' and any particular 'community'- are constituted. But we are running ahead of ourselves here. Let us approach this issue from three different angles. Let me, in other words, assemble three images. I'll circulate them, and their assemblage, in the next three sections. We'll then hopefully be able to pull together the threads - *to draw these things together* (this phrase again !) - and see where it takes our (yours and mine) scientific or theoretical 'self' and 'community'.

Fashion: The Abbot and 'Noble Simplicity'

Abbot Suger was a peculiar man. Born in 1081 and appointed Abbot of St. Denis (the abbey of St. Denis was just north of Paris), Abbot Suger had a penchant for gold, jewels, and all things shiny and glittering. Light too, lots of it, was high on the abbot's wish list. Now whether or not the abbot's taste for jewelry and suchlike things to some extent expressed something of his essential self, or his sense of community, or whether indeed his taste is only a sign of his *becoming* a different self, or a member of a different community, is of no great import here. We do know that Suger was born to a very humble family and ultimately ended up in those diplomatic circles that were closest to the French king himself. So yes, one might argue that the abbot's taste for gold and silver and gemstones simply expressed something of a nagging desire to transcend embarrassingly humble origins. Or, on the other hand, it might also have indicated something of the aspirations of the emerging, *becoming* parvenu. But that would not lead us very far. The issue is not so much about whether the abbot's taste, or anyone's taste, for that matter, expresses some essence or betrays some process of becoming or other. One could say that things human that express themselves *as* essence do so through aspiration, that is, they will somehow betray an aspiration to do so, i.e. to express themselves *as* essence. And the other side of this coin is equally arguable, namely, that for anything to *become*, to aspire towards difference, change, why not 'newness', something of this 'newness' must already be present - let's not use the word 'essence' to denote it - to fuel the process of *becoming* newness. So we won't be wasting any more time here on this issue of expressive becoming (on the Nietzschean and existentialist notion of *becoming* and its importance for criminology, see e.g. Lippens and Crewe, 2009; and Lippens, 2009). Let us go back to Abbot Suger instead.

We do know that the abbot was fond of glitter and shiny valuables. He actually made the effort, near the end of his life, to meticulously record, describe, and account for all the valuables he managed to procure or collect for the benefit of the abbey. The phrase 'for the benefit of the abbey' is not coincidental here. Suger himself always adopted a fairly humble, or, if not, a certain temperate lifestyle. No luxury for Suger's own person, then. Moderation, temperance, and a very balanced sense of diplomacy, were his. In his account of the abbey's glittering riches, the abbot made sure he listed and expanded on the very many architectural changes which he had made to the buildings of the abbey, the church, and the estate. Huge windows, in various shapes, that allowed the daylight to flood inside the church, bathing the many shiny treasures inside in a sea of bright sparkle, for example, were introduced. And wider, more spacious halls and rooms. We know of all these treasures and architectural innovations because the abbot made sure they were recorded and written down. One of the foremost twentieth-century scholars of art history, Erwin Panofsky, came across the abbot's inventory, edited, translated, and annotated it. The information for this section, by the way, comes from a reprint, in *Meaning in the Visual Arts* (1955), of Panofsky's 'Introduction' to Suger's inventory. Little did Abbot Suger know that all the changes he had made to his church and his estate would, much later, lead art historians such as Panofsky to classify the abbey of St. Denis, just north of Paris, as the first medieval gothic building. Suger himself seems to have been unaware of the 'newness' which he expressed/became, and which the ecclesiastical community of monks embodied and lived out within the walls of the estate. But he did know that his project, if ever it was a consciously conceived and planned project, to some considerable extent, went against the grain of the day. For instance, he often uses the word 'modern' to describe his architectural vision. But there is more. The dominant atmosphere in religious communities, at the time, was one that was proscribed by Bernard, later Saint Bernard of Clairvaux. The atmosphere of religious worship, Panofsky tells us, was one of obligatory austerity and asceticism, of dark, moist cloisters and grey shadows on bleak walls. Suger, on many occasions, had to muster all his diplomatic skills -of which he had many, perhaps not by mere accident-in order to be able to proceed with the ongoing production, indeed assemblage, of *deviant knowledge* which he, and his monks at St. Denis, were circulating. Suger's was a kind of knowledge that, at least to some extent, expressed a becoming self as well as a becoming community, or, in other words, became an expressive self and an expressive community of change and newness. And yes, here are the two words again: deviant knowledge. That the abbot's taste for brightness and for glittery gold did tend to be perceived by his fellow clerics - Bernard of Clairvaux amongst them- as deviant, should perhaps come as not too big a surprise, and indeed the importance of the very fact of the abbot's effort to record and, above all, justify his deviancy in a long, annotated inventory, might perhaps go without saying. But why do we call this taste, here, in this contribution, why do we call the abbot's desire *knowledge*? The Abbot of Saint-Denis himself would probably have agreed to consider knowledge as a deeply sensual matter, as a matter of the senses, of emotion and of desire. Panofsky, who by the way is not directly interested in the issues that concern us here, tells us how Suger came across translations of the neo-Platonist writings of Dionysius the Areopagite, one of the church fathers who, it was assumed at the time, was the real St. Denis. In there he finds a most appropriate justification for his 'modern' desires: the neo-Platonist doctrine of divine light. "But we profess", he writes in his inventory, "that we must do homage also through the outward ornaments of sacred vessels. (...) For it behooves us most becomingly to serve our Saviour in all things in a universal way", in other words, in and through the circulation (and admiration) of materials that embody a knowledge that knows that universal, divine Truth is in God ("the superessential Light") and Christ (the "first radiance"), and that we, devout mortals, must attempt to partake in that divine light, in Suger's words, to get "transported from this inferior to that higher world in an anagogical manner", in and through "the delight in the beauty of the house of God" (Panofsky, 1955, p. 133-9). And by "the house of God" Suger meant something quite literal and tangible. So, what have we got here. We have a monk, of very humble origins, and perhaps a little "vain" (Panofsky surmises), who, while in high places, assembles together very partial bits and pieces of found, indeed stumbled upon fragments of neo-Platonist theology, with gold, gemstones, and flows of sparkling light, as well as with particular desires, tastes, and diplomatic sensitivities, and who then circulates this assemblage, thus expressing/becoming something that might be called newness; newness of *self*, and newness of *community*. Whether this process of assemblage and circulation of new, deviant knowledge resulted from Suger's biography or from context, or from both, is not the issue here. The issue is to recognise how, in particular contexts involving particular biographies, 'new' knowledge gets to be assembled from available bits and pieces, embodied, and circulated, and how in and through this very process of assemblage and circulation, *self* (e.g. Suger's sensuous and therefore contradictory neo-Platonist self) and *community* (e.g. an emerging community of sensuous, gothic worship) emerge, better still: are constituted, or, as we have argued, are simultaneously expressed and becoming.

Self and community are not eternal. The knowledge assemblages and circulations in and through which they are constituted aren't either. For reasons that are yet to be explored in subsequent sections, they are bound to fragment, disintegrate even, leaving bits and pieces to scatter around, possibly to be re-used in other bouts of knowledge assemblage and circulation. It is interesting to note, with Ernst Gombrich (1962), how Suger's gothic knowledge, and how gothic selves and communities, gradually gave way to other, more fashionable forms of knowledge, self, and community. In his classic essay on 'Visual Metaphors of Value in Art' (1962, p. 12-29), Gombrich tells us how, at the cradle of the Renaissance, in the writings of Leone Battista Alberti, the "mere surface attractions of sparkle" gave way to an emerging knowledge that knows vulgar abundance from "noble simplicity", the fake "sprinkling of gold" from "dignified purity", superficiality from "sincerity", excess from "moral restraint", irrational disorder from rational order, in short low from high (1962, p. 17.). Soon this knowledge, newly assembled from available bits and pieces, and circulating in and between emerging, 'deviant' selves and communities, would end up on canvasses, in architecture, in theological and philosophical tracts, and in the black-and-white, that is: strict and restrained and 'sincere' dress code of a newly emerging cultural elite whose *perspective* (indeed !) on life, whose knowledge of life expressed/became a certain 'newness'. For a while. But that is another story (see e.g. in Lippens, 2004). Let us now go to the tribes of Papua New Guinea.

Tribe: In Papua New Guinea

In her book, *Partial Connections* (1991), Marilyn Strathern, one of the most prominent representatives of ANT, describes and analyses how tribesmen in the jungle and foothills of Papua New Guinea, when applying or adjusting adornments, used as extensions of the body, do a number of things simultaneously. They would, in assembling and then applying extensions, negotiate tribal custom, or, using our phraseology here, tribal knowledge. They would, in applying these extensions (negotiated embodiments of tribal knowledge), simultaneously assemble their own selves. In other words, when applying extensions, and when circulating them while they are walking about the village, or, in yet other words, when they are evoking and mobilising and gauging and negotiating tribal knowledge during such parades, tribesmen help constitute both self and tribal community at the same time. The ramifications of this insight cannot be underestimated: self and tribal community emerge in and through the assemblage and circulation of (embodied) knowledge; the assemblage and circulation of tribal knowledge is in turn a matter of self and community, a matter, that is, of gauging and negotiating the boundary between self and community.

As this has been elaborated upon elsewhere (Lippens, 2003 and 2006) let us now focus on one issue in particular. Just like the embodiments of tribal knowledge themselves, i.e. the extensions that get assembled and circulated, their expressive products or becoming source, that is: self and community, too, are always, and inevitably so, a matter of *partial connections*. This means that knowledge, self, and community (we feel we have now reached the stage where these three words can be uttered in one breath) are always partial, ultimately unstable, and inevitably shot through with the potential for change, for 'newness' to occur. Let us unpack this idea to its very basics.

Picture one of our tribesmen's adornments. It's made out of feathers, pieces of carved wood, and string. It is an assemblage. It's going to be used as an extension. When that happens, it will be part of another assemblage, one that expresses/becomes self and community. But have another look at this tribesman's assemblage. It has been *fashioned*, not unlike Suger's sparkling crucifixes and other adornments, not unlike Alberti's 'sincere' architecture. It has been fashioned out of a number of bits and pieces, out of fragments found or stumbled upon. It is therefore, as any assemblage would be hybrid, inevitably hybrid. But there's more. Like any other assemblage, it is full of empty spaces, let's call them 'holes'. Indeed, for any assemblage to exist at all, there must be emptiness -holes- around which the assemblage is ... assembled. In short, without hybridity and without emptiness, there can be no assemblage. Assemblages, in other words, by their very nature, are assemblages of hybrid fragments and holes. The holes are absolutely necessary. In a way, it's the holes that keep assemblages apart/together. An assemblage that has no holes in it, is either no assemblage, or an impossible one, i.e. one that somehow would have managed to assemble all and everything. So let us recapitulate, using Strathern's words: assemblages, by their very nature, are assemblages of partially connected fragments, connected as they are in hybrid assemblages around holes that keep them apart/together. Now we have seen that assemblages, fashioned thus, tend to circulate (as extensions) and, in this very process, constitute self and community. But that means that the outcomes, and in turn again the source of circulating assemblages, i.e. self and community, will themselves, out of necessity, be hybrid assemblages of fragments and holes. The self, then, is, it too, an assemblage of partially connected fragments. Let us illustrate. Here are two very differently assembled knowing selves: 1) a critical criminologist, X, is reading Jacques Derrida's *Positions* in 1975; 2) the very same critical criminologist, X, is reading the very same book, *Positions* in 2009. These are very different assemblages. But there's more. The self as such is partially connected to the community, or better, to the communities it circulates in, and the latter, the communities, are in turn hybrid assemblages of partially connected selves and the holes in-between them that keep them apart/together.

Now let us substitute 'knowledge' for 'extension'. Knowledge, that which circulates as extensions in, through and between selves and communities, or again, that which constitutes, indeed *fashions* self and community, is inevitably hybrid, partially connected, fragmentary, and shot through with holes that keep it apart/together. It may, for a while, constitute selves and communities. But only for a while. Its connections, that is, its internal connections (it is after all an assembled extension), as well as the connections of self and community which it constitutes during its circulations, are always partial, and inevitably so. And it is there, in this very 'partiality', in the hybridity of knowledge and its outcomes, in the 'empty' holes that keep it as well as its outcomes apart/together, that the ever-present potential for change, indeed for newness, resides. Let us now try and answer a number of questions.

Where does scientific or theoretical change, or newness, come from, one might ask. The answer might sound something like this: it comes from the hybridity and the holes knowledge assemblages are made of. The more hybridity, the higher the odds that particular materials, when happened upon, may suddenly 'stick' and cause some disturbance or other, and that, in turn, may lead to change, or newness. The more 'holes', the greater the space for change, or newness, coming from the 'outside', to slip within. Change, and newness, are, as potentiality, already embedded in the hybridity and the holes which knowledge extensions consist of. They lurk in the hybridity and the 'emptiness' of *knowers* who circulate knowledge extensions, and who, on their wanderings through knowledge communities, or, more importantly, across knowledge communities, stumble or happen upon bits and pieces of other extensions which they may decide, or not, as the case may be, to adopt, and thus introduce change, and possibly newness. Indeed, the circulating knower may, at any point, decide to either ignore any disturbance caused by circulating knowledge extensions (or fragments thereof) or use it to adjust the current knowing self, possibly expressing/becoming newness. We will return to this issue later. Suffice to say for now that the potential for change and newness (*deviance*, if you wish) resides inexorably in the porosity that marks the twin results of knowledge assemblage and circulation, i.e. the knowing self and the knowledge community. Change and newness in science and theory therefore is that which needs no explanation. It's what should be expected. The absence of change and newness in and through knowledge assemblage and circulation is what one should be wondering about. When, one might ask, do knowing selves and their knowledge extensions stop circulating (and thus prevent knowers from 'stumbling upon' disturbing knowledge extensions)? Or, even if they do keep circulating, when, and why would knowers prefer to ignore any disturbance? That is the more important question. But before we deal with that issue, let us ask ourselves one more question. If change in science and theory is a matter of knowledge assemblages, or at least bits and pieces of them, circulating and crossing each other, then scientific or theoretical change, possibly newness, is something that *takes place*. It therefore must be particular, i.e. it must be the particular result of particular knowing selves who, adorned with particular knowledge extensions, circulate in particular places at particular times, only to stumble across a particular set of knowledge assemblages that 'happen' to circulate in those particular places and at those particular moments in time. If all these conditions are met, then it will be the particularities of the knowing self, of the knowledge communities involved, and of the knowledge assemblages that circulate, that, together with the particularities of the time and place of the 'disturbance', that will determine whether or not a particular scientific or theoretical change, possibly even newness, occurs. It should be clear that ultimately it is impossible to predict whether or not particular disturbances will result in scientific or theoretical change. Not just because the particularities of selves, communities, extensions, and times and places are always too vast to even begin to contemplate. But also because, indeed, any such prediction itself can be no more than a particular extension/assemblage, fashioned by a knowing self who, having circulated in or across a particular series of particular knowledge communities, will have come across, in the course of its particular life-trajectory, only a limited number of knowledge assemblages. Any such prediction, in other words, can be no more than the result of a particular assemblage of particular hybridities and holes.

However, having said that, one can say something about all this and indeed many ideas and concepts have been floated in the past few decades to denote the occurrence of scientific or theoretical change. We've touched upon a few of those in our introduction and this paper is not the place to expand on them. Let us just note that there is something *tribal* about scientific or theoretical change. Now this idea (i.e.: 'scientific or theoretical change is like tribal change, indeed *is* tribal change') is in itself not all that new (see e.g. Becher, 1989). And Bruno Latour, perhaps *the* foremost of actor-network theorists, once famously exclaimed that, when it comes to science and theory, and modernity as such, 'We Have Never Been Modern !' (Latour, 1993). The production of scientific knowledge, says Latour (who originally came from anthropology), is still a very tribal affair of *drawing things together* (at last! the phrase is Latour's: Latour, 1990), in and by tribal groups of scientists *together*, in the hope that this process of *drawing things together* and then circulating those things might *draw* the like-minded *together*, on the road to victory. Strathern's tribesmen, Panofsky's Abbot Suger, Gombrich's emerging Renaissance *elite*, Latour's scientists, ... 'we have never been modern' when it comes to the process of knowledge assemblage and circulation, certainly not in an age such as ours which Michel Maffesoli recently (1996) called a *neo-tribal* age. Latour's notion of *drawing* things together, just like Strathern's notion of *extension*, has also something of the visual about it. It's not just Suger's knowledge or the budding Renaissance man's, or a Papuan tribesman's, that was or is all about the taste of image. In the final analysis, it seems to be images that circulate as knowledge assemblages which, as extensions, in that very process of circulation constitute knowing selves and knowledge communities who in turn will further assemble and circulate image-extensions. In other words, *image* seems to be crucially important in the assemblage and circulation of knowledge -literally as well as figuratively.

Image: Drawing Criminological Things Together Distinctively

The word 'image', in the previous sentence, can be read quite literally. That which circulates as knowledge extensions, says Latour (1990), can be called 'immutable mobiles'. Those are often two-dimensional and very visual hybrids such as textbooks, articles, images, graphs, and so on, *drawn together* from ambition, ideas, motivation, strings of words, desire, experience, insight, ink, paper, and so on. In Papuan jungles they tend to be extensions that are fashioned out of feathers and forest materials. These hybrids are 'immutable' in the sense that they seem to express a certain coherence and stability, but they are highly mobile in the sense that they tend to circulate through networks of actors for other actors to 'happen upon' and, possibly, to pick up. Latour's *immutable mobiles* are *drawn* together (there are certainly connotations here with notions such as *force*). They are then often used, in a process of circulation, to mobilise other actors, in order to start drawing things *together*, that is, to act collectively, for example, to maintain or expand an existing knowledge community, or to emerge, in all deviancy, as a separate knowledge community. *Immutable mobiles* are never completely immutable though. Once assembled, once *drawn together*, they will of course continue to circulate as such throughout the actor-network. Simultaneously however, cracks will appear, and will start to cut across the *immutable mobile*, only to scatter its fragments across the actor-network, for others to visibly notice, and to make use of in further bouts of *drawing things together*.

But the word 'image' in the last sentence of the previous section can also be read figuratively. Fashioning knowledge assemblages or noticing them, perhaps even adopt them when happening upon them, is also a matter of image. Desire of, or desire for community is always involved in the process of knowledge assemblage and circulation. Imagine the critical criminologist who, after his initial rejection of Derrida's writings and of 'deconstruction' in the 1970s and 1980s, his enthusiasm about it during the 1990s, and then his mixed feelings about deconstruction in 2009, might recall how a measure of *image* was involved in this process of fashioning fashionable knowledge assemblages and drawing together knowledge communities. Suppose he has now achieved the following cascade of images when he considers himself to be part of a knowledge community where the 'us' are 'those who know a bit about Derrida, but have never been able to ditch all other assemblages stumbled upon, such as Sartre, Bloch, Levinas, Foucault, Deleuze, and many more, and who now firmly realize that they have gotten themselves into a pretty fine mess, but who have equally realized that this is basically OK, that, in other words, this mess is both proof and promise of theoretical fruitfulness (doesn't Gayatri Spivak come to mind here?), albeit that this notion of 'fruitfulness' is a highly problematic one, that, if one comes to think of it, could also be claimed by the strict Derridians who continue to make assemblages and extensions from bits and pieces of Derrida's writings ... yes, that's a pretty accurate *picture* of *us*, those who are in the know. *Us*, those who are *in'*. Then, there are the *others*, of course, those who haven't grasped any of this; them, 'the rest', those who are 'out'. Adopting knowledge, maintaining knowledge communities, or *drawing together* deviant *new* ones, to a considerable extent, is also about *drawing together* image, sensuous image, fashionable image. The world of knowledge is the world of tribesmen, gothic abbots, and Renaissance men. Anthropologists such as Quentin Bell (1947) and Pierre Bourdieu (1984) have often analyzed the desire that seems to be so conspicuous, particularly in the 'cultured' elites, indeed the 'knowledge class' as they are sometimes called in a somewhat different, more militant vein, to culturally distinguish themselves from others through the manifestation of cultural taste. It's not just about 'cultural' taste though. That should perhaps come as no surprise to criminologists who are well aware of the extent to which groups often emerge in and through processes of cultural, moral, intellectual, or social *subjectification*, processes whereby images of cultural, moral, intellectual, and social inferiority and superiority are assembled, circulated, adopted, and, as the case may be, rejected. They are very often prepared to mount, as Joseph Gusfield (1986) has been at pains to demonstrate, *symbolic crusades* in order to mark out others and distinguish themselves. In the words of Tony Kearon (2005), the bourgeois has never been truly liberal but, quite on the contrary, always dependent on the desire to distinguish. There is no reason to assume that the image of distinction and the distinction of image would be any less important when it comes to the assemblage and circulation of knowledge, and the establishment, or, as the case may be, the contestation of knowing selves (those who are *in the know*) and knowledge communities.

Now, back to criminology. Take gang life. Let us note how the boundary between 'in' and 'out' is a recurring theme of gang life, where so much of gang members' energy goes towards defining and maintaining correct or stable *knowledge* of signs, practices, methods, threats, defenses, and, more generally, behaviours. Or consider the example of a community of crack dealers in *El Barrio* (Bourgois, 1995). How much of Primo's, Candy's, and Caesar's (Philippe Bourgois's protagonists) efforts goes into establishing correct or stable knowledge of life in East Harlem, into acquiring stable and reliable knowledge about social codes (dress codes not in the least) for them to be able to venture into the world of regular employment, or into attempts to produce correct knowledge about the fashionably deviant dynamics of the retail crack trade. Or let us take the example of a board of directors (e.g. ENRON's) where good knowledge about what constitutes 'good' (i.e. acceptable, or in a sense, internally legitimate) *accounts* is paramount in any decision which the board may take. In a situation like this one (e.g. during a board room meeting), one has to be either very foolish or very brave (depending on your viewpoint) to produce alternative 'good' accounts. Or imagine a professional group of mediators who spend a lot of time acquiring stable knowledge about criminal aetiology, about 'restorative justice' and about interpersonal dynamics and standards of professional practice. Imagine how they will tend to demonstrate their 'good' knowledge of these issues, circulating it amongst their colleagues through talk and visual display, hoping perhaps (whether consciously or not) to be accepted by their fellow mediators as 'one of us', or, as the case may be, hoping to be recognized as an 'innovator' instead, a 'risk taker', or, why not, simply as an 'outsider'. Now picture yourself a criminology department where faculty as well as students will tend to be eager to acquire good and stable knowledge about gangs and gang members, about crack dealers in *El Barrio*, about ENRON's board room dynamics, about restorative justice, about mediators and their professional standards, about who or what counts as 'in' and who or what counts as 'out', and so on. Like the gang member, the crack dealer, the board member, the mediator, or the tribesman, the criminology faculty member will venture into the forest of knowledge assemblages that are already available in libraries, in scholarly publications, in the biographies of gang members and board members, in the thoughts of mediators who have tried to express them during interviews, in what can be observed in neighbourhoods or read in the press. The faculty member will then select a number of splinters from these assemblages in order to produce his or her fashionably deviant assemblage. He or she will adorn him or herself with it, not unlike the Papuan tribesman actually. This assemblage in turn will end up circulating amongst the criminologist's fellow faculty members, or amongst criminologists more generally, where, in various places, processes of assessment and negotiation of some sort may then ensue in order to ascertain whether, and to what extent, the criminologist is 'one of us' or an 'innovator', and whether or not, *as an innovator,* he or she merits scorn or praise. Ultimately this particular assemblage will join the flood of knowledge assemblages which the world 'out there' is made of. This criminologist's assemblage will be particular; it will be partial. Its articulation will depend not just on the few connections he or she has managed to make between a limited number of materials, but also on the vast and sheer limitless number of possible alternative connections which he or she, for a dizzying number of reasons, has been *unable* to make. And that, i.e. this dizzying number of alternatives, this 'hole', is where the promise of change and newness lurks. Countless knowledge extensions, marks of distinction, images of desire, are resting there, as potentiality, waiting to get assembled and circulated. The raw materials for an almost unlimited number of potential tribal knowledge selves and knowledge communities are stored there, waiting to emerge.

Conclusion

Our focus in this contribution was on the emergence and therefore *change* of *accounts* of how behaviours or groups come to be defined 'in', or, as the case may be, 'out'. Our intention was to provide an answer to the question 'Where does newness, or change, in such criminological accounts come from?'. This contribution, in short, set out to say something about the origins of scientific and theoretical change. It has hopefully become clear that here we consider scientific or theoretical newness as the result of a tribal process of assemblage and fashionable circulation of images, indeed: of *image*. This process of assemblage and circulation, as we have argued, is at the very same time also a process of formation of self and community. Now, allow us to be a little self-reflexive here. As such, this very contribution cannot be anything but a tribally fashioned knowledge extension which expresses/becomes a desiring knowing self and a ditto knowledge community. Its destiny is unsure. It will join the countless other extensions and their fragmented bits and pieces that are already circulating throughout the actor-network. What tribesman will happen upon it, stumblingly, or upon fragments of it? What will happen when this stumbling occurs? Indeed, as we have argued, any such prediction itself can be no more than a particular extension/assemblage. Any such prediction can be no more than the result of a particular assemblage of particular hybridities and holes. The ways of tribal image, fashionable deviance, and cultural distinction, that is, the ways of criminological change and newness, are ultimately unpredictable.

Acknowledgements

Some ideas in this paper were first presented at the 'Teaching Theory' symposium at Birkbeck College's Law Department, University of London (September 24th, 2004). Thanks go to those who offered remarks, both critical and supportive, on that occasion: Phil Carney, Costas Douzinas, Simon Hallsworth, Keith Hayward, Gordon Hughes, Paul Kiff, George Pavlich and Claire Grant. Thanks also to Tony Kearon for fine comments on the final draft of this paper. An earlier and shorter version of this paper was published in H. Kania, T. Serassis, and H.-J. Albrecht (eds) (2009) *Images of Crime III*. Berlin: Duncker & Humblot (pp. 45-56). Thanks go to Duncker & Humblot, to the Max Planck Institute for Foreign and International Criminal Law in Germany (to Michael Knecht in particular), and to the editors of the aforementioned volume for allowing me to reprint a revised and extended version of that paper here.

References

Becher, T. (1989) *Academic Tribes and Territories: Intellectual Inquiry and the Cultures of Disciplines*. Buckingham: Open University Press.

Bell, Q. (1947) *On Human Finery*. London: The Hogarth Press.

Bourdieu, P. (1984) *Distinction. A Social Critique of the Judgement of Taste*. Cambridge, Mass.: Harvard University Press.

Bourgois, Ph. (1995) *In Search of Respect*. Cambridge: Cambridge University Press.

Cohen, S. (1988) *Against Criminology*. New York: Transaction Books.

Fish, S. (1989) *Doing What Comes Naturally*. Durham: Duke University Press

Gombrich, E. (1962) *Meditations on a Hobby Horse and Other Essays on the Theory of Art*. London: Phaidon Press.

Gusfield, J. (1986) *Symbolic Crusade. Status Politics and the American Temperance Movement*. Champaign: University of Illinois Press.

Kearon, T. (2005) 'We Have Never Been Liberal. Bourgeois Identity and the Criminal(ized) Other', *Social Justice*, 32, 1, 5-19.

Kuhn, T. (1970) *The Structure of Scientific Revolutions*. Chicago: University of Chicago Press.

Latour, B. (1993) *We Have Never Been Modern*. Cambridge: Harvard University Press.

Latour, B. (1990) 'Drawing Things Together' in M. Lynch and S. Woolgar (eds) *Representation in Scientific Practice* (pp. 19-68). Cambridge: MIT Press

Lippens, R. (2003) 'Imagining Lines, Assembling Criminologies, Towards Negotiation.', in K.L. Kunz and C. Besozzi (eds), *Soziale Reflexivitaet und Qualitative Methodik* (pp. 167-188). Bern: Verlag Paul Haupt.

Lippens, R. (2004) (Ed.) *Imaginary Boundaries of Justice*. Oxford, Hart.

Lippens, R. (2006) 'Crime, Criminology and Epistemology: Tribal Considerations' in: B. Arrigo and C. Williams (eds), *Philosophy, Crime, and Criminology* (pp. 103-133). Chicago: University of Illinois Press.

Lippens, R. (2009) *A Very Short, Fairly Interesting and Reasonably Cheap Book about Studying Criminology*. London: Sage.

Lippens, R. & Crewe, D. (Eds) (2009) *Existentialist Criminology*. London: Routledge

Maffesoli, M. (1996) *The Time of the Tribes*. London: Sage

Panofsky, E. (1955) *Meaning in the Visual Arts*. New York: Doubleday Anchor.

Strathern, M. (1991) *Partial Connections*. Lanham: Rowman and Littlefield.

Index

List of Contributors

Don Crewe is Senior Lecturer in Criminology at Leeds Metropolitan University (UK). He recently completed his PhD 'Will, Power, Constraint, and Change: Prolegomena to a Study of Self and the Emergence of Structure in Young Offender Institutions' (2007). He is co-editor, with Ronnie Lippens, of 'Existentialist Criminology' (Routledge 2009). His research interests entail the philosophical critique of the topoi of criminological discourse and of human rights and criminal justice ethics.

Ronnie Lippens is Professor of Criminology at Keele University (UK). His research interests include critical criminology and organizational criminology. Latterly his research interests have focused also on the imaginary of law and order in art and literature. The author of numerous scholarly contributions on these topics in criminological as well as socio-legal studies journals and other venues, he recently published a textbook for undergraduates, 'A Very Short, Fairly Interesting and Reasonably Cheap Book about Studying Criminology' (Sage, 2009).

Luis Lobo-Guerrero is Lecturer in International Relations at Keele University (UK). He completed his PhD thesis on the biopolitics of insurance in 2007. His intellectual interests revolve around understanding the ways in which liberal ways of life are promoted and protected through the very processes that make them possible. He has meanwhile published on the biopolitics of security in a variety of specialized and reputed journal series and collections, including e.g. Theory, Culture & Society; International Political Sociology, Review of International Studies, and Security Dialogue.

Claudius Messner is Associate Professor of the Philosophy and Sociology of Law at the University of Salento (Lecce, Italy). The author of a great number of publications – books, articles, as well as chapters – in a wide variety of venues, on philosophical issues and problems pertaining to law and jurisprudence, his research also includes work on migration and citizenship, on mediation and justice, as well as theoretical reflections on systems theory, and on phenomenology.

Jamie Murray is Lecturer in Law at Liverpool John Moores University (UK). His research concerns Lacanian and Deleuze & Guattari perspectives on legality and social organisation. His book 'Deleuze & Guattari: Emergent Law' is due out with Routledge in 2010.

Luciano Nuzzo is Lecturer in Legal Theory and Philosophy of Law at the University of Salento (Lecce, Italy). His doctoral thesis on the philosophical work of Giorgio Agamben, Michel Foucault and Carl Schmitt was published under the title 'Le Anticamere del Diritto' [The Antechamber of Law] by Pensa Multimedia, Lecce, in 2008.

Marc Schuilenburg is Lecturer in Criminology at the Free University of Amsterdam (the Netherlands). A lawyer and philosopher by training, his work focuses on the control society and 'crime & punishment'. His publications include numerous articles and chapters on law, philosophy and popular culture. In 'Studio Popcorn' he researches, with architect Alex de Jong the effects of popular media on urbanization processes. Their book, 'Mediapolis. Popular Culture and the City' (2007) was published by 010-Publishers.

Patrick Van Calster is Associate Professor of Criminology at the University of Leyden (the Netherlands). A philosopher and criminologist by training, his research interests include the interface between organizational criminology, policing and complexity theory, as well as the cultural analysis of (representations of) crime and control. He has published prolifically on these issues in a wide variety of venues.

Gijs van Oenen is Lecturer in Legal, Social, and Political Theory at the Department of Philosophy at Erasmus University Rotterdam (the Netherlands). He has also been affiliated with the University of Amsterdam and the Rotterdam Academy of Architecture and Urban Design. His main research interests include citizenship, rule of law, democracy, art and public space, urban design, and interpassivity. He has previously published in journals such as Theory & Event, Law & Critique, Citizenship Studies, and Open: Cahier on Art and the Public Domain.

Veronique Voruz is Lecturer in Law and Criminology at the University of Leicester (UK), Guest Lecturer in Criminology at the Université Catholique de Louvain la Neuve (Belgium) and a practising psychoanalyst. An internationally renowned expert in the Lacanian psychoanalytical analysis of law and punishment, she has published widely on that topic. Her book, 'Foucault and Criminology', is due out with Routledge in 2010.